Tom
Benson

Tom Benson
A Billionaire's Journey

Kathy Finn

Kathy Finn (signature)

PELICAN PUBLISHING COMPANY
Gretna 2017

Copyright © 2017
By Kathy Finn
All rights reserved

The word "Pelican" and the depiction of a pelican are trademarks of Pelican Publishing Company, Inc., and are registered in the U.S. Patent and Trademark Office.

ISBN 9781455622320
E-book ISBN 9781455622337

Printed in the United States of America

Published by Pelican Publishing Company, Inc.
1000 Burmaster Street, Gretna, Louisiana 70053

The difference between a successful
person and others is not a lack of strength,
not a lack of knowledge, but rather a lack of will.
—*Vince Lombardi*

Contents

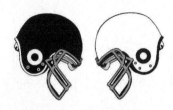

Introduction	. . . .	9
Chapter 1	Loved or Loathed?	13
Chapter 2	The Feel of Money	20
Chapter 3	Who Is Tom Benson?	26
Chapter 4	Cars Paved the Way	38
Chapter 5	Bankshot	50
Chapter 6	Call to Sports	56
Chapter 7	Investors Cry Foul	65
Chapter 8	Benson's Saints, the Early Years	76
Chapter 9	Hardnosed or Competitive?	81
Chapter 10	Born Rich, Part One	88
Chapter 11	Born Rich, Part Two	103
Chapter 12	The Grace Years	111
Chapter 13	Making Money in the NFL	119
Chapter 14	Walloped by Katrina	133
Chapter 15	Bad Day in Baton Rouge	145
Chapter 16	Big Easy Business	159
Chapter 17	Rough Going for Rita	165
Chapter 18	Gayle: Behind the Smile	178
Chapter 19	San Antonio	194
Chapter 20	Subsidized Billionaires	202
Chapter 21	Benson Gets a Makeover	216
Chapter 22	Historic Climb, Hard Stumble	225

Chapter 23	Basketball and a TV Station	234
Chapter 24	Anatomy of a Feud	243
Chapter 25	A Family Implodes	255
Chapter 26	The Gloves Come Off	266
Chapter 27	In Search of Stability	277
Chapter 28	Gauging Benson's Legacy	282
	Appendix	287
	Notes	293
	Index	308

Introduction

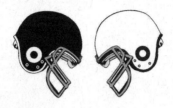

The first time I met Tom Benson—it was sometime in 1990, I think—I could not have imagined that I would one day write his story. I was a young New Orleans business reporter, and I covered the banking industry. It was a productive news beat, as the economy of the region had soured during the 1980s national recession, and it was pretty obvious that a lot of banks had feet of clay.

Troubled financial institutions provided plenty of fodder for news coverage, and one of the banks on my radar was Pontchartrain State Bank. The small suburban New Orleans bank had grown quickly by acquiring other institutions that had fallen on hard times, and it was becoming clear that the purchases had not been a good idea. I needed to interview the owner of the bank, and the owner was Tom Benson.

Though his bread-and-butter business was automobile retailing, Benson had owned banks, fairly successfully, in Texas for some years. And in 1985, he decided to try the business in his hometown of New Orleans.

The fact that Benson had also put together a $70 million deal to buy the New Orleans Saints football team in that year probably was no coincidence. As I learned through my later research, the man has a thing about keeping his plate piled high with complex deals. He mastered the art of "extreme" multitasking long before it was cool.

My 1990 interview with Benson was pretty forgettable—based on my current memory, anyhow. I had interviewed quite a few worried bank owners in those days, and the discussions came to have a familiar ring. The owner or CEO would sit behind his desk, generally with the bank's attorney and a public-relations aide nearby, and for an hour or so they would give vague answers to pointed questions about the bank's future.

The only clear memories I have from that interview are my impressions of Benson. He was not cordial, even at the moment I entered the room and we shook hands. Throughout the interview, in fact, he was kind of cranky. I wasn't offended. His bank was in trouble, after all. But it struck me that most people I interviewed, even in difficult circumstances, at least made an attempt at good humor.

The other thing that I noticed, and that many reporters have since learned, is that Tom Benson is not especially quotable. He does not have much fondness for words, and he spends little time searching for the right ones to use in a given situation. Mostly, he tosses out short, simple answers that he clearly hopes will help put the interview in his rearview mirror.

In the years since that interview, I have had only brief contacts with Benson, generally at press conferences and once at the Saints training camp during a photo shoot for an article about him and his granddaughter Rita that we were running in the magazine I then edited. None of the encounters changed my initial impressions of him.

Nevertheless, when Pelican Publishing Company asked me in 2015 if I would be interested in writing this biography, I didn't have to think about it for long. During thirty years of NFL team ownership, Benson had become one of the most unpredictable and controversial public figures in Louisiana. And that was *before* his relationships with family members exploded in courtrooms and news headlines. How could I resist?

I wrote a hurried initial outline for the book—essentially a wish list of everything that I would like to include. Benson's family situation and the future of his sports teams were at the top of my mind, of course, but his life held much more.

He had come from virtually nothing, and he had become one of the richest people in a several-state area through his financial acumen and extraordinary negotiating skills. Though automobile dealerships launched his career, his public profile soared after he acquired an NFL team. As the owner of the New Orleans Saints, and later the NBA's New Orleans Pelicans, he has felt both the wrath and the gratitude of the teams' fans.

During his journey across the decades, Benson has also suffered tremendous personal loss. And the resilience he has shown in the face of tragedies is enough to give the average person pause.

Tom Benson has experienced higher highs and lower lows than have most other people, even those who have lived as long as he has. I believed that his experiences were worth the telling, and I hope that readers will agree.

Because of the sensitivity of litigation among the family members, and perhaps because of his advancing age and health issues, Benson's lawyers and handlers have sharply limited his exposure and availability for interviews. Attorneys for Benson's daughter and two of his grandchildren, who brought suits against him, also have closely controlled their clients' contact with the press. All parties to the lawsuits declined interview requests for this book.

But through extensive research of news articles, public records, and interviews with other family members, friends, and acquaintances of the Benson family, I have compiled what I think is the most thorough story of Tom Benson's life written to date. I believe that the story is not only interesting, and at times entertaining, but instructive for a wide range of people for diverse reasons. Benson's life holds lessons for families, whether or not they are wealthy; for business owners and entrepreneurs; for cities that are home to major-league sports teams and the fans who love the teams; and for anyone whose life has been touched by tragedy and has had to figure out how to move ahead.

Chapter 1
Loved or Loathed?

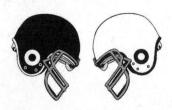

Tensions always ran high in the owner's suite during the hour before kickoff. And guests of Tom Benson had the added frustration of knowing that during the next few hours, they would have no chance to cut loose.

Benson, oddly enough, had little tolerance for the screams and bellows that reverberate in a stadium during a professional football matchup. He expected his guests to keep their spirits in check throughout the game, and that created an air of forced calm in a room positioned high above the fifty-yard line, overlooking thousands of fans who were itching to erupt in raucous emotion.

So it was when Benson's family and friends gathered in a suite at Sun Life Stadium in Miami Gardens, Florida, on February 7, 2010. Along with his wife, Gayle, Benson's granddaughter Rita, the heir apparent to his sports empire, was on hand, as was his daughter Renee and his grandson, Ryan. In line with Benson's tradition of holding a Catholic Mass for friends, family, and staff before every New Orleans Saints game, members of the clergy were also among his guests, including his close friend, retired New Orleans archbishop Philip Hannan.

The scene was no doubt sharply different in a suite on the opposite side of the stadium where Indianapolis Colts owner Jim Irsay had gathered with his entourage.

Irsay, then a voluble fifty-year-old with a taste for fashion, rock music, and the writings of Jack Kerouac, was known as a free spirit who had a penchant for waxing philosophical at the drop of a hat.

He had inherited the Colts from his father, Robert Irsay, in

1997 and ten years later experienced the thrill of bringing the NFL's championship trophy home to Indianapolis. That win had in no way dampened Jim Irsay's yearning for another.

Tom Benson, meanwhile, had owned the Saints for twenty-five years and had struggled during much of that time to put together a winning mix of front-office leadership and football talent. While the Saints had several times made it into the playoffs, the team had never reached a Super Bowl in its forty-four-year history.

That quiet time before Super Bowl XLIV likely had Tom Benson reflecting on the rollercoaster of a life that had brought him to this point. During his eighty-two years, he had built extraordinary success in business, and he had experienced deep personal loss.

He had sweated through countless white-knuckle moments in deals where the risks were steep and the potential rewards were great. But never had the stakes seemed as high as they did on that night in 2010.

This was not merely a watershed moment for a football team that had struggled for decades. The game's outcome could become the linchpin that would seal Tom Benson's legacy. The prospect was enough to put even the tough-minded Benson on edge.

The two weeks since the Saints' thrilling playoff win against the Minnesota Vikings had been a frenzy of celebration and planning for the trip to the Super Bowl. And since arriving in Miami, he had been through several days of NFL socializing and pregame hoopla. Benson was ready for the show to get started.

When kickoff time finally arrived, he and everyone else in the suite grew hyper-focused on the field below. As it turned out, the first two quarters would do little to calm their nerves.

The Saints had won the coin toss, but the Drew Brees-led offense got off to a sluggish start. Dropped balls and lost footing thwarted their attempts to make a break down the field.

The Saints defense, meanwhile, had trouble reining in powerful Colts quarterback Peyton Manning, who got his team into position for a thirty-eight-yard field goal and then led a ninety-six-yard drive for a touchdown, all in the first quarter. In response, the

Saints could muster only field goals, and they left the field at halftime trailing the Colts, 10-6.

If spirited banter eluded the guests in Tom Benson's suite before the game, easy chat was out of the question during the halftime break. Benson's guests quietly nibbled snacks and fretted over what tricks Manning and company might concoct in the second half.

But the smoke from the halftime fireworks had barely cleared when it was the Saints—not the Colts—who took the entire stadium by surprise.

Head coach Sean Payton had alerted the game officials in advance that the Saints might try an onside kick at some point during the second half, and at the beginning of the third quarter he dialed up the play he called "Ambush."[1] Rookie punter Thomas Morstead executed the kick perfectly, drawing a collective gasp from 76,000 fans in the stadium and millions more seeing it on television. The ball wobbled ten yards to Morstead's left and glanced off the facemask of a Colts player, then bumped Saints special teamer Chris Reis, who threw himself on the football and held on through the brutal pileup that followed. When the officials finished peeling off all the players, the Saints had the pigskin.

The onside kick stunned the Colts and ignited the Saints offense. Quarterback Drew Brees next threw a bullet downfield to Pierre Thomas, who followed an artful catch-and-run with a dive into the end zone, giving the Saints their first lead of the game and sparking thoughts across the football universe that an upset could be at hand.

The momentum shift even drew gasps in the normally controlled Benson suite, while thousands of Saints fans in the surrounding stands launched into an earsplitting rendition of "Who dat," the team's signature chant.

As shocked as the Colts were by the turn of events, Manning kept his cool, and he quickly responded with a seventy-six-yard touchdown drive.[2] But the Saints' aggressive second-half start had energized Brees. He mounted drives that would lead to another Garrett Hartley field goal and a Jeremy Shockey touchdown, followed by a nail-biting two-point conversion that ended with a dramatic Lance Moore catch-and-dive.[3] The Saints were up 24-17.

Though Manning stayed calm, serving up laser passes that put the Colts within thirty yards of the goal line, the Saints defense was bent on engineering a turnover. As Manning cocked his arm for another assault, cornerback Tracy Porter spotted an opening. By the time Manning released the ball, Porter had scrambled into position in front of Colts receiver Reggie Wayne and—wham!—Porter picked off the pass, tucked the ball, and sprinted seventy-four yards for a touchdown.

Dumbfounded and on their heels, the Colts stumbled through the final minutes of the game. On the Saints' last possession, Brees took a knee. New Orleans and Tom Benson had their first Super Bowl win.[4]

The elation of the Saints and their fans was boundless, not just in Miami but also in New Orleans, where ecstatic locals who had watched the game on barroom television screens spilled into the streets of the city's famous French Quarter. Their screams joined blaring car horns that echoed through the city. Spontaneous parties erupted on front lawns, and ad hoc jazz bands swung into home-cooked renditions of "When the Saints Go Marching In."

New Orleans was headed into full-tilt celebration by the time

New Orleans Saints fans celebrate on Bourbon Street in the city's French Quarter after the Saints win Super Bowl XLIV on February 7, 2010. (AP Photo)

Tom Benson and family made their way onto the field in Sun Life Stadium for the Vince Lombardi Trophy presentation.

As he stood there, blanketed by confetti and hugging players, coaches, and family, Benson likely felt transported by this crowning achievement. He had come a long way since leaving his boyhood home in the Seventh Ward of New Orleans some seven decades earlier. His life had turned into a journey he could never have imagined, and the experience of this night certainly was one for the books. As Benson hoisted the Lombardi Trophy and beamed his smile in every direction, an observer couldn't help wondering: could it be the happiest moment of his life?

Redemption?

The night had not merely brought the culmination of Tom Benson's dream to own a championship football team. It had also made him the bearer of a huge gift to his hometown as New Orleans struggled to recover from the worst disaster in its nearly three-hundred-year history.

The city at the time was more than four years removed from the flood that had inundated it following Hurricane Katrina in 2005, but devastation was still visible, and questions remained about whether a full comeback was possible. Benson, however, showed no doubt on that night in Miami as he basked under the stadium lights. "New Orleans is back, and we showed the whole world!" he shouted into a reporter's microphone.[5]

Some people who watched the scene may have questioned whether he was strong enough to withstand the thrill, but Benson probably had no such thoughts. Ignoring his age, the automobile dealership magnate, bank chairman, and professional sports-team owner was continuing much the same work routine he had followed throughout his life. He still put in full days at his office overlooking the Saints practice field in suburban New Orleans, and he kept an eagle eye on an array of balance sheets and cash-flow analyses.

But health issues had cropped up. In 2001, he underwent quadruple heart bypass surgery[6] and a year later had a surgical procedure to relieve back pain.[7] In 2008, surgeons removed a cancerous mass from his left kidney,[8] and while he would later declare himself fully recovered from his stint on "injured reserve,"[9] that hospitalization would not be his last.

His advancing age also had Benson attuned to matters of legacy. Bringing the Lombardi Trophy home from Miami could mean everything in terms of the mark that he eventually would leave on the city where he was born, grew up, began a family, and planted the roots of a large fortune.

The businesses he built over decades had enlarged his net worth and brought him the respect of powerful people. But Benson had also drawn the ire of many New Orleans and Gulf Coast residents, some of whom saw him as a calculating opportunist who had too easily shown a willingness to abandon them at a critical time.

Several days after the Saints' Super Bowl win, New Orleans formally welcomed the team home in a grand fashion that only the Big Easy could pull off, featuring a Mardi Gras-style parade that drew thousands of cheering fans into the streets. Sean Payton, Drew Brees, and dozens of other players and coaches rode atop colorful Carnival floats, swaying to the tunes of marching bands and tossing trinkets to the crowds. Tom and Gayle Benson sat enthroned on the lead float, flashing delighted smiles.

But even as people in the streets gleefully waved back to Benson, they had not forgotten his actions of just a few years earlier. Local news and op-ed pages in late 2006 brimmed with anger over speculation that, in the wake of the Katrina disaster, Benson might move his football team to another city, and New Orleans residents were outraged. "Mr. Benson's first allegiance has always been to his bottom line, rather than to the community that has supported him so loyally for many years," a resident wrote in a letter to the editor[10] that appeared shortly after the rumors began circulating.

Was Benson's seeming willingness to consider leaving New Orleans indicative of his approach to other relationships as well? Had bottom-line considerations, as the letter writer suggested, always underwritten his decision-making, not only in business but in personal matters?

If so, perhaps it should not have been surprising. Benson had come from almost nothing, in terms of his family's material resources, and through his own efforts he had built a business empire that few, even among his close friends, could have envisioned decades earlier.

He had turned a job as a bookkeeper for a car retailer into an automobile dealership empire. He also stepped into the banking business and accumulated institutions whose assets totaled hundreds of millions of dollars.

Benson had a keen eye for business opportunities and sharp negotiating skills that seldom left him on the losing side of a deal. He turned land and building purchases into high-dollar developments and built a valuable portfolio of properties in several states.

But a major-league sports team is a business of another color. A team's value is closely tied to its ability to win the loyalty of local people and capitalize on their support. Players and coaches count for plenty in the equation, but it is the owner, as the one who controls the organization, who becomes its most important face.

Benson at times seemed not to perceive that owning the New Orleans Saints created certain expectations of him, personally. He didn't understand that local football fans believed he should return the loyalty they had shown his team and that some distrusted his motives.

Now, on a field in Miami in 2010, with the Saints' Super Bowl victory still echoing through the stadium, Benson realized that the night could mean everything in terms of how New Orleans would remember him.

Standing there, surrounded by loved ones, he savored the extraordinary moment. But he had no way of knowing how much trouble lay ahead.

During the next few days, he and his family would revel in the joy of bringing the Super Bowl-winning Saints home to New Orleans. But in the coming years the city's beloved team would take a blow to its image that no one saw coming, Benson would face more criticism and personal loss, and the family that stood united in the glory of victory on that memorable night in Miami would begin to come unglued.

Chapter 2
The Feel of Money

People who grow up in middle-class families generally don't give much thought to the downsides of being rich. From the perspective of a person with limited means, after all, the idea of never having to face financial stress practically defines life on Easy Street.

But in fact, accumulating a fortune can make life difficult in some respects.

"Very wealthy people can feel isolated, and they can be quite lonely," says Thayer Willis, a writer and educator who specializes in counseling wealthy clients on the psychological challenges of dealing with money.

Willis says routine social interactions that most people take for granted can be more difficult for people with abundant assets.

The prospect of meeting new friends and doing such ordinary things as inviting them over for dinner, for instance, is complicated by a fear that socioeconomic disparity will make everyone uneasy. Will people of average income feel comfortable visiting a wealthy friend's mansion? Is it likely that anyone would feel at ease with a reciprocal invitation?

Such seemingly small concerns can have the effect over time of making wealthy people wary of developing relationships outside of tightly controlled circumstances. A hyper-awareness of their own elevated socioeconomic status can impair their ability to interact spontaneously on a personal level.

For that and other reasons, they may limit social interactions to circles of financial peers. Private clubs become the stomping grounds of some rich people, while others tend to hunker down with relatives and close associates in vacation homes or family enclaves.

"Having a great deal of money can actually create a lack of motivation to get out in the world," Willis says.

Social isolation often goes hand in hand with a general sense of distrust. Rich people may be wary of anyone who shows a personal interest in them because they worry they are liked or loved only for their money.

The concern is particularly keen when it comes to romantic relationships. Even in a time when prenuptial agreements are routine, fear that a prospective life partner's interest may arise more from money than love leads many wealthy individuals to search for a spouse only among financial equals.

Wealth can also give rise to control issues. While money may imbue the rich with a feeling of power, they often feel frustrated by an inability to control the behavior or life choices of their loved ones. A rebellious son or daughter can present big challenges to parents at any socioeconomic level, but teenage angst can take on epic proportions when the kids have ample funds at their disposal. Their choice of friends and, eventually, a life partner can also spark family fireworks.

On top of the personal challenges that money can produce, people who have amassed great wealth must figure out how to preserve it and pass it on. Financial and estate planning can be a nightmarish prospect for someone whose assets total in the billions.

The wealthy tend to spend a great deal of time and money on legal and other professional services aimed at managing their assets and ensuring that their wealth will be distributed precisely as they wish after their death. Yet sometimes, even with all that attention, a well-laid estate plan can go awry if an heir or would-be beneficiary chooses to mount a legal challenge.

In short, while money makes for an easy and enjoyable lifestyle, it can also seriously complicate one's life.

Business, Family Intertwined

As is the case for most individuals who earn their way into the financial stratosphere, the challenges that come with wealth dawned on Tom Benson gradually.

Always driven to make money, in the early stages of his career he directed his increasing net worth into better homes and family vacations and showering his kids with amenities he had no inkling of during his own childhood.

Benson also enjoyed his growing ability to introduce his relatives, including his siblings, cousins, and their families, to business opportunities.

In doing this, he put into practice family values he had learned early on. He credits his mother, Carmelite Marie Pintado Benson, with instilling in him a responsibility to share any success with those closest to him.

"My father ran the show, but she was the wheel behind him," Benson said of his mother in a 2001 interview. "She thought that if you did well, certainly everybody in the family ought to do well."[1]

Benson followed his mother's rule, routinely bringing into his automobile and other businesses his brothers and any cousins, nephews, and nieces who showed an interest. From working in the service department to becoming dealership managers, Benson family members tested the waters of car retailing. In many cases over the years, Benson helped launch relatives into their own lucrative careers.

His brother Augustin, for instance, would follow Benson's lead into the automobile business in the 1960s, as would his father, Tom Benson, Sr., who moved from New Orleans to San Antonio with his wife in 1964 and worked at Tom Benson Chevrolet.[2] Until his death, the elder Benson remained active in the company that oversaw his son's automotive, banking, and real-estate holdings in Louisiana and Texas.

Another brother of Tom Benson, Jr., Jerome Benson, would come to head Suzuki and Pontiac dealerships, among others, before eventually taking over Benson Automotive World from Tom in the 1990s.[3]

Even their youngest brother, Larry, who was eighteen years younger than Tom and had earned a law degree from St. Mary's University in the early 1970s, came to focus his law practice on Tom Benson's automobile businesses, becoming what Benson called the "legal mind" behind Benson Automotive.[4] In time Larry, too, would hold automotive assets, becoming owner of Ingram Park Auto Center, which included Nissan, Chrysler, Mazda, and other franchises in San Antonio.[5]

Tom Benson also brought his cousin Robert W. Benson, Jr., into the business.

Bob Benson, as most knew him, had considered becoming a professional baseball player after starring in the sport at Loyola University of New Orleans and being offered a minor-league contract. But he instead chose to put his pharmacy degree to work and eventually went into pharmaceutical sales.[6]

After he retired from that thirty-five-year career, Bob Benson went on to manage several Benson dealerships in San Antonio, and his son Mark would later become manager of Benson Honda.[7]

Tom Benson did not limit his career influence to blood relatives.

At the time he married his second wife, Grace, in 1982, her four adult children from her first marriage had started on various career paths. But in time, Grace's two daughters would become car dealers as Tom phased himself out of the business and offered them opportunities to buy dealerships.

Grace's daughter Miriam "Mimi" Walker for a time worked in human resources for Benson Automotive before marrying then-Benson employee Martin Peake. The couple eventually would acquire Benson's BMW dealership, now known as Peake BMW, in Kenner.

Later, Mimi's sister, Susan Walker, who was a registered nurse with a degree from the University of Texas at San Antonio, made a career shift and became owner of Benson's local Volkswagen and Acura dealerships. Both of Susan's children, who received their college educations courtesy of Benson, now work in management and marketing at Walker Volkswagen.

"Tom took care of everybody in his family," including the children and grandchildren of his second wife, Walker says. "He has been nothing but generous to us."

While his car dealerships, which at one time numbered more than two dozen in three states, provided many opportunities for Benson to boost his relatives' wealth, it didn't stop there. As he grew his real-estate holdings in Texas and Louisiana, he involved his brothers and some of their family members in completing the transactions or managing the properties.

When Benson got into the financial services business through the acquisition of several banks in the 1970s, and when he returned to the business in 2003, close family members became trustees or advisory-board members and received stock in the companies.[8]

"Tom just always had his family involved with him," says Miriam Whitman, a cousin to the billionaire.

She adds that Benson's generosity has held up through every football season. "Ever since he's owned the Saints, he's invited us to the [owner's] suite for almost every game," she says.

Place of Refuge

As Benson's wealth grew, life became easier for his family. The Bensons moved into larger homes and acquired second and third residences. The Benson children enrolled in private, Catholic schools in San Antonio, and they enjoyed the attention of a live-in housekeeper. The family took vacations to one or another coast, often accompanied by close friends and relatives.

Sooner or later, any individual whose net worth hits a critical mass will look to invest in real estate, and Benson was no exception. He began to scout land and commercial property in the Texas Hill Country.

He put a large chunk of cash at risk on a deal to purchase a tract of land in north San Antonio that he envisioned as an expansion site for his automobile business. He also started amassing land near Johnson City, an hour north of San Antonio, which eventually would become the site of the Benson Farm and Ranch. That purchase would become increasingly important to Benson as his wealth grew.

As Benson's money and business success raised his profile and made him a magnet for social and charitable solicitations, the naturally shy and socially awkward businessman needed a place to escape and sink into the comfort of familiarity. He held a membership in San Antonio's most exclusive private club, but the country-club set was not his cup of tea. The Johnson City ranch became a retreat where he could surround himself with the people he knew best.

Benson delighted in driving a Jeep full of kids around the Hill Country landscapes. And he loved hosting friends for fishing and hunting weekends that included big barbecue spreads laid out by the ranch staff.

The Benson Farm and Ranch became both a beloved residence and a symbol of Benson family unity. Not only was it a summer and weekend home for Tom Benson's immediate family, it was also a gathering spot for his parents, siblings, cousins, nieces, nephews, and their friends. It was a hub for holiday dinners and family celebrations.

Most importantly, the ranch gave Benson a place where he could be himself. The stone ranch house at the end of a dirt road was a homey and unpretentious abode set amid hills populated with cattle, horses, and wild game. In a trophy room used as a den, the heads of animals killed in hunts lined the walls, and a large, sunny dining room accommodated family dinners that sometimes brought twenty or more Bensons together.[9]

Benson's ranch was an inherently casual gathering spot where his growing wealth was not the elephant in the room.

"I think the ranch was a refuge for Tom," says New Orleans lawyer Maury Herman, who for many years was a legal adviser and close friend to Benson.

Over time, Benson would acquire more of the obvious trappings associated with a high net worth. Particularly after he became an NFL team owner, such amenities as a private jet, a yacht, and vacation homes in tony locales became must-haves. And Benson and his family traveled abroad more frequently.

But for years the Texas ranch remained the preferred place for Benson to retreat and entertain friends. And when he was there, he expected family to be there as well.

Even as Tom Benson's three children grew up and got married, he clung to the belief that they would stay close to home or maybe even settle into a home on the ranch.

But in time he would bump up against the fact that, despite having accumulated great wealth and influence, he could not control the feelings or inclinations of those closest to him. In the end, only one of his three children would make the ranch a long-term home. And as his family relationships became strained, the time would come when Benson himself would no longer feel comfortable in what was once his favorite retreat.

Chapter 3

Who Is Tom Benson?

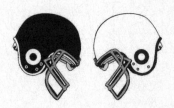

It was not an auspicious time to begin a life. The Roaring Twenties had brought prosperity and a cultural awakening to much of the United States, but the excesses of the decade began to reach a tipping point as the years wore on.

Thomas Milton Benson, Jr., came into the world on July 12, 1927, just two years before a bubble of euphoria that had engulfed the country exploded into the most devastating stock market crash in the nation's history. The bloodbath on Wall Street marked the beginning of the longest economic downturn the Western industrialized world had ever known. High unemployment, bank failures, and food shortages became facts of life during the Great Depression for millions of people across the country.

In New Orleans, the period also brought challenges from Mother Nature. The unprecedented spring rains that swelled rivers throughout the Midwest in 1927 brought the Great Mississippi River Flood to the Crescent City in April, with the gushing waters compromising levees upriver from New Orleans and setting the stage for a drastic decision by local authorities to blow open downriver levees in order to prevent an inundation of the city.

Even with that, it would take months for the water to completely recede, and area residents were still shoveling mud when Thomas Milton Benson, Sr., and his wife, Carmelite, brought their firstborn from the hospital to their rented shotgun house on Elysian Fields Avenue.

Worries about money formed an undercurrent of most families' lives in those days, and the Bensons were no exception. The birth of their son would be followed in quick succession by two more boys, Jerome and Augustin.

The family moved to a slightly larger house, on North Johnson Street, where the boys would spend most of their childhood. When they were old enough, they all would do their part to support the household, which expanded again when a fourth son, Lawrence, came along fifteen years after Augustin's birth.

Throughout those years, Tom Benson, Sr., struggled to cover the family's needs with the paycheck he earned as a floorwalker and manager at the Gus Mayer Department Store on Canal Street in New Orleans.[1]

The Benson sons saw many friends and families around them who were steeped in similarly difficult economic circumstances, but Tom Benson, Jr., did not find the company comforting. In the far reaches of the boy's mind, visions of something better had begun to take shape, and as he grew up and took on responsibilities for helping to support his family, he began to plan how he would paint a different picture with his own life.

Working-Class Roots

Some people who accumulate great wealth through their own efforts recall that, during the years when they struggled to build businesses, they sometimes felt disrespected or even shunned by individuals who had been born to money. Writer Shaun Rein took note of the phenomenon in a 2010 *Forbes* article for which he interviewed dozens of wealthy business owners about their early lives. "Nearly all the self-made billionaires I interviewed told me they had faced contempt from people born rich," he wrote.

Pointing to a Chinese Internet billionaire who encountered repeated rejections when he first tried to raise money from Silicon Valley venture capitalists, Rein said: "They pooh-poohed him because of his shabby clothes, broken English and lack of a Western education."[2]

Tom Benson may have seemed similarly undistinguished in the 1950s, as he began to lay the foundation for what would become an automobile dealership empire.

Benson had grown up in New Orleans' Seventh Ward, in a small home on North Johnson Street that was crowded with relatives, including his parents, his three younger brothers, and his grandmother.[3] Everyone in the household, including the kids, worked to support the family. Tom's first paying gig, while attending Our Lady Star of the Sea Elementary School, was a newspaper delivery route.[4]

The family's budget could never have covered private-school tuition for the Benson boys. But thanks to a kindly member of the Brothers of the Sacred Heart who became acquainted with the family and believed that the boys were promising students, they got to attend the well-regarded St. Aloysius High School.

"Pay what you can for the boys," Brother Martin Hernandez told Tom Benson, Sr.[5]

As young Tom grew up and finished high school at St. Aloysius, he seemed destined to become a typical working-class guy, and he looked the part. Of medium build, with rounded facial features and a pasty complexion, he would not have stood out in a crowd. In social settings he remained on the periphery, where he had a better chance of avoiding chitchat. He was neither an easy conversationalist nor a trendsetter. While his suits may not have been shabby in the manner of the businessman Rein wrote about, they certainly were not custom-tailored.

In contrast, many of the locally prominent businesspeople of the time hailed from the "old money" families who populated grand homes along St. Charles Avenue in Uptown New Orleans. The young men of these ranks wore their breeding and Ivy League educations on their sleeve. They married young women of similarly privileged backgrounds, lived in stately homes handed to them by parents or grandparents, and in many cases worked in family-owned businesses that they would one day inherit.

Benson had no illusions that the future he envisioned for himself would get a kick-start from family money. His maternal grandfather—the son of a man who immigrated to New Orleans from Havana, Cuba in 1836—supported his wife and seven children by working as a steamboat pilot on the Mississippi River.[6] Benson's paternal granddad, whose father immigrated from Sicily and fought with the New Orleans infantry in the Civil War, worked as a clerk in a local post office.[7] One of his sons, Thomas Milton Benson, Sr., would later support a wife and four children by working at a department store.

Growing up in that household, Tom Benson, Jr., and his three younger brothers were expected to help support the family. In addition to his newspaper route, young Tom sometimes worked with his dad at the Gus Mayer store. Later, when his father opened a dry-goods store on Claiborne Avenue, Tom manned the shop while living in an apartment above the store.[8]

"When he was young, we didn't have anything," his mother, Carmelite Marie Pintado Benson, said of her oldest son in 1987.[9]

She described Tom as hardworking and more driven to get ahead than his younger brothers. "He was serious at an early age," she said.[10]

Benson had a knack and taste for earning money, and his enthusiastic pursuit of the dollar showed that he envisioned a life for himself that was different from the one he and his family had known.

It wasn't so much that he hungered for the social status and accoutrements enjoyed by the young men who lived across town. Rather, he simply liked the challenge of making money.

Tom Benson saw that the process of amassing wealth would require being not only financially astute but persistently and aggressively competitive. As many business associates and rivals would eventually learn, Benson had the goods.

"If there's a nickel on the corner of Gravier and Baronne, and Tom Benson wants that nickel, I would suggest you get out of the way," New Orleans lawyer Michael Little, who once represented a client sued by Benson, told a reporter in 2001.[11]

For Benson, the reward for his pursuit of money would be the personal satisfaction that would come with an ever-increasing net worth. The lifestyle he would be able to buy for himself and his family would be icing on the cake.

"He was always a hardworking person, and he was a financial whiz," says Ledoux Chastant, Jr., one of Benson's best friends since high school.

The two, along with their friend Roy Hock, who died in 2007, were constant companions in the days when some of Benson's friends knew him by his middle name.

"I always called him Thomas, but a lot of people called him Milton," Chastant says.

Chastant remembers the weekend drives he and Benson used to take from New Orleans eastward along the Gulf Coast, stopping in barrooms along the way and hitting up clubs as far away as Miami. After both men married, they and their wives socialized often, and their entertainment frequently included dancing, as Tom and Shirley Landry Benson loved to dance.

The Chastants were eyewitnesses to Tom Benson's rapid climb toward wealth. They saw him ply his job at a local auto dealership into an ownership position that would launch him toward a dealership empire, and they watched him dive into the banking business, growing his banks' assets into the hundreds of millions of dollars.

Decades later, after Benson bought the New Orleans Saints, the Chastants were regulars in the owner's suite on game days. Ledoux Chastant and Tom Benson remained so close that Chastant joined Benson on the team plane for almost every away game during football season, even as both men advanced into their late eighties.

Through all that time, Chastant says, Benson has not changed. "He's still a lot of fun, and he can still do anything he puts his mind to," he says.

Not all of Benson's early friends continued to hold him in high regard over the years. Three of Benson's high-school buddies who eventually went to work for him parted company with the car dealer when they all were in their thirties.

The four had initially become close as children when they gathered for regular Friday-night meetings of the Boy Scouts, Troop 31. They stayed in close touch after high school, but as one of the former scouts, Harold Frederick, told a reporter years later, their relationship suffered as Benson's fortunes rose.

During the early years of Benson's automobile career, he hired all three of his old friends to work in his dealership. But when they didn't measure up to his expectations, he fired two of them, including Frederick, and the third man quit shortly thereafter.

"The three of us used to sit around and wonder what happened," Frederick said.[12]

All subsequently cut their personal ties with Benson.

The path Benson followed into his business career was, to an extent, shaped by the times. As a teenager during the years leading to World War II, he was part of a generation of young people whose lives and career development would be interrupted by military service.

After graduating from St. Aloysius High School in 1944, Benson enrolled at Loyola University of New Orleans, intending to study business. But he soon left his classes to enlist in the U.S. Navy. He had hoped to join the Naval Air Forces but ended up being assigned as a seaman. Because he'd been studying accounting at Loyola, he said, "They put me on the USS *South Dakota,* where I worked on accounting for the ship."[13]

The start of his military service coincided with the culmination of a high-school romance.

Growing up in a devoutly Catholic family, it was no surprise that Tom met his future wife at church. He had first noticed Shirley Mae Landry as she sang in the choir at Our Lady Star of the Sea Catholic Church on St. Roch Avenue. The teenagers struck up a friendship.

In 1944, as Tom graduated from St. Aloysius, Shirley received her diploma from nearby Annunciation High School. A year later, when Tom returned from Navy boot camp, the two married, with Shirley dressed in white and Tom in his Navy blues.[14]

After the war ended, Benson returned to New Orleans and went back to Loyola, this time with help from the GI Bill. He attended classes for a few years, majoring in business administration, while also working part-time at a local accounting firm.

The work was a good fit with his college studies, but Benson grew impatient with school. Anxious to get on with his life and career, he left Loyola without earning a degree.[15]

Despite lacking a diploma, he believed he could become a certified public accountant, and he decided to sit for the CPA exam. But his hopes of leveraging his earning power with a professional certificate fizzled when he failed the CPA test.[16]

Nevertheless, Benson soon landed a job offer as a bookkeeper at Cathey Chevrolet Company on North Rampart Street, at the edge of the French Quarter. He signed on with the dealership at a salary of $300 a month.[17]

Fatherhood

Building a family was always part of Tom and Shirley Benson's plans, and they got an early introduction to the responsibilities when, not long after they married, they took on raising a nephew, Leonard. Later, when they learned that they could not have children biologically, they decided to adopt.[18]

In 1948, the couple brought home their newly adopted infant son. Robert Carter Benson's first home was the family's rented apartment on Claiborne Avenue. But he would not live there long, for it was around this time that a car dealer named Mike Persia became Tom Benson's employer.[19]

Persia, who had become a car-retailing dynamo in San Antonio, expanded into New Orleans by acquiring Cathey Chevrolet, and Benson stayed on to work for the new owner. In no time, Persia began to heavily rely on the young accountant.

By the time Benson was twenty-seven, he had moved his family out of their rental apartment and purchased a modest home on Florida Avenue. That's where the Bensons lived in 1956 when they decided to adopt another child.[20]

The baby girl was born in New Orleans, and later Renee Elaine Benson joined her adoptive parents and brother in their Florida Avenue home. But soon, the family would be on the move again, as Persia had tapped Benson for a bigger job.

Persia had acquired a Chevrolet dealership in San Antonio that was in need of a strong hand, and he asked Benson to take over its management.[21] Benson agreed, and the family packed off to Texas.

They found the move invigorating. Benson welcomed the challenge of having control over a dealership and the freedom to manage it into a more profitable operation. And he and Shirley were excited about the change of scene. They liked the feel of the countryside surrounding San Antonio, and they saw it as a good place to raise their growing family.

In 1959, the Bensons adopted their third child, daughter Jeanne

Marie Benson, whom they immediately nicknamed "Tootsie."[22]

As Shirley managed the Benson household, now with two little girls at home and a boy in elementary school, Tom Benson flexed his muscle at the Chevrolet dealership in downtown San Antonio. He made rapid progress in growing revenues by following in the footsteps of his mentor, Mike Persia, Sr., who was known for pushing his sales people hard.

"Tom's never satisfied, and that's the way the old man was," former car salesman Pete Rizzo, who had worked for both Benson and Persia, said in 2001. "If we sold 200 cars, he wanted you to sell 250. If we sold 300, he wanted 350. Never, never, never satisfied," he said.[23]

But Benson was finding satisfaction in his burgeoning net worth. As the automobile business grew, so did his financial profile.

He began looking for ways to make his family feel even more at home in the landscape of the Texas Hill Country. He found his answer in the hills near Johnson City, about sixty miles north of San Antonio. There, in the early 1960s, he began buying land parcels that eventually would become the Benson Farm and Ranch. The spread not only would come to house hundreds of animals, including exotic deer, antelope, Longhorn cattle, and racehorses, across its 2,300 acres but would for decades be the favorite home and gathering spot of the Bensons, their extended family, and friends.

His purchase of the ranch warmed Tom Benson up for a venture into commercial property development, and he took his first stab at it when he was still in an early stage of his automobile career. In 1966, with his children then ranging in age from seven to eighteen, he took a financial risk on a land deal in north San Antonio that he envisioned as the future home of his business.

Benson rolled the dice on a million-dollar loan, which he knew he would have trouble paying off should his car business begin to falter. During a visit to New Orleans before he concluded the deal, he confided his fears to a close friend, Father John Sokolski, at St. Anthony's Seminary.

"Pray for me, Padre," Benson told him.[24]

Promising to continue his support of St. Anthony's as long as his own good fortune held up, Benson added: "If this works, we're all in clover."[25]

Neither Benson nor the priest would be disappointed. Coming years brought many retailers to the suburban San Antonio commercial site, which would come to house the headquarters of Benson's automobile empire.

Acquiring the San Pedro Avenue site anchored the Benson family even more solidly in the San Antonio area, and they became accustomed to dividing their time between their home in the city and the Johnson City ranch, with occasional trips back to New Orleans to visit family and friends. The family was happy, and Tom Benson thrived on the wheeling and dealing required to build his automobile business.

As the Benson children grew up, the father they knew was a confident and hardworking man who had the wherewithal to give them just about anything they wanted. They attended private schools, went on frequent family vacations, and invited their school friends to spend weekends and summers at the ranch. The kids rode horses and learned about the care of thoroughbreds. They lived in nice homes and had a housekeeper who constantly looked after them. When they were old enough to drive, they had their pick of new cars.

Yet, despite his burgeoning wealth, Tom Benson and his family maintained a relatively simple lifestyle. He provided everything the family needed and plenty of what they wanted, but the Bensons did not steep themselves in luxury.

Their various homes were comfortable but not palatial, lovely but not exquisite. While they traveled abroad and visited famous places around the world, some of their favorite vacations were driving trips they took across several states with friends.

Tom Benson for years relied on his Chevy Caprice to get him from the Bensons' suburban San Antonio home to his office and out to Johnson City on weekends. The Bensons liked to dine out but seldom chose gourmet restaurants. More often, they invited friends and extended family for weekends of hunting, fishing, swimming, and barbecues at the ranch.

"We live in a very normal way," Benson once told a reporter.[26]

Still, the Bensons' life in the 1960s was a far cry from what Tom Benson had known as a child, and their various homes in Texas and Louisiana seemed light years away from the little shotgun house on North Johnson Street in New Orleans.

Back to the Big Easy

Throughout the years that Tom Benson spent building his business, the family maintained close ties to New Orleans, where both Tom and Shirley had grown up. But much of the Benson clan made a geographic shift to the west over time, as Tom brought his younger brothers, Jerome and Augustin, into the auto retailing business. Both relocated their families to San Antonio from New Orleans in the 1950s.

Eventually, Benson's parents and his youngest brother, Larry, also would end up in Texas, all living within close range of Tom's family and businesses.

While some members of the family would become permanent residents of Texas, in the 1970s Benson got a hankering to renew his business ties to New Orleans. It was a notion that in years to come would have an impact on the city that no one could have foreseen.

Benson's reach back to the Big Easy came as he sought to further expand his auto business. With eight dealerships then operating in Texas, he cast his eye on the old Mike Persia dealership at the edge of the French Quarter, where he had begun his auto career. His plan was to buy the dealership and move it to a suburban location, much as he had expanded his San Antonio business from downtown to San Pedro Avenue several years before.

He had no idea that executing the plan would lead him into an expensive, yearlong court battle with the Louisiana Motor Vehicle Commission.

The litigation, brought by the New Orleans law firm Herman & Herman, became a landmark case that cracked open the automobile retailing market not only for Benson but for other auto dealers to come.

"You learn an awful lot about somebody when you work that closely," says New Orleans lawyer Maury Herman, who with his partners fought the legal battle side by side with Benson.

Herman was impressed not only with how Benson took up a complicated fight against a state agency but also with the fact that he continued to scout new business deals as he did so.

On top of it all, the litigation coincided with one of the saddest periods of Benson's life. His wife, Shirley, was slowly succumbing to complications from lupus, a chronic inflammatory disease that can affect many parts of the body.

Even as Shirley weakened and lost her ability to walk, she was at her husband's side through his fight to expand his New Orleans business.

"Shirley came to court practically every day," Herman says.

Herman was struck by Tom Benson's devotion to his wife as he pushed her wheelchair into the courtroom each day of the trial, positioning her next to his own chair at the plaintiff's table.

"She wanted to be there and he wanted her to be there," Herman says. "He was very attentive to her."

Shirley's death several months after the trial brought an end to their thirty-six-year marriage and an event-filled journey that had taken the couple a long way from their humble beginnings.

The loss of his wife would test Tom Benson's resilience, and in time he would rebound. But it was far from the last such test he would face.

Over and over during his life, the ambitious and driven Benson would retreat into his work to comfort himself in times of pain or to shield himself from a world of awkward and difficult human relationships. Work put him at ease, and he was happy when surrounded by family and close friends who knew him well and made him the focus of their attention.

But life was tougher for Benson when his views clashed those of with loved ones or when his efforts to control their behavior or feelings toward him failed.

A person who was once close to the family lauds Benson as a self-made man who earned his wealth and deserves respect for his achievements but adds that Benson is insecure in some respects and prone to showing outright disdain for anyone who disagrees with him or is distinctly unlike him.[27]

Though Benson became a famously shrewd businessman, throughout his life he remained a plainspoken person who sometimes felt uncomfortable around people who were more articulate or socially adept. His fear of being disrespected may have planted a chip on his shoulder that helped drive his quest for wealth: if he could amass enough money, he would not have to kowtow to anyone.

"He had an inferiority complex around certain people, but by having more money, he was the powerful one," the acquaintance says of Benson. "He liked to be the biggest man in everybody's life."[28]

Power was perhaps the aspect of wealth that Benson found most appealing. While his money afforded a lifestyle he and his family could not otherwise have known, the ability to get people to do what he wanted and to make things happen by wielding money was the wealth amenity that appealed to him most.

Benson was not above bringing that power to bear on people who clashed with him.

"He could be astonishingly generous and then astonishingly hateful," the acquaintance says.[29]

The opposing aspects of Tom Benson's character would be in evidence throughout his life.

Chapter 4

Cars Paved the Way

Tom Benson could have built a career in just about any of the industries that shaped the New Orleans economy in the 1950s and '60s. Given his inherent financial savvy and training in accounting, he might have gone into the insurance business or become a chief financial officer in a maritime transportation company. His skills would have been a good fit on the financial side of the oil and gas industry, which then was poised to become the state's biggest employer and a fortune-maker for scores of Louisiana businesspeople.

But the "help wanted" ad that drew Benson's attention in 1946 was one placed by a car dealer. It's possible that the location appealed to him: the Chevrolet showroom was within walking distance of the little Florida Avenue shotgun-style house Benson had recently moved into with his wife, Shirley.

In any case, Benson landed the accounting job with Cathey Chevrolet on North Rampart Street and soon began learning the automobile business from a back-office perspective.

He could not have known that the dealership at the edge of New Orleans' French Quarter would become the launching pad for a lifelong career, but he took his first steps in that direction a few years later when a Texas auto dealer came to town.

Mike Persia, Sr., was a native of San Antonio and owner of an automobile business that he founded in that city and was running with his son, Mike Persia, Jr. The Persias were focused on growing the business from central Texas eastward into Houston, and as they laid the groundwork to become the largest Chevrolet franchise in the South, New Orleans became an expansion target. Cathey Chevrolet would be their first local acquisition.[1]

Known as hardnosed businessmen, the Persias had a reputation for pressuring their salespeople and aggressively gobbling market share.

The Persias brought their take-no-prisoners mindset to New Orleans as they set out to dominate Chevy sales in southeast Louisiana. And it didn't take them long to see that the young Tom Benson, Jr., who had stayed on in the dealership's business office after the acquisition, could be an asset.

Benson liked the Persias and their way of doing business. Like them, he had little patience for people who lacked ambition or energy or had no feel for how to make money. He was just fine with working ten-hour days and seven-day weeks. And he loved the answer Mike Persia, Sr., would give when asked whether he had any hobbies: "My hobby is making money."[2]

As the elder Persia became Benson's mentor, Mike Jr. became his best friend, and Benson soaked up their guidance. He learned the importance of building sales volume across multiple locations in order to benefit from cost-sharing in such areas as advertising, insurance, and bank credit.

It became clear to him that revenue from service and parts departments could help offset narrow margins in new and used car sales. He learned marketing and cost-control techniques and how to improve inventory management. He also learned how to drive sales staff to juice up revenue.

As the Persias built up their New Orleans-area business, adding dealerships on Canal Street, St. Claude Avenue, and Metairie Road, they leaned heavily on Benson for help in every part of the company. First they made him office manager, and later, sales manager—not based on any demonstration of slick-talking salesmanship but rather on his intuitive understanding of how to improve financial results through better management of operations.[3]

Of particular value was Benson's ability to see weak spots when reviewing monthly profit-and-loss sheets. He was adept at reading cash-flow statements and extracting critical information that could lead to a change in operations.

In Benson's mind, every action in every department should translate to improvement in the dealership's bottom line.

First Big Deals

A decade after Benson stepped into the automobile business, he got a chance to make a big leap. The Persias, who then had operations in several cities, had enlarged their San Antonio holdings by acquiring Ormsby Chevrolet, a faltering dealership in the downtown area.

Mike Persia, Sr., asked Benson to move to San Antonio to manage the dealership and told him that if he could turn the business around, Persia would finance Benson's purchase of a partial interest. It was a watershed moment.[4]

Benson and his wife, Shirley—now with two adopted children—made the move to San Antonio, where Tom dived into his new role as a dealership manager and owner.

Within just a few years, Benson not only grew sales but was able to borrow enough money to purchase the entire dealership from Persia. In 1962, the Tom Benson Chevrolet Company was born.[5]

As Benson built sales at his downtown San Antonio dealership, he began to think about other possibilities. In the early 1960s, businesses in many cities were starting to shift out of downtown areas and into suburban locations that offered more space and easier access for customers.

Benson understood the retailing shift and believed that the north side of San Antonio held promise not only for a car dealership but other types of business as well. He consulted with some real estate and banking professionals, and he commissioned a marketing study of the area to get a fix on traffic patterns and the direction of residential growth.

What Benson had in mind was to buy twenty-five acres of undeveloped land along San Pedro Avenue, in a part of town where farmers still grew crops and goats grazed on sparse vegetation. Benson believed he could plop down his auto dealership there and it would become an anchor for additional commercial and retail development that would draw homeowners to the area as well.[6]

This dream was not just about selling more cars, though that was a perennial goal. It was also about taking risks and proving that he could do big deals. He aimed to make people sit up and take notice.

At the time he started contemplating the north San Antonio land deal, Benson was selling about three hundred cars a month and living well, in a house valued at about $400,000. He had come a long way, but he believed he could do better, and he felt that veering into real-estate development would get him where he wanted to go.[7]

The deal he envisioned would be complicated, though. Not only would he have to borrow around $1 million in order to swing it, but he would have to convince several different owners who held the land that selling to him was a good idea. One owner dug in hard.

Recognizing that Benson wanted the land badly, the owner said he would only sell if Benson agreed to cover the tax on the deal and buy the owner a comparable piece of land somewhere else. Benson found and bought the man a piece of land and eventually concluded the acquisition with help from several friends.[8]

San Antonio lawyer Stanley Rosenberg, who had previously witnessed Benson's ability to juggle many moving parts of a deal, said the San Pedro Avenue land acquisition pushed his respect for Benson to a new level. Numerous times as the talks proceeded, Rosenberg believed that the deal would collapse, but Benson always found a way to keep it alive.

"It was one of the most complicated negotiations I have ever participated in," Rosenberg said, recalling the deal years later.[9]

Time would show that Benson had guessed right as to the promise of the San Pedro Avenue tract. The corridor would become one of the most high-demand commercial areas in San Antonio, sporting shopping centers, restaurants, and office buildings, anchored by six Tom Benson car dealerships.

According to Bexar County property records, the three dealerships that Benson still owns along San Pedro Avenue had an assessed value north of $45 million in 2015.

"Tom Benson always was able to watch the markets and hit it right," says Todd Gold, who owns a San Antonio commercial real-estate business and whose father was Benson's business partner for many years. "His goal was to move all the dealerships out to the [Highway] 281 area, and it was a fantastic idea. There was probably not a better tract of land in town."

Benson moved the headquarters of his San Antonio Chevrolet business to his suburban property in 1968, and in subsequent years he embraced the trend of diversifying his automobile holdings. Being able to offer more than one franchise would help protect his business in the face of market changes that might dampen sales of one type of vehicle while boosting demand for another.

Foreign imports were rapidly gaining ground across the country, and Benson brought Honda, Mazda, and Nissan franchises into his product line, while also developing a relationship with Mercedes-Benz.

He followed these affiliations with additional domestic franchises, including Jeep/Eagle, Chrysler/Plymouth, Cadillac, Oldsmobile, and Pontiac.

His goal was to become one of the biggest auto dealers in Texas, if not the entire country, and he cultivated close relationships with Detroit honchos to help pave the way. One of his most important connections was Edward Cole, then president of General Motors.

Benson credits Cole with teaching him how to put Detroit's marketing strategies to work in a local market and how to tailor his offerings to meet local demand.[10] They became close friends and entertained one another's families at their respective ranches in Michigan and Texas. In time, Cole would name Benson to a national GM advisory council.

Ten years after shifting his business to north San Antonio, where he eventually established eight dealerships, Benson found himself pulled homeward. He was itching to get a toehold in Louisiana, and he came up with an acquisition target that would bring him full circle.

The dealership on North Rampart Street in New Orleans, where he had begun his career, had seen big changes since Benson had left town. Mike Persia, Jr., had died suddenly in 1968, at the age of forty-one. At the time, the youngest of his four children, thirteen-year-old Mike Persia III, was already being seen as the likely successor to the business built by his father and grandfather.[11]

Worried about the future of the Chevrolet dealership after his son's death, Mike Persia, Sr., who had been paring down his work schedule in anticipation of retirement, stepped back in to take charge. His aim was to keep the dealership thriving and allow time for his grandson to complete his education and take over the business.

In the subsequent years, Mike Persia III, who had spent summers and weekends working in the dealership as a youngster, completed high school and went on earn a degree in automotive management at Texas Christian University and study finance at San Francisco University. He returned to New Orleans after college and rejoined the dealership. He worked with his grandfather for about two years when suddenly, personal loss struck again: in 1976, Mike Persia, Sr., passed away at the age of seventy-four.

What followed, according to Mike Persia III, who now lives in Beaumont, Texas, was a money grab that would rob him of the future his father and grandfather had envisioned for him.

Mike Persia, Sr., was survived by his much younger second wife, Mary Bradford Persia, And because he had not made specific legal provisions for his grandson to inherit the Chevrolet dealership, the bulk of the business landed in her hands, with young Mike holding a small percentage that he had inherited from his father's estate.

Following his grandfather's death, young Mike found his situation much changed. Mary Persia had taken charge, and her stepson now was merely an employee working under her command. By all appearances, she had no intention of keeping him on a future ownership track.

In fact, according to Persia, not long after her husband died, Mary began urging Mike to sell his ownership stake to her, which would have enabled her to sell the company. The young man repeatedly refused, and Mary responded by moving him into positions of lesser stature and responsibility, ultimately relegating him to selling used cars from a remote car lot. He believed that it was an effort to force him to sell his shares.

Mike Persia says that during this period, he stayed in touch with his father's best friend, Tom Benson, Jr. He phoned Benson in San Antonio regularly to let him know about the problems with Mary Persia, and he sought Benson's advice.

"He'd always say, 'Just hang in there, Mike. We'll figure something out,'" Persia recalls.

Bait and Switch

During the two decades that Benson had spent building up his business in San Antonio, one of his most trusted associates was Arnold Gold, a man two years younger than Benson who had started selling cars at Ormsby Chevrolet shortly before Mike Persia, Sr., bought that dealership and moved Benson over from New Orleans to take charge of it.

Gold and Benson became fast friends, and Gold rose quickly through the dealership ranks as Benson expanded the business. Gold eventually became general manager of Benson Chevrolet.[12]

In the late 1970s, when Benson got a hankering to expand his business back to New Orleans, he knew he wanted Gold to be a part of it. That's when he got in touch with the twenty-three-year-old Mike Persia III.

As Persia remembers it, Benson called him and said: "I've got an idea: you sell your stock back to your [step-]grandmother, and I'm going to work a deal where I will buy her out, then I'll finance the dealership back to you. I'm going to do for you exactly what your grandfather did for me in San Antonio."

Persia did as Benson suggested, finally agreeing to sell his stake to Mary Persia. But after that, the scenario did not play out as he had expected.

Though Benson did, indeed, buy the dealership from Mary Persia, he took no steps to put Mike Persia III in charge. Instead, he brought Gold in from San Antonio as a co-owner and general manager of the New Orleans dealership.

Persia was devastated.

"I trusted him to take care of me, and he didn't," he says of Benson. "He took advantage of a young guy that didn't know what was going on."

In recounting his story in 2001 to a New Orleans reporter who was writing about Benson and his car businesses, Persia said that for two weeks after the sale, he heard nothing from Benson. When Persia finally called him to ask what was up, Benson simply replied, "There's been a change in plans," and he offered to send Persia to a dealership in Texas.[13]

Persia, who as a child had often played with Benson's children during visits to the Texas ranch, and who as an adult had viewed Benson as a friend and mentor, said he felt duped.

When the reporter asked Benson to respond to Persia's comments about the deal, Benson answered: "If his grandfather wanted him to have the dealership . . . you go through a certain process to do that. If he's blaming me for something, maybe he should be thinking about how his grandfather set it up."[14]

Making Peace?

Persia says he seethed over Benson's actions for years, but gradually he has come to feel that losing his chance at the car dealership was actually a stroke of good fortune.

"At the time it happened I truly was devastated, because I didn't understand why Tom did what he did," Persia says, recalling how he felt when he left the Mike Persia Chevrolet showroom for the last time.

But he says his life took a good turn after he and his wife moved to Beaumont, and he began a new career in investment advising with UBS Financial Services, Inc.

"I've got a wonderful business, and I did it on my own, and that was a good thing," he says.

Now a grandfather, Persia says that he even sees his step-grandmother's action years ago, in forcing him into used-car sales, as a blessing in disguise. "I didn't realize until I got down to that used-car lot that I was a good salesman," he says with a laugh.

He still says that it was difficult for him to see the Mike Persia name removed from the New Orleans dealership and be replaced by Benson & Gold Chevrolet. But he bears no ill will toward Tom Benson—a fact he shared with Benson in early 2015.

Until that time, Persia says, he and Benson had not spoken since their final unpleasant exchange in 1978. Suddenly, nearly forty years later, Persia received a phone call, and Tom Benson was on the line.

Exactly what prompted Benson to track down Persia decades after they had parted company is anybody's guess. But given the turmoil in Benson's life at the time, perhaps the call was not so mysterious. Persia says it occurred around the time when conflicts between Benson and his daughter and grandchildren were erupting into public view.

"He just called and said, 'I've been thinking about you.' He said, 'I've been sitting here looking at pictures of your dad and granddad, and I'd like to see you sometime.'"

Persia says the call shook him up. "It truly got me. I was very emotional about it."

Three days later, Persia headed for New Orleans to visit Benson. He won't discuss many details of the meeting but says he feels he made his peace with the man who had once been his mentor, his grandfather's protégé, and his father's best friend. "I hugged him and told him I loved him and that I have no hard feelings for anything that happened, and then I left."

A few days later, Persia tried to speak with Benson again by phone. "I left a couple of messages, but he didn't call back," he says.

High-Court Fight

If Benson feels any regret today over those long-ago events, he showed little remorse as things unfolded at the time. Rather, he appeared focused on aggressively expanding his New Orleans-area footprint, using his success in San Antonio as a guide.

As it turned out, his plan all along had been to buy the North Rampart Street dealership and, as soon as he could also acquire the right piece of land, move the business from New Orleans to a suburban location in neighboring Jefferson Parish.

In fact, before the Benson & Gold name went up on the old Persia dealership, Benson signed a conditional franchise agreement with the Chevrolet Division of General Motors Corporation that required the relocation of the business to a site near a specific intersection about twelve miles outside of downtown New Orleans, in Kenner, Louisiana.[15]

It was no coincidence that the target area shared many of the attributes that had made Benson's land acquisition along San Pedro Avenue in north San Antonio so successful—room to grow, easy access for customers, and the potential for future ancillary commercial development in the area that would enhance the dealership's growth prospects.

"The reason Tom bought that dealership was so he could relocate it to Veterans Boulevard in Kenner," says New Orleans lawyer Maury Herman, who learned of the plan when he received an unexpected call for help not long after Benson and Gold acquired the downtown dealership.

Herman and his brothers in the New Orleans law firm of Herman & Herman had been recommended to Benson to handle a hitch that had cropped up with his planned move into Jefferson Parish.

While Benson had had no problem in obtaining a license from the Louisiana Motor Vehicle Commission to operate a dealership in New Orleans, and had signed an option to purchase a piece of property in Kenner, opposition to his suburban expansion had surfaced, and the commission had come under pressure to deny Benson's application for a new license at the Jefferson Parish site.

In January 1980, the commission formally nixed the application, concluding that "it would not be in the public interest to license a new Chevrolet dealership in such close proximity to a presently existing" Chevy dealer.[16]

The primary competing dealer was Bryan Chevrolet, Inc., which had operated for twenty years at a location on Airline Highway, less than three miles away from Benson's targeted site for his Chevy dealership.

As it happened, Bryan Chevrolet's owner, James Bryan, was a member of the Motor Vehicle Commission. And though he recused himself from the proceedings related to Benson & Gold, he opposed Benson's application in a court filing.

As the clock ticked on Benson's agreement with Chevrolet, which required that the relocation of his dealership be completed by October 31, 1980, Benson also was running up against the expiration of his lease on the downtown property where Benson & Gold operated.

"He would have been left with nowhere to move that dealership, and he had millions of dollars on the line," Herman says.

Days after the Motor Vehicle Commission denied Benson the license, his lawyers initiated an administrative proceeding against the commission. They spent weeks gathering evidence and taking depositions in order to make a second application to the commission, and when they did, the commission again refused to issue a license.

"It was obvious that the deck was stacked" against Benson, Herman says.

So the lawyers ratcheted up the pressure. They immediately filed an appeal in state court. After a three-week court battle during which Maury Herman, his brother Russ Herman, and their client Tom Benson brought their case against the Motor Vehicle Commission, the judge ruled in their favor. But still, the matter was not settled.

The commission appealed the decision to the Louisiana Supreme Court.

Benson and his lawyers fought back. Given Benson's time-sensitive circumstances, they asked the court to hear the case quickly. A few weeks later, the court ruled that the Motor Vehicle Commission had erred in refusing Benson a license to operate in Jefferson Parish.

To the chagrin of James Bryan and a few other southeast Louisiana car dealers, Tom Benson was in the suburban market to stay, and he immediately began signing deals for additional New Orleans-area dealerships.

In time Benson would amass an automobile empire that sold thirty-three brands from twenty-seven dealerships in Texas, Louisiana, and South Carolina. The franchises ran the gamut from Chevrolet to Isuzu, BMW, Jeep/Eagle, Toyota, Volkswagen, Nissan, Honda, Mercedes-Benz/Land Rover, Acura, Dodge, Lincoln/Mercury, and Mitsubishi, among others.

At its peak, the Benson auto business sold more than 25,000 new and used vehicles a year and had gross revenue of about $600 million.[17]

In the late 1990s, after divesting much of his auto business in order to focus on his football team, Benson owned a core of just five dealerships—three offering Mercedes-Benz, Chevrolet, and Honda in San Antonio and two in New Orleans, selling Mercedes-Benz and Chevrolet.[18]

Maury Herman says the wheels of business never stop turning for Tom Benson. If anything, the more he is challenged, the harder he is likely to fight.

Herman and Benson became close friends through their battle with the Louisiana Motor Vehicle Commission, and they developed a long-term professional and personal relationship. Herman says that Benson's fight with the commission was not only an important victory for the car dealer but also helped the Herman law firm gain stature and respect in the New Orleans business community.

"If Tom Benson has a goal in mind, he doesn't want to hear much about the complexities," Herman states. "He just says, 'I know this can be done,' and you begin to believe that you can do it. That meant a lot to this firm."

During the next decade, the law firm would handle many legal matters for Benson and his businesses, and the Hermans would remain close to him.

"I enjoyed those years very much, although it was a tremendous strain on the firm," Maury Herman says with a laugh. "When Tom Benson wants you to get something done, he insists that you drop everything, so you do it."

Though both Maury and Russ Herman say they are grateful for the opportunities that Benson brought to their door years ago, a day would come when they—like some others who came to know and trust Tom Benson—would decide to cut their ties with the businessman and leave both their personal and professional relationships with him in the past.

Chapter 5

Bankshot

Many people who have done business with Tom Benson note his ability to multitask at a high level. Throughout his life, each time he reached an important business benchmark, it seemed he was also managing one or more crises or big transactions in another area. In the late 1970s, he arrived at one such convergence.

Benson decided it was a good time to make his debut in an entirely different business line in Texas. In late 1977, he filed an application with the Texas Banking Commission to acquire control of San Pedro State Bank, a small San Antonio institution whose bread and butter was small-business and mortgage lending in the region.[1] Benson, at age fifty, instinctively felt that the banking business would be a good fit for him, as making money in banking essentially required being able to scout good business prospects and design financings that minimized risk—areas in which Benson had proven his skills.

The Texas banking commissioner approved his application in 1978, and Benson became the owner of San Pedro State Bank. Four years later, even as his automobile business was taking off in New Orleans, he teamed with other local business leaders to buy Groos National Bank, one of the oldest financial institutions in San Antonio.[2] It was through that transaction that he met a man who would become one of his most trusted business associates.

Tom Roddy hit it off with Benson initially because both were Louisiana natives. Roddy's roots were in Houma, Louisiana, an hour south of New Orleans, though he had grown up largely around Austin, Texas.

Roddy, who had worked in his dad's seafood market as a

teenager, did not enter the banking business until he was married and in his twenties. In 1974, he added a graduate certificate in banking from Southern Methodist University to his undergraduate business degree, and after stints at two other local banks, he signed on at Groos National Bank in the same year that Benson bought the company.[3]

Benson named Roddy president and CEO of Groos Bank, and the two went on to collaborate on an expansion in which Benson acquired three more institutions: Kelly Field National Bank, Commercial Bank, and Exchange National Bank.[4]

For someone who understands the basic needs of growing businesses and has good judgment when it comes to evaluating the reliability of borrowers, the community banking business, at least in the early 1980s, was pretty straightforward: keep your institution well capitalized and your loan portfolio diversified among different types of business clients, and you would likely make good money in a decent economy.

But the late 1980s brought challenges for bankers in many states and, more particularly, in areas vulnerable to volatility in the oil and gas industry.

As plunging oil prices battered the Texas energy industry, problems stacked up in real-estate lending as well. Loans and mortgages, even to high-quality borrowers, began to go south. Turmoil descended on the savings and loan industry, which focused on mortgage lending, and the conditions soon spread to commercial banks such as those Benson owned.

Roddy and Benson adapted by consolidating their holdings and cutting costs. They folded several of the smaller institutions into either Kelly Field National or Groos Bank and reduced expenses by sharing certain functions across the institutions.

"So many banks failed, and we had major problems, but we worked our way out of those problems," Roddy recalled in a 2003 interview.[5]

Later, they placed both banks under the umbrella of Benson Financial Corporation, creating a holding company with about $450 million in assets, and in 1994 they took Benson Financial public through a stock offering that raised $17 million from investors.[6]

While the capital infusion enabled more growth and helped

the company reduce its problem loans, regulatory and market pressures on smaller banks remained stiff, and two years after the public offering Benson decided he'd had enough of the competitive struggle. "We had to withdraw from banking, otherwise the [pressures] may have put us out of business," he said later.[7]

He sold Benson Financial in 1996 to Minneapolis-based Norwest Banks in a stock deal valued at $76 million. The Benson family, who held 40 percent of Benson Financial, took $30 million worth of stock away from the deal.[8] Norwest would later merge with Wells Fargo, and the Texas institutions would take the Wells Fargo name.

Bad Bet

Years before Benson exited the banking business in Texas, he got a yen to add a bank to his Louisiana business portfolio as well. In 1984, a year when he added four banks to the two he already owned in Texas, he signed an agreement to acquire Pontchartrain State Bank, an unprofitable $40 million-asset bank located in suburban New Orleans.

In June 1985, less than three weeks after announcing that he had completed the purchase of the New Orleans Saints, Benson made his debut in the New Orleans banking market. He purchased Pontchartrain State Bank with help from some of the same investors who had signed on as limited partners in the Saints deal, including Benson's brother Jerome Benson; his cousin Bob Benson; lawyer Maury Herman; businessman Bernard Frischertz; and local physician Nathan Goldstein.[9]

Benson at the time vowed to restore the little bank to profitability and grow it into a $100 million institution. But in fact the Louisiana banking market was headed toward the same economic downturn that was affecting Texas.

Fred Lay signed on as executive vice president and senior lender with Benson's new acquisition. "Tom had bought the bank and capitalized it well, and it was doing very well," he recalls. "It had just about doubled in size during the first couple of years and was making money."

But then Benson made an error. He tried to grow the bank by buying the assets of other institutions that were failing, and he paid too much for them.

Federal banking regulators at the time, along with the deposit insurers who guaranteed the security of up to $100,000 deposited in every federally insured account, were clamoring for help from bankers who would take over failing institutions and ease the pressure on the federal insurance fund. Many previously healthy banks around the country answered the call, and some of the owners soon regretted doing so, as they found that the bad loans and foreclosed real estate they took on with those acquisitions would be nearly impossible to dispose of through the prolonged economic downturn.

Benson in 1988 put in a bid on three failed banks in the New Orleans area that fell into the category of "dirty banks"—the industry's term for institutions that were riddled with bad loans and real estate for which it would be difficult to find buyers. Banking regulators typically offered dirty banks for sale at a discount in order to entice buyers to take on the bad assets.

But Lay says the discount the Federal Deposit Insurance Corporation (FDIC) gave Benson on the purchases was not deep enough to offset the costs of resolving the banks' trouble. "There just wasn't enough money there to cover all the problems that existed."

Pontchartrain Bank could not digest the failed institutions it had gobbled.

Hoping for a remedy, Benson tried to plead his case with the Comptroller of the Currency. He made a rescue proposal that included injecting $7 million of his own money on top of the $15 million he and the other investors had previously put into the bank, and he requested additional help from the FDIC. But the regulators gave him a thumbs down.

Benson watched Pontchartrain Bank rack up three years of losses before regulatory officials arrived at the bank one morning in July 1991. They closed the bank, took over most of its "bad" assets, and sold the healthier portion of the bank's portfolio to First National Bank of Commerce in New Orleans, providing First NBC with a $100 million cash subsidy to take over Pontchartrain's deposit accounts.[10]

Benson released a statement that was tinged with bitterness. "Our plan represented a much less costly solution to the government and taxpayers than the alternative to which the FDIC has agreed," it said.[11]

He blamed the bank's problems in part on 1986 changes in federal tax law.

"Pontchartrain State Bank has approximately 130 parcels of real estate to sell because of the negative impact on investment caused by the Tax Reform Act," his release said.[12]

Down, Not Out

His 1991 bank failure in New Orleans may have helped push Benson toward his decision to sell Benson Financial Corporation to Norwest in 1996, but the experience wasn't enough to kill his taste for banking. As the Texas economy improved, he began to see opportunity in financial services once again.

After a seven-year hiatus, Benson, then seventy-six, returned to the game, purchasing a small bank in San Antonio that had fallen on hard times. He bolstered the institution, Clear Lake National Bank, with a $1.5 million capital injection and installed his old friend Tom Roddy as chairman.

"I think San Antonio has a need for a bank with local ownership," Benson said, promising that Clear Lake would grow.[13]

Benson's motivation to return to banking may have arisen from a need to redeploy the proceeds from the spinoff of some of his other businesses.

In the mid-1990s, he had publicly announced his intention to sell most of his car dealerships in order to focus more closely on his ownership of the New Orleans Saints. By the end of the decade, he had scaled his auto holdings back to just five dealerships in New Orleans and San Antonio.

Benson sold the businesses to various parties, including his brother Jerome Benson, with help from Roddy, who had left the banking business after the sale of Benson Financial and signed on with Benson as president of Benson Motors Company. Roddy managed the car business from San Antonio, while Jerome Benson headed up the New Orleans operations.

Once they had downsized Tom Benson's auto holdings, they searched for other places to put his money while also looking to involve members of Benson's family more closely in his businesses.

With the patriarch in his seventies, his succession planning was becoming more focused.

Roddy, who had briefly been a member of Houston-based Clear Lake National Bank's board a few years earlier,[14] put the institution in Benson's sights as an acquisition target. Once they completed the deal, they moved directly on to their next purchase, Mission National Bank.

In June 2003, Benson merged both banks into a single, new entity, Lone Star Capital Bank. He populated his new board of directors with a tight circle of family and friends that included, along with Roddy, Benson's longtime lawyer, Stanley Rosenberg, and his daughter Renee Benson, who lived on the Benson ranch outside of Johnson City.

Three years later he would add his grandchildren, Rita Benson LeBlanc and Ryan LeBlanc, who were still in their twenties, to the board.

Benson in 2012 expanded Lone Star Capital Bank outside of San Antonio and into the Texas Hill Country by acquiring Cattleman's National Bank in Johnson City. By 2015, Lone Star had $230 million in assets and operated eight branches around central Texas.[15]

While the bank seemed a promising place for Benson to invest his money and a good vehicle for passing part of his fortune on to his family, it would become one of many assets at the core of an escalating fight with his relatives in years to come. In 2015, his control of the institution would come under assault when he sought to remove his daughter and two of his grandchildren from all of his businesses.

Chapter 6

Call to Sports

It came as a surprise to some that a man who had previously shown little interest in professional sports and had built his wealth in the automobile and banking businesses suddenly was setting his sights on a National Football League franchise. But insiders say that once Tom Benson raised the money to buy the New Orleans Saints, he became intensely focused on doing the deal and relied heavily on Louisiana's most famous politician to make it happen.

Edwin Edwards, the charismatic Cajun from Marksville, Louisiana, who became a U.S. congressman and served four terms as governor, eventually would also serve eight years in a federal prison on racketeering charges stemming from the 1990s startup of casino gambling in the state. But in 1984, during his third term in the governor's mansion, Edwards was still in his political prime and capable of wielding a deft hand in the legislature. He hadn't yet met Benson when the Saints went up for sale, but the two would soon become close allies.

Louisiana at the time was awash in red ink, thanks to a severe downturn in the market for the state's most important commodity—oil. When a supply glut sent the price of oil plunging more than 60 percent in a single year, the energy industry sank into a deep recession that dragged everything else down as well. Bankruptcies became the stuff of daily news as businesses around the state struggled to stay alive.

In New Orleans' Central Business District, which housed thousands of energy industry employees, the office towers that lined Poydras Street began to echo with empty space as Big Oil slashed payrolls.

Meanwhile, at the upper end of Poydras, it appeared the Louisiana Superdome might also soon sport a "vacancy" sign. The future of the New Orleans Saints had gone cloudy during the previous year when word got out that the team's owner, Houston oilman John W. Mecom, Jr., had an itch to sell.

Mecom, whose father had made a fortune in the oil patch, was just twenty-seven years old in 1966 when he paid a $7.5 million league expansion fee to launch the New Orleans Saints. NFL Commissioner Pete Rozelle had announced the birth of the franchise in a news conference at the Pontchartrain Hotel, not far from the Tulane University campus where the Saints would play their first season.[1] It was a big day for the city.

Local residents were excited to think that a day might come when New Orleans could boast a winning NFL team. More than eighty thousand fans were on hand at Tulane Stadium when the team took the field for its first regular-season game.[2]

The Saints lost that match to the Los Angeles Rams and went on to post a 3-11 record for the season, but the fans shook off the losses. It was hardly unusual, after all, for a new franchise to get off to a rocky start.

Besides, fans could now look forward to the day when they could watch their team play in one of the country's biggest domed stadiums. The legislature in 1966 had approved a measure that would help fund construction of the Louisiana Superdome. Construction began several years later along upper Poydras Street.

In 1975, the completed Superdome opened its doors to cheering crowds, but the fans soon realized that the Dome wasn't the cure for the team's continuing mediocre performance. The Saints lost their first game in the new stadium to the Cincinnati Bengals, 21-0.[3]

It was beginning to look as though the team would struggle indefinitely. During its first decade, Mecom burned through a string of head coaches, and the Saints won only a handful of games.

Even the talents of a popular young quarterback named Archie

Manning couldn't turn the tide. Manning set passing records and became a two-time Pro-Bowler during his eleven-year stint with the Saints, but the team still languished.

Mecom continued to shuffle the deck in search of answers. He brought in former Kansas City Chiefs head coach Hank Stram, then dumped him two losing seasons later. Stram's successor, Dick Nolan, met the same fate at the end of his third season—a pitiful affair during which the Saints went 1-15.

By 1980, those bitterly frustrated Saints fans who continued to show up at games took to covering their heads with brown paper bags labeled with the word *Aints*. The "bag heads" became a favorite with game-day photographers, who helped ensure that memories of this sad chapter in the team's history would endure.

New Game Plan

Increasingly desperate to put the era of the Aints behind him, Mecom scouted for yet another new coach and found one in Texas. The beefy, Stetson-wearing O. A. "Bum" Phillips had won praise for rebuilding the downtrodden Houston Oilers in the mid-1970s, and he had put the team on a hot streak. Perhaps he could do the same for the Saints.

The Saints did show improvement on Phillips' watch but still couldn't pull out a winning season, and by mid-1984 Mecom decided he'd had enough. He put out the word that he would entertain purchase offers for the team.

Among several parties that came courting, the A. N. Pritzker family of Chicago, who owned the company that operated the Superdome and nearby Hyatt Hotel, seemed the most serious.[4] The Pritzkers mounted a bid that reportedly neared Mecom's $75 million asking price. But the deal would have required the state to kick in millions in cash, and even Louisiana's top politician couldn't sell lawmakers on it.

Edwards—now living near Baton Rouge with his third wife, a son, and a new career in real estate—still vividly recalls those days in early 1985 when the Saints' future stood on a foundation of shifting sands. The key problem, as he remembers it, was that neither the Pritzker family nor any other bidder was willing to assure lawmakers that the Saints would stay put.

"I was dealing with three or four different prospects but never was able to put anything together because none of them wanted to commit to keep the team in New Orleans," Edwards says. "I was reluctant to sign off on an agreement that did not have that kind of commitment."

Scrambling to find a prospect who was wealthy enough to do a deal and also solidly rooted in Louisiana, Edwards sought advice from a close friend and political ally, Jefferson Parish Sheriff Harry Lee. It was the locally famous lawman who suggested a possible buyer: a successful automobile dealership owner named Benson.

"Harry said Tom Benson might be interested, so I called him, and he was interested, but he said he didn't know whether he could raise the money or just how much it would cost," Edwards recalls.

Edwards offered to do some preliminary legwork. He went to Mecom, who also was a friend of the governor, and got Mecom to provide "a bottom-line" price he would be willing to accept.

The governor passed the word back to Benson, who immediately began tapping relatives and business associates to help him raise the money. One of the first calls Benson made was to New Orleans lawyer Russ Herman.

Benson was well acquainted with the firm of Herman & Herman, whose attorneys had represented him and his dealerships in big cases. Now the firm would also take the legal reins in his bid to buy the Saints.

"Tom Benson called and said, 'Look, fellas, I've arranged this deal, and I'd like you to raise $25 million in the next forty-eight hours,'" Russ Herman remembers.

At first, the lawyers were incredulous. "What?" Herman recalls sputtering into the phone.

But he and his brothers, Maury and Fred Herman, and their partner, Morton Katz, shed their shock and soon decided to throw their own hats in as investors. Then they made a list of clients and friends they believed also might want a piece of the action.

"The calls would go like this," Herman says. "'Mr. Benson is going to own this franchise. . . . Have you ever wanted to own part of an NFL team?'"

The lawyers warned each prospect that key details were fuzzy. No one was sure what the team was worth, for instance. And the tax implications, if any, of buying into the team were unknown. But the investors didn't seem to care.

"Everybody we contacted wanted to be a part owner," Herman says. "In less than twenty-four hours, we were oversubscribed."

Herman says no one on the list raised questions typical of a normal business deal. Discussions of risks, downsides, timetables for recouping the investment—none of it ever came up.

"This wasn't the type of thing where you weighed upsides and downsides," he says. "All the people we talked with were good businesspeople, but nobody we talked to spent a lot of time analyzing the economics—except Tom Benson."

Herman, who no longer has a business relationship with Benson, says he thinks Benson had been eyeing the Saints for as much as a year before he started pursuing the team in earnest. He says that Benson accurately predicted that neither the Pritzkers nor any other active bidder would be able to conclude a deal.

"He reads tea leaves better than anyone I've come in contact with in fifty years of trial practice," Herman says of Benson. "He has an unusual quality that allows him to see around the corner. He knows what can happen and he prepares in advance to deal with it."

Herman believes that Benson simply bided his time, waiting for Mecom to realize that he would never get a deal without legislative help and that lawmakers would not support any deal that failed to keep the Saints in Louisiana. By the time that fact dawned on Mecom, Benson was ready to jump in.

His brothers, Jerome and Larry Benson, had already signed on as investors. With the help of the Herman brothers and others, he lined up additional players, including personal injury lawyer Wendell Gauthier; dental practices owner Peter Glaser; United Distributors, Inc. president Paul Rosenblum; owners of contracting firm Frischhertz Electric Company; and Joe Yaeger, president of construction services firm the MCC Group.

Benson's close advisor, San Antonio lawyer Stanley Rosenberg, also anteed up, while wealthy Houston entrepreneur Fred Schneider bought in for 10 percent, as did San Antonio businesswoman Elizabeth "Libba" Barnes and her parents.

With commitments from more than two dozen investors, Benson turned back to Edwards. The deal Benson had proposed would require support from the state that hadn't materialized for other bidders.

Benson had made his purchase offer contingent on the state agreeing to build additional suites in the Louisiana Superdome, upgrade existing seats, and grant to Benson the right to all suite and game-day concessions revenue. In addition, he demanded a forty-year lease on the Dome.

The governor would need to work some magic. As Edwards notes, few lawmakers in the 1980s were as enamored with the Saints as many would become decades later. Not only did the team have a "dismal" record on the field, he says, but "at the time there was great controversy as to whether the state should make concessions and whether it was worth keeping the Saints."

The economic ripple effect of having 50,000 or more people coming to New Orleans on game days was clear in tax revenues that the state realized from hotels, restaurants, and other visitor services, Edwards told them.

In addition, he pitched to lawmakers the value of the team to the state's image.

"The prestige of owning a team was very important," he says. "I remember that Oakland made a $300 million concession to get a team moved from Los Angeles, and cities that didn't have teams were offering all kinds of incentives to prospective owners to move teams."

Selling the idea to legislators who represented areas outside of New Orleans was tough. Lawmakers from conservative jurisdictions in North Louisiana, in particular, had long frowned on laidback New Orleans as a hub of decadence that consumed more than its share of state support.

But in working the halls and backrooms of the state capitol, the governor turned up the heat. Trading favors here and promises there, he soon felt he was close to sealing the deal.

Edwards would need to line up just a few more supporters before the bill came to a vote on the House floor. During an informal meeting in the Speaker's office, four representatives told the governor that if Benson would remove one relatively inconsequential provision from his proposal, they would back it. Edwards believed that Benson would agree.

"So I went to him and I said, 'Tom, I think you're going to have to give up on this particular issue,'" Edwards recalls. "Well, he looked me straight in the face and said, 'No. Either I get the team with these concessions or I give it up.'"

Benson told the governor that he had dealt with politicians often enough to know that "if I concede on this, they'll want me to concede on something else." Then he gave Edwards his marching orders: "You go in there and tell them that Tom Benson is on the ten-yard line, and either they vote for it or I'm gonna walk."

Edwards says he was taken aback, but when he returned to the lawmakers, he repeated Benson's football metaphor. "We're either gonna make a goal here, or we're going to give up the team," he told them. The threat won him five more votes.

In the end, under intense lobbying by Edwards, the Louisiana Senate approved the Superdome lease and other provisions by a one-vote margin. The measure also squeaked by in the House, which barely provided the two-thirds majority needed for passage. Benson had a deal.

Attorney Russ Herman says the agreement could not have happened without Edwards' touch in the legislature, but he adds: "It was Tom's deal from beginning to end."

Herman also says the Saints bill landed on the governor's desk not a moment too soon. Minutes after Edwards signed it, the Benson group was served with an injunction issued by a judge in Missouri. A group that wanted to move the Saints to St. Louis, which appeared close to losing the Cardinals to another city, wanted to halt Benson's purchase and start new negotiations with Mecom.

But the injunction was moot because Benson's deal had legally concluded fifteen minutes earlier, Herman says. The St. Louis group did not raise a challenge.

Mecom, who initially had said he wouldn't sell the team for a penny less than $75 million, ultimately agreed to a deal valued at $72 million in cash, debt, and assumed liabilities.

It was a big premium over his original investment. But the sum was well below the reported $83 million price that H. R. "Bum"

Bright had paid for the much more successful Dallas Cowboys in 1984.⁵

Meanwhile, Tom Benson, then fifty-seven, came away with all the concessions he had sought from the state and a 31 percent interest in the Saints. At a news conference called in New Orleans to announce the sale, Benson and Edwards stood side by side in a room crowded with Benson's family members, fellow investors, and friends.

"Knowing Tom Benson, I know he'll bring about the next great miracle in the life of this city—a winning season," Edwards said, according to a news report that also noted the Saints had never managed better than a break-even season in eighteen years.⁶

For his part, Benson took note of Louisiana's contributions to the deal, including a long-term lease at the Superdome, a donation of state land for a training facility, and exemption from state taxes for Dome events. "We just want what other major-league cities are doing for their teams," he said.⁷

Benson went on to announce that to help pay for the deal, ticket prices at the Dome would rise immediately. Then he added that the Saints almost certainly would have left New Orleans had his deal not won approval, because interests in Jacksonville, Phoenix, Baltimore, and Oakland were ready to pounce if it had fallen through.

Nonstop Partying

For Benson's extended family, his purchase of the Saints was a huge thrill. He had been married to his second wife, Grace, for only a few years when he began putting the investor group together. Now, he and Grace were the "first couple" of professional sports in New Orleans.

Celebrations rippled through branches of the Benson family from New Orleans to San Antonio.

"It was pure euphoria," says Marillyn Barbot, the sister of Grace Benson, who died in 2002. Barbot recalls the period as one of nonstop celebration. "It was one party after another. There were parties to celebrate and then parties to calm down," she says with a laugh. The men in the family, in particular, were in "hog heaven," Barbot says.

Naturally, the family looked forward to game days and especially to home games. Benson was generous with tickets for the family, though spaces in the owner's suite tended to be taken up by the many individuals who had invested in the team.

The squeeze in the suite would ease up about eight years later, after Benson bought out his minority partners to become the sole owner of the Saints.

Several months after completing his original purchase of the team, Benson reflected on some of the factors that influenced his decision to buy it, in an interview with the *San Francisco Chronicle*. He pointed out that he had substantial business interests in New Orleans and Louisiana. "I just thought that if the Saints left New Orleans, it would be a disaster," he told the reporter.[8]

The irony of his statement would surface more than once in years to come.

Chapter 7

Investors Cry Foul

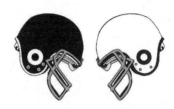

When he decided he wanted to own the New Orleans Saints, Tom Benson tapped a lot of people for help in doing the deal. Close to three dozen individuals in 1985 committed amounts ranging from a few hundred thousand dollars to more than $6 million to acquire interests in the New Orleans Louisiana Saints Limited Partnership, a business organized in Texas.[1] The partner agreements stipulated that Benson would hold a controlling stake in the business.

Because of NFL policy regarding the number of individuals who could be involved in team ownership, Saints investors who individually committed to buying interests of less than 3 percent were made part of larger groups that collectively took interests ranging from 5 to 10 percent.

Benson Football, Inc., also a Texas business entity, was the sole general partner of the Saints limited partnership. Tom Benson, as president, CEO, and majority shareholder of Benson Football, controlled the team.[2]

Villanova University sociology professor Rick Eckstein says Benson's purchase of the Saints through such a large investor consortium was an "old-school" approach that is virtually unheard of in contemporary major league sports. An expert in the area of professional sports and stadium financing, Eckstein notes that with team values soaring during the past few decades and purchases subject to the approval of a league and its owners, an investment group such as the one Benson amassed in 1985 likely would not get a nod in a time when the league places heavy emphasis on stability and longevity in team ownership.

"A Tom Benson-type buyer today probably wouldn't be allowed to buy a franchise because other owners might see it as too much of a risk," Eckstein says. "Benson got in when he could get in. You've got to be in a different class now to buy a sports franchise."

The reality, of course, is that thanks to the appreciating value of his team, Benson long ago graduated into "a different class." In fact, whereas he told his original investors in 1985 that he needed them because he was financially unable to buy the team on his own, just seven years later he was prepared to raise his ownership stake to 100 percent.

Disposable Partners?

In July 1992, Benson sent copies of a letter to all of his minority limited partners offering to purchase their interests in the Saints. His letter did not clearly state his reasons for wanting to raise his stake but made vague references to "the NFL's continuing problems with their players" and to tax law changes that made it "apparent to most sport franchises that it is best if they are wholly owned by one person."[3]

His letter said that the team, which the group had purchased for $72 million in 1985, had appreciated to a gross value of $92 million, based on an analysis he commissioned.[4]

During that seven-year period, Benson bought out a small number of investors who indicated they were ready to cash out, thus raising his own stake in the team to 51 percent.

Negotiations with the remaining investors began in August, with Benson insisting that unless he could get agreements to buy out all of the partners, he would not buy any of their interests.

Pressed along the way for more specific reasons for making the offer, Benson told investors, according to court documents, that he needed to own 100 percent of the team in order to have the freedom to do such things as "paying my wife a salary."[5]

Documents show that he also acknowledged he wished to be rid of obligations to open the team's records to his partners and to free himself from arranging perks such as game tickets, suite seats, and rides to away games on the team plane, as stipulated in the investors' original partnership agreements.[6]

One of Benson's former partners in the Saints says that it

became clear that dealing with his limited partners had gotten under Benson's skin during the early years of their co-ownership. "I don't think he really liked to have meetings with the minority partners," says Elizabeth "Libba" Barnes, a San Antonio businesswoman who, with her parents, bought a 10 percent stake in the Saints in 1985.

Barnes had become acquainted with Benson after his lawyer, Stanley Rosenberg, suggested her as a board member for the Texas-based Groos Bank, which Benson had purchased in 1982. Barnes was a director of the bank until Benson folded it into the holding company that he eventually sold to Norwest Banks.

Early in 1985, Benson phoned Barnes and said he wanted to gauge her interest in his latest business plan.

"He said, 'Let's buy us a football team,'" she recalls.

Barnes' father, Chalmer McClelland, Jr., was a military man who had built a successful second career in trucking, launching a small line of refrigerated carriers that he turned into one of the largest such businesses in the Southwest. He was also involved in ranching and banking in the San Antonio area.

When Benson called Barnes about the Saints proposal, he suggested she bring her parents in. "Get your family together and see if they would be interested in doing it," he told her.

Barnes says she and her parents were excited about the prospect. After discussions with their lawyers and Benson, the McClellands and Barnes together committed to buying a 10 percent interest in the Saints.

The only single limited partner to hold an interest of that size was Fred Schneider, owner of several Houston automobile dealerships, who also bought 10 percent.[7] Schneider passed away in 2006.

Barnes says she and her parents loved being a part of the Saints and making trips to New Orleans for every home game, which they enjoyed from the owners' suite in the Superdome. Their ownership also entitled Barnes to one flight per year on the team plane to an away game.

"I was the only woman on the plane, and it was really fun. Even in the days when people were wearing sacks over their heads, it was fun," Barnes says.

But Barnes and her family developed concerns about their investment. For one thing, they heard through the grapevine that Benson had taken certain actions without consulting them.

"He borrowed $5 million from the team and none of us knew it," Barnes says.

In addition, word leaked out that Benson was making plans to put one or more of his family members on the Saints executive committee.

The potential for the Saints to fall into the hands of Benson family members should something happen to him was a point of concern among the limited partners before they signed the original purchase deal. According to a court document filed later, "the investors required assurance that a Benson family member would not automatically assume control of the Saints" if Tom Benson should become unable to continue to manage the team as president.[8]

To address their concern, Benson signed a management succession agreement stipulating that if he should die or become incapacitated, the investors would be well represented in "a bona fide effort" to sell the team on advantageous terms.[9]

But some investors later would accuse Benson of arbitrarily attempting to change the succession agreement "so that he could unilaterally select his successor," court documents show.[10]

Barnes says investors learned about the attempt through a memo that was inadvertently sent to investor Fred Schneider. She says that when her dad got wind of the information, he became concerned that Benson was not communicating adequately with the limited partners. "We didn't know what was going on," she says.

In addition to Benson's purported attempts to change the succession agreement, she says: "We didn't have any idea how much those TV contracts and everything else was worth, and we wouldn't see a financial statement."

Her father requested meetings with Benson and was ignored, Barnes says. "It really angered me that he [Benson] didn't have the courtesy to answer my father, but what could we do?" she says, noting that by this point Benson had raised his own stake to 51 percent of the team.

Barnes' father—by this time in ill health and using a wheelchair but still attending every Saints home game—became increasingly worried about the partnership. So when Benson's offer of a buyout came along, though the family had hoped to continue being owners, they thought it safer to accept the terms.

"We decided, if this man's going to do this, we'd better just cut and run," Barnes says. "We all made money on it, though we didn't make anything close to what it's valued at today, of course."

Barnes says that Benson showed signs early on that he didn't wish to be involved with the people who had helped him buy the team. Not long after acquiring the Saints, he moved out of what had been the owners' suite in the Superdome and established his own suite on the opposite side of the field—a long walk away. Barnes says that made it more difficult to stroll over and have a discussion with him on game days.

"It didn't bother me because I was young, and I could walk, but my parents didn't like it," Barnes recalls. "Tom wasn't an easy partner."

Investors Dig In

Of several clusters of investors who participated in the purchase of the Saints, the largest was a nine-member group based in New Orleans and organized by the Herman, Herman & Katz law firm. Maury Herman, his brother Russ Herman, and their law partner, Morton Katz, each bought small interests in the team. Collectively, their group owned 10 percent of the Saints.

When Benson decided to buy out his limited partners in 1992, he asked the Hermans to manage the legal arrangements. They agreed, knowing that they, too, would no longer own a piece of the Saints once a buyout was concluded.

But not all the partners were easily persuaded to part with their fractional piece of the NFL. Two sub-partners from the Herman group, Peter Glaser and Wendell Gauthier, though they owned less than 3 percent of the team between them, had no intention of forking over their interests to Benson.

Gauthier, a high-profile personal injury lawyer in New Orleans, was well known for representing plaintiffs in some of the biggest class-action lawsuits of the 1970s and '80s, winning large judgments for victims in the crash of a Pan American World Airways plane near New Orleans and hotel fires at the MGM Grand Hotel in Las Vegas and the Dupont Plaza in San Juan, Puerto Rico. Before his death in 2001, Gauthier would also prevail in a massive liability case against U.S. tobacco companies. In 1985 he used a chunk of his proceeds from such cases to buy a 1 percent interest in the New Orleans Saints.[11]

Glaser, meanwhile, was a dentist and owner of dental practices associated with Touro Infirmary in New Orleans. When his longtime friends, the Herman brothers, invited him to join the Saints ownership group, he bought a 1.7 percent interest.[12]

Both Glaser and Gauthier, and their families, for several years enjoyed the benefits of Saints ownership, including ticket and suite privileges in proportion to their percentage stake. When the letter came from Tom Benson in 1992 explaining his intention to buy out all his limited partners, both men took offense.

"Did I want to stay in? Yes. But everybody was forced out," Glaser says. "He [Benson] made it very difficult for people."

Glaser and Gauthier reiterated their intention to hold on to their stakes, but even as a battle of letters ensued, Benson proceeded to sign buyout agreements with other partners. Finally, Glaser and Gauthier sued Benson for damages in federal court in San Antonio, where Benson Football was incorporated. They would also subsequently file a related suit in both state and federal court in New Orleans.

The case dragged on for many months until a Texas judge forced the parties into mediation. They settled the matter shortly before it was slated to go to trial, later also settling the New Orleans case.

A confidentiality agreement signed by the parties prevents them from discussing the outcome. But records of the proceedings leading up to mediation show that Gauthier and Glaser took issue with what they considered underhanded tactics on Benson's part not only to remove them from Saints ownership but to ensure that they would never hold a stake in the team.[13]

Glaser and Gauthier did not necessarily object to the buyout terms that Benson had offered; they simply did not want to sell. Benson's insistence that he would not purchase the stakes of any limited partners unless all of them agreed to sell made it harder for the two to hold out, because their stance interfered with the wishes of others who wanted to shed their shares. Still, when Benson tried to get their case dropped, the two fought back.

Court records show that as an end-of-year deadline approached for Benson to complete the buyout in 1992, and as Glaser and Gauthier remained recalcitrant, he came up with a new proposal. If they would agree to divest their interests in the Saints, he would grant them an option to buy back into the team after an eighteen-month waiting period, a term that he said was necessary to establish a more favorable tax status for the organization under a single owner.[14]

The investors accepted his proposal and sold their stake to Benson—at a premium that reflected a $20 million appreciation in the team's value—after signing an option agreement that specified the terms of their deal to buy back in later.

But in June 1994, when they attempted to exercise the option Benson had offered, they discovered that he had made changes in the organization that dramatically altered the picture. According to court records, after buying out his limited partners, Benson had reorganized the Saints business and "transferred substantially all of the income-producing assets of the Saints" to a new corporation known as Benz-Saints, which Benson owned and controlled.[15] The transfer moved millions of dollars of income received by the Saints under the team's Superdome lease, including ticket, suite, club, parking, and concessions revenues, to the new entity and left the original Saints organization with almost no assets.

When the former investors learned of the change and told Benson they wanted to buy into the new organization rather than the devalued old one, he refused, they said.

In court filings, they charged that he "intentionally and with full knowledge of the consequences reorganized the structure of the Saints in order to substantially lower the value of the partnership interest" that he had agreed to sell back to them. They said Benson's actions constituted malice and fraud.[16]

As part of their filings, Glaser and Gauthier presented an independent accountant's analysis of Saints revenue to prove their case. It showed that while the Saints organization realized annual net income of more than $7 million during the years before Benson bought out his investors, the business plunged to a $400,000 loss in 1994. For the same period, the new Benz-Saints organization showed profits of $5.5 million and $7.7 million in 1994 and 1995, respectively.

"Benz-Saints is a shell which exists solely to capture and transfer to Benson revenue which otherwise would be paid to the Saints," the accountant stated in his analysis. He said that money received by Benz-Saints was "paid to or on behalf of Benson as management fees or to repay" a personal loan from Citicorp.[17]

In court filings, Glaser and Gauthier suggested that even before Benson had signed buyout agreements calling for him to make an upfront cash payment to the minority partners and installments over five years, he became dissatisfied with the restrictions the notes imposed on him. His lawyer acknowledged that Benson began negotiating with Citicorp for financing to prepay the promissory notes so that he could quickly own the team outright.

Benson borrowed $25 million from Citicorp in the spring of 1993, court records show, and shortly thereafter he prepaid his debt to all of the minority partners. His lawyer, Stanley Rosenberg, cited Citicorp's requirement that Benson be the "sole owner" of the Saints in order to secure the loan as the reason for insisting that all the limited partners had to sell him their interests.

While Benson's offer took some of his partners by surprise, he claimed in a 1996 deposition that he made it only after some of the limited partners had said they wanted to be bought out. He told lawyers that a few of the original investors had experienced changes or financial difficulties—an expensive divorce in one instance, a loss on an unrelated investment in another—that made them want to exit the Saints deal. Benson said that it was after hearing from these investors that he wrote to all the remaining limited partners stating that he was prepared to purchase all or none of their interests.

Glaser and Gauthier claimed in their court filings that, even before Benson offered them an option to buy back into the Saints if they would just agree to sell their interests in 1992, he already knew that the option would be virtually worthless by the time the two attempted to exercise it.

"I didn't have any idea what had gone on until I saw what we were getting for our money," Glaser recalls. "What we were getting was a shadow of what we originally owned."

When the two took Benson to court, they demanded that he either transfer to them partnership holdings that were identical to those they purchased initially or pay them damages to offset the profits they lost as a result of not holding their original shares. In addition, they demanded that Benson pay punitive damages of $5 million to each of them.[18]

In a countersuit in Texas, Benson maintained that he owed Glaser and Gauthier no obligations under their option agreements. He said that transferring assets out of the original Saints organization and into a new entity was both legal and allowed under the provisions of the option. He also claimed that he was not obligated to them as "limited partners" because they were merely sub-partners of a limited partner in the business.

In a deposition, Benson was matter-of-fact about having transferred valuable assets out of the Saints organization and into Benz-Saints without informing Gauthier or Glaser. In answer to a lawyer's question about a face-to-face meeting he had had with Glaser about reinvesting in the Saints, Benson said: "When he came to see me, I learned that he knew everything. . . . Not only the fact that it was Benz-Saints, but the fact that the football business as it was before, where he made a lot of money on it, was quite different now, and that there would not be any type of return like that, and that I didn't see where . . . it would be a very good investment."[19]

Benson settled with Gauthier and Glaser several months later.

Not all the investors were upset by Benson's decision to buy them out. Karl Singer, who had an insurance business in Dallas at the time Benson bought the team, became a 1 percent owner when he invested as a member of a subgroup that included Benson's brother, Jerome Benson, who acquired a 2-percent interest in the team.

Singer had been a director at Kelly Field National Bank, one of the institutions Tom Benson purchased in the 1980s, but their relationship reached back to the 1960s, when Singer did business with auto dealers around the country.

"Tom has always been somebody I held in high regard, and I still do," Singer says.

When Benson asked him to participate in the Saints deal, Singer jumped in. "He called me and said, 'We need some help to get this done,' so I invested, and I found some other investors for him."

Seven years later, when Benson approached his limited partners about selling their interests to him, Singer says he believed that most of the partners were willing to sell. "I know there are a couple of significant shareholders who did want to sell, for their own particular reasons . . . and I know there were a couple of dissidents . . . but I think Tom handled it right."

Still, he concedes that, given the choice, he would love to have remained an owner of the Saints.

"Well, sure, who wouldn't want to be involved in an NFL franchise if you're a sports fan and an ex-football player in college, as I was? It was a thrill, and it was fun," he says.

No Love Lost

Whatever their take on Benson, the original investors all seemed to agree that owning a piece of the New Orleans Saints was a once-in-a-lifetime thrill. And no matter how they felt about being bought out, with the team today valued north of $1 billion, the former limited partners who are still around surely yearn a bit for what might have been. It's certainly no secret that Tom Benson's net worth skyrocketed through his decades of owning the team.

In 1989, *Texas Monthly* magazine, in its annual look at the state's wealthiest residents, pegged Benson's net worth at $160 million. Three years later, when he made his move to buy out his limited partners, his fortune had grown to $180 million, according to the magazine.

The next two decades would see the figure soar. In 2015, *Forbes* magazine estimated the value of the New Orleans Saints at $1.51 billion. In the same year, *Forbes* named Benson to the magazine's list of the country's wealthiest people, pegging his fortune at $2.2 billion.

Benson, during the 1970s and '80s, had become a millionaire

hundreds of times over by selling cars, owning banks, and plying his own resources and business savvy. But he made the leap into the world of the NFL by convincing others to enable his deal, and once he was in—and his partners were out—his net worth launched toward a much higher plateau.

Wendell Gauthier said in his original 1993 lawsuit against the Saints owner that when Benson agreed to pay John Mecom $72 million for the Saints in 1985, he admitted that he wasn't able to swing the deal on his own, which is why he tapped dozens of investors to help him out. "Benson was successful in acquiring the Saints because of his own acknowledged business ability and also because he was able to attract investors . . . who were willing to take a major financial risk," Gauthier stated in the complaint he filed.[20]

In years to come, Benson would push off much more financial risk onto the taxpayers of Louisiana. He cajoled city and state officials into giving his sports teams and other businesses tax breaks and other subsidies totaling hundreds of millions of dollars, all of which would have the effect of increasing the teams' value and fattening Benson's personal fortune.

Meanwhile, former limited partner Peter Glaser, whose 1.7 percent stake in the New Orleans Saints would be worth more than $25 million if he still held it, says he "absolutely" wishes he were still an owner of the team—though he never made another attempt to get back in. "To be honest, I've never talked with Mr. Benson since those days, even though he lived in the same building that I lived in."

For some years, both Benson and Glaser were residents of the swanky One River Place condominium tower that stands along the Mississippi River in downtown New Orleans. The proximity of their living quarters made for some awkward encounters, Glaser says, and not one of those moments resulted in a friendly turn of conversation.

"It was not a very nice conclusion to our business relationship," Glaser says.

Chapter 8

Benson's Saints, the Early Years

As he sought to shed the headaches he had taken on by partnering with so many investors to buy the Saints, Tom Benson also had to tackle responsibilities he had never faced before.

By his own admission, he didn't know much about football, but he had bought a team with a decidedly unimpressive record, and he had to do something about it.

Several months after Benson purchased the team, Bum Phillips, the head coach Benson inherited from John Mecom, resigned before the season ended, knowing that Benson was preparing to clean house.

The following year, Benson won praise throughout the league when he hired Jim Finks, a general manager who had helped build Super Bowl teams in Minnesota and hire star players in Chicago. Well liked and respected throughout the sport, Finks brought new credibility to Saints management.

While the Saints roster in those days didn't give New Orleans a lot to brag about, it had a few bright spots. One was Rickey Jackson, at the time one of the best outside linebackers in the league. Jack Del Rio, then a rookie linebacker, was showing promise. And the team could generally plan on racking up field-goal points with one of the NFL's most reliable kickers, Danish-born Morten Andersen.

"I've seen clubs with less material become a club and win, and I think that's the number-one objective here," Finks said during a press conference announcing his hiring.[1]

Finks told Tom Benson he had his eye on a coach who could make it happen. In 1986, the Saints hired Jim Mora, who had made a name in Philadelphia as one of the best coaches in the short-lived U.S. Football League.

Meanwhile, as Finks began fleshing out the front office, he made a call to Jim Miller, who then worked for the NFL in New York, administering the players' collective bargaining agreement. Finks asked Miller to consider signing on with the Saints, and they arranged to meet in New Orleans in January 1986, as the city hosted Super Bowl XX.

Miller clearly recalls what happened when he arrived.

"I was to meet Finks in the office at the Superdome on Super Bowl Sunday, so I went to the receptionist and said, 'I'm here to see Mr. Finks.' So this older guy walks out, and he looks kind of rumpled, and I'm wondering who he is. Then he comes over and says, 'I'm Tom Benson.'"

The inauspicious introduction did not dampen Miller's interest. Finks hired him as vice president of administration, and Miller shortly joined what he would come to see as a dream team of football management. With Finks in the driver's seat and Mora developing the talent on the field, the Saints seemed poised to turn a corner.

Miller says the team appeared to be a good fit for Benson too. "A good owner is one who knows what he doesn't know and keeps good people in position," he says. "Jim Finks was the guy, and Tom was smart enough to let him run it. You can't always rely on getting that type of ownership, someone who lets the people who know what they're doing run the ship."

Jim Finks exuded a confidence that seemed to make Benson comfortable. They liked each other, Miller says, and as Finks did with nearly everyone around him, he assigned Benson a nickname, referring to him in private conversation as "the tire kicker," in a nod to Benson's automobile background.

"Finks would say things like, 'Straighten up your office; the tire kicker's coming in.' And it wasn't meant as disrespect. Jim just had nicknames for everybody," Miller says.

Coach Mora began living up to Finks' predictions of a turnaround right off the bat. With Bobby Hebert as quarterback, a strong defense helped carry the team to a 12-3 season, and the Saints headed for their first-ever playoff game.

It was such a good season that speculation arose as to whether the team had received help from "above." In the deeply Catholic city of New Orleans, some suggested that a September 1987 appearance by Pope John Paul II in the Superdome might have had something to do with it. "He blessed the Saints and we've been winning since—this is unbelievable," famed New Orleans jazz clarinetist Pete Fountain declared.[2]

While the team made the playoffs four more times under Mora, the Saints didn't win a single playoff game. In 1996, bowed by frustration, the coach stepped down.

Mora's tenure likely was shortened in part by unexpected events.

Finks, who had become one of the most highly regarded front-office execs in the NFL, nearly became the league's commissioner in 1989, to succeed Pete Rozelle. After the league hired Paul Tagliabue instead, it appeared Finks would remain at the helm of football operations in New Orleans for the long term.

But in 1993, Finks learned that he had lung cancer, and he pared back his workload as he underwent treatment. He died in the following year.

Filling his shoes would have been tough for almost anyone, but when Tom Benson turned to football operations vice president Bill Kuharich to fill the job, it may have been a mistake.

Mora was not particularly fond of Kuharich to begin with and did not take well to him becoming general manager. The team's on-field performance had begun to falter, and as personality clashes off the field became more common, frustrations started to boil over in the front office.

Miller says, "I remember a meeting early in the '95 season, when we had started out 0 and 5, and Tom calls us in and tells Mora, 'You're going to fire two coaches,' and he tells Kuharich, 'You're going to fire two scouts.' And he tells me, 'You're going to fire the junior member in every department.' And then he tells Mora he's also going to cut a couple players. Tom was furious, and he was beating on the table. He thought change would shake us all up and make the team play better."

The heated meeting went on for about three hours until "we finally talked him off the ceiling," Miller says.

After Benson cooled off, he did not follow through on the personnel cuts. Miller says that was the only time he ever saw Benson threaten to get involved in football operations.

"Tom never interfered," he says. "Anytime we wanted to sign a free agent or do something that would help the team, he never gave us any pushback."

Benson was able to give coaches and managers what they wanted because he made it his own mission to see that the team did well financially. The Saints were seeing an operating income of about 10 percent of revenue during the first decade of Benson's ownership, and he incentivized his executives by offering bonuses based on profit growth.

"Tom always wanted to be in the top ten [among NFL teams] in profit, and I think we were close to that," Miller says.

Nevertheless, Benson's frustration with the team grew after a disappointing 1995 season, and in the spring he decided someone should go. It would be Miller.

"For some reason, Tom decided that the non-football guy would be the first to go," Miller says. The move didn't make sense to him, but he adds: "It was fine. If you're in the business long enough, you know that NFL stands for Not For Long."

Miller, who moved on to the front office of the Buffalo Bills, bumped into Benson at a league meeting in 1997. He was surprised when Benson waved to him from across a room and walked over to shake hands.

"I just wanted you to know that I fired the wrong guy," Benson said to Miller.

The stunned Miller didn't ask Benson whom he thought he should have fired instead. "I still don't know if he meant Mora or Kuharich, but I assumed he meant Mora because Jim walked out on him in the '96 season," Miller says.

Miller, who has since moved back to New Orleans, was amazed that Benson, in a manner of speaking, apologized to him for his firing. "I thought that took a lot of guts," he says, adding that he still respects Benson and admires what he has done for the Saints.

The years after the Finks-Mora era were tough ones for the Saints and Benson. Some in New Orleans found it difficult to fathom how the team owner decided on his next head coach, but for better or worse, Benson announced in 1997 that he had hired Mike Ditka. Without Finks' advice in his ear, and feeling the pressure to reengineer the team, Benson may simply have reached for a big name.

Though Ditka had stacked up a string of successes during a decade as head coach of the Chicago Bears, and the team had won a Super Bowl on his watch, the Bears owners fired him in 1992 after a humiliating season.[3] He had been away from coaching for five years when Tom Benson brought him in to lead the New Orleans Saints.

Ditka's unapologetic swagger and his bull-in-a-china-shop persona never fit well in New Orleans, and his coaching and management decisions rankled Saints fans. After the team went 6-10 in his first two seasons, Ditka seemed to flail about, looking for answers. Some fans couldn't believe it when he traded all of the team's 1999 draft picks and a first-round pick in 2000 in order to sign Texas running back Ricky Williams, a talented player who would become best known for his bizarre behavior on and off the field.

Ditka took the move to an absurd level when he agreed to appear in a magazine cover photo with Williams, who was wearing a wedding dress.

The Saints went 3-13 in that year, and Tom Benson had had enough. At the end of the season, he cleaned house, firing not only Ditka but also Kuharich and most of the coaching staff.

Chapter 9

Hardnosed or Competitive?

"Some people like to play golf. I like to come to the office."[1]

Tom Benson has made that comment more than once over the years when asked why, even though he surrounded himself with capable people who could take the reins, he continued to maintain a schedule that would tire a younger man. Benson just seems to be more comfortable when he is at work, in whatever setting, than almost anywhere else. And after his net worth crossed the billion-dollar mark, he gave no indication that he was ready to sit back and enjoy the view. Even into his eighties, his habit of going to work and spending full days at his office did not change.

While his facility with numbers makes easy work of reviewing balance sheets and profit-and-loss statements, Benson realized early in his life that what really gets him revved up is an opportunity to do a deal. Big transactions give him a chance to flex his negotiating muscles to get what he wants on the most favorable terms.

His skills served him well over a nearly a half-century of deal-making, including his many negotiations with the state of Louisiana over stadium lease agreements for the New Orleans Saints.

Former Saints front-office chief Jim Miller recalls watching Benson in action in the early 1990s, when Edwin Edwards was governor and Benson wanted the state to pay for more luxury suites in the Superdome. "I was in meetings at the governor's office, and we'd sit at a long conference table. Edwards would sit at the end and put his feet up on the table, and Tom would tell him what he wanted," Miller says. "Tom would start banging on the table, and shouting, 'We need to do this!' But Edwards was cool as a cucumber. He'd just chuckle at Tom and say, 'Settle down, Benson; we'll get this done.' And they did."

At age eighty-eight, Benson was still pursuing deals in 2015, working on yet another potential real-estate transaction near the Superdome that he said could result in a new luxury hotel and retail space coming to the area.[2] Benson had his eye on the Freeport-McMoRan office building, which stands across the street from the Dome and likely was priced well given that its namesake company, Freeport-McMoRan, Inc., had fallen on hard times.

New Orleans attorney Russ Herman says his former client is one of the best people he knows at putting together such transactions. "He knows how to structure a deal, and he can see what the risks and opportunities are far in advance."

Even people who have criticized Benson over the years as being insensitive or outright ruthless in his dealings will grudgingly concede that he is skilled at what he does. "He's a good businessman, and he works hard, I'll give him that," says one.

Because Benson had built his skills in the automobile business, associates note that when he entered the banking arena, he turned to others who had the expertise he needed.

"He was not a banker per se but he understood what made a good loan and what made sense to invest in, and that's really what you're doing when you're running a bank," says Fred Lay, who became executive vice president of Pontchartrain Bank in Metairie after Benson bought it in 1985.

Lay says he got to know Benson well as they grew the bank and struggled to keep it above water after a banking crisis weighed it down. "Tom was a good businessman. He aligned himself with good people that were honest, hardworking, and smart," Lay says. "He had a lot of good, common sense."

But no one who has worked with or for Tom Benson could miss the fact that he is toughminded and stubborn. Throughout his career, he has shown an intolerance for people who do not live up to his expectations, and he does not hesitate to get rid of them if they don't measure up.

Benson expects people who work for him to keep their nose to the grindstone, which at times has led some to complain privately about his policies regarding paid leave and holiday time off. Some employees viewed Benson as almost Scrooge-like in his insistence that workers be at their posts at such times as Christmas Eve and other days that many companies routinely regard as holidays.

Sometimes Benson could be almost shockingly insensitive, as became clear to a handful of senior executives one day in 2001.

It was the morning of September 11, a day that would burn into the memories of people around the world. Many can recall exactly what they were doing when they heard the news that two commercial airliners had crashed into the twin towers of the World Trade Center in New York.

In offices throughout the country, workers clustered around whatever television screens they could find, anxious to glean details of what had happened and why. But at Saints headquarters in Metairie, there was work to be done. So when Benson walked by an office where several executives had gathered for a meeting, and he saw that they were watching television, he let loose.

"Shut that goddamned television off," he barked, ordering the executives to get back to work.

If Benson ruled his realm with a heavy hand, he also managed to earn the loyalty of many employees who stayed with him for decades and enjoyed the rewards of playing key roles in his businesses.

Todd Gold, who owns a commercial real estate company in San Antonio, is the son of Arnold Gold, a longtime business partner of Benson. Arnold Gold, who died in 2015, worked with Benson for many years in San Antonio and co-owned Benson & Gold Chevrolet in New Orleans, the dealership that in the 1970s marked Tom Benson's return to business in the city after a twenty-year absence. Some years later, Gold and his family would go back to Texas, again at Benson's suggestion.

"Tom gave my dad the opportunity to run what was at that time the only Mercedes-Benz dealership in San Antonio," Todd Gold recalls.

Todd Gold and his two brothers all worked for Benson at some point in their business careers, and he says that both his dad and

Benson could be tough. "My dad was a spare-the-rod-spoil-the-child kind of guy. He was a hard man to love . . . and he and Tom had a very similar persona."

Both men "watched every number" and were demanding of their employees. "But they also had some of the most loyal employees you could ever find," Gold says, taking note of some who stayed with the dealerships for decades.

In Arnold Gold's partnership with Benson, Gold ran the operations while Benson was the strategist and risk taker. "My dad got put in situations where he had to fire certain family members who were relatives of Tom," Todd Gold says.

Terming Benson "about as shrewd a guy as I know," he says the reason some people find Benson tough to work for is that he is a perfectionist. "He has high expectations of everybody around him."

When Arnold Gold became ill in his mid-eighties and was hospitalized in San Antonio, Benson called him in the intensive care unit several times. And after Arnold passed away, Benson, then on crutches due to a knee surgery, attended the funeral, Todd Gold says.

"I told him I was surprised to see him, and he just said, 'Why wouldn't I come to your dad's funeral?'" Todd recalls.

Over the years, Benson sometimes showed his loyalty to friends and family by offering financial help. But occasionally his business and family relationships became so entangled that it was difficult to say exactly who benefited.

In the late 1980s, a business deal with his youngest brother, Larry, drew Tom Benson into litigation with a real-estate firm in San Antonio. The case stemmed from a lease agreement that Larry Benson had signed for office space in a building owned by One Oak Park, Ltd. According to a complaint the company filed in a state court in 1989, Larry Benson, a lawyer who also played a role in his brother's automobile business, had fallen behind on his office rent and had failed to comply with One Oak Park's demands for payment.[3]

Around the same time that the lease problem arose, Larry Benson had become the controlling owner of the San Antonio Riders, a new franchise in the World League of American Football. His ownership of the team became an issue at court as One Oak Park pursued its case against him over a period of three years.

During that time, Larry Benson's debt to his landlord—pegged at about $18,000 in the original complaint—burgeoned to more than $300,000. In 1992, a district court judge ordered that Benson transfer his 45 percent ownership stake in the Riders to One Oak Park to satisfy a judgment against him.[4]

At that point, Tom Benson intervened in the case, asking that the court set aside its order because he had a "security interest" in the Riders.[5] In a series of filings that followed, One Oak Park fired back at the Benson brothers, claiming that Larry's ownership of the football team was a sham.

Lawyers for the company maintained that Tom Benson actually had wanted to buy a WLAF franchise himself, but he already owned the New Orleans Saints, and NFL bylaws at the time prohibited him from owning another sports franchise.

"To circumvent the NFL Constitution and Bylaws, Tom Benson turned to his brother . . . to act as a front for Tom Benson's wishes," One Oak Park's attorneys alleged in a filing. The lawyers said that Tom pursued the arrangement even though he knew that Larry "was already deeply in debt and was rapidly approaching insolvency."[6]

Tom, through Benson Motors Company, arranged loans totaling $2.4 million to his brother and paid Larry $150,000 a year as general manager of the team, according to court documents.[7]

Filings by Tom Benson stated that Tom, because of his loans to Larry, held a first lien on Larry's stock in the Riders. Among other steps, Tom at one point attempted to foreclose on his loans to Larry in an effort to hold on to the team.[8]

Eventually, the court forced the Bensons and One Oak Park into mediation over the matters, and in July 1992, the parties reached an agreement.[9] The terms of the settlement remained confidential, but Larry Benson came away holding a faltering Riders team, only to see the World League of American Football fold a short time later.[10]

Larry Benson briefly gained entrance for the Riders into the Canadian Football League, but he pulled the plug on the team before its 1993 season began. Several years later, he retired from his law practice to become owner of Ingram Park Auto Center in northwest San Antonio.

After Larry's sudden death in 2013 while he was traveling in Italy, his son, Larry Benson, Jr., became owner and CEO of the dealership.[11]

Tom Benson, who briefly addressed mourners during Larry's funeral, said that the brothers had been close throughout their lives despite the eighteen-year difference in their ages. "I talked to him almost every day," Benson noted. "I'm sure gonna miss him."[12]

It is not unusual in business circles to hear an individual described as hardnosed and at the same time lauded for being financially successful, which may help explain why high achievers in business sometimes develop problems with family members. Opportunism can morph into ruthlessness, and that toughminded behavior can infuse one's personal relationships as well.

"Tough" is often the first word that people who know him use to describe Tom Benson. While he enjoys the company of close friends and relatives, who have often witnessed the fun-loving side of his personality, some say an underlying aggressiveness permeates his demeanor and lends a hard edge to his interactions, even in social settings.

Benson used to enjoy dancing, for instance, but women he whisked around the dancefloor sometimes felt more driven than guided. "When he would touch you, he always pushed; he didn't pull. And when you danced with him, you'd be all over the floor," says Marillyn Barbot, the sister of Tom's second wife, Grace Benson.

Tom Benson likes to feel that he is in control of events and people around him, and if compassion and sensitivity were sometimes lacking, close family members were the ones most likely to feel the chill.

When bitter differences erupted publicly between Tom Benson, his daughter, and two of his grandchildren in 2015, outsiders could only wonder: was Benson as tough and unforgiving with his family as he sometimes was with employees or people on the opposite side of a business deal?

Had his heirs embraced that same tough approach to dealing with the people around them, and would Benson now come to know the other side of ruthlessness?

Chapter 10

Born Rich, Part One

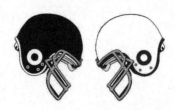

For most parents who grew up in modest circumstances, the desire to give their own children a better start in life comes naturally, as it did to Tom and Shirley Benson. Both were products of working-class families that struggled through tough economic times. Neither grew up expecting to receive anything they did not earn.

Therein lies a potential minefield of problems for parents who become rich in adulthood. Having no idea what it is like to be a child who has everything, they can miss signs that their good intentions toward their own children may not be having the desired effect.

In Tom Benson's case, some of the family problems that erupted late in his life may have stemmed from early assumptions he made about his children, on whom he showered his money and influence. Chances are that he thought the kids would be as driven to make money as he was.

Wealth counselor Thayer Willis says it's a common misconception. Self-made wealthy people tend to attribute their own values to their offspring, she says.

"They think, 'Wow, if I had had access to this kind of money when I was twenty-five or thirty, imagine what I could have done with it.' They assume that the rising generation will behave the same way they did—at least that's what their hope is."

Willis, a psychotherapist and author of *Navigating the Dark Side of Wealth*, was, herself, a child of wealth, born into the family who founded Georgia-Pacific Corporation. She says she managed to thwart "spoiled brat" tendencies in her own life because she took a hard look at herself when she was in her twenties and realized that if she were to have a meaningful life, she needed to change. "There's a crucial period of time in your twenties and maybe early thirties when you may be willing to learn to give up these spoiled behaviors, but once you get past that, these things become very habitual, and it's pretty hard to give them up," she says.

Willis says that billionaire parents who built their own fortunes often fail to recognize "attitudes of entitlement" developing in their children. Self-made individuals may not realize that their kids don't understand or relate to money in the same way the parents did.

The kids don't always see that while money can make life easy in many respects, it can actually make things too easy. "The problem is, money can create a lack of motivation," Willis says. When a young person does not feel motivated to do well at school or at work, that individual does not learn how to strive and reap the rewards that come with trying and failing, she adds.

As an example, she points to the college student who quits a class or even drops out of school just because the work got a little too challenging or the student received a bad grade. "Or maybe you're in a job and you don't get the promotion you thought you should have had, so you just quit."

Willis continues, "For the wealthy person, there are no financial consequences to these decisions. You live in a world where if things get difficult, you can just bail, and you miss some very significant maturing experiences."

She says the freedom to quit when the going gets tough carries a high cost. "The only way any of us develops competence is to stick it out through the tough times. If you live in a cushioned world where there are no consequences to quitting whenever life gets a little tough, then you never develop competence—or confidence."

People who earned their way to a high net worth know that their own difficult experiences made them wiser and stronger. But transferring an understanding of the importance of striving to their offspring is often easier said than done.

Educating their children about the challenges and hazards of wealth was not a top concern for Tom and Shirley Benson in the 1950s. Like many young couples starting a family, they were focused on providing for their kids' basic needs.

Unable to have children biologically but anxious to build a family, they turned to adoption, and over a period of eleven years they adopted three children.

Their first child, Robert Carter Benson, likely would be the only Benson child who, in adulthood, would retain any memory of his family's early working-class life.

In 1948, when Tom and Shirley brought their baby boy home, they lived in a hardscrabble neighborhood of New Orleans, in an apartment located above a dry-goods store that Tom operated with his father.[1]

A few years later, when Tom went to work for a local automobile dealer, he moved the family to a small house just around the corner, on Florida Avenue, where they would live until Robert was eight years old.[2]

These were years when Tom Benson was learning the ropes of automobile retailing and figuring out how to apply his accounting savvy to squeeze bigger profits out of a dealership. By 1956, he had become a valued employee of Mike Persia Chevrolet.

In that year, Tom and Shirley brought home their second baby, Renee Elaine Benson, from the St. Vincent de Paul Orphanage.[3] A short time later, Persia offered Tom the opportunity to manage and become a part owner of a dealership Persia had acquired in San Antonio,[4] and Benson accepted.

By the time Renee Benson started kindergarten, her father owned Tom Benson Chevrolet in San Antonio, and the family was more financially secure. Private school and big vacations lay ahead for the Benson children, as their father focused on ever-larger business opportunities. In just a few years, he would buy the land on San Antonio's north side that would enable the expansion of his dealership into one of the largest auto retailing companies in the South.[5]

By the time he and Shirley adopted their third child in 1959, Benson's net worth was in a steep climb, ensuring that baby Jeanne Marie "Tootsie" Benson would grow up with no inkling of the financial challenges her parents had faced in the early years of their marriage. The Bensons had beautiful homes and a live-in housekeeper, Viola Searcy, who not only cooked and cleaned for them but became a beloved member of the family. Through the luck of the draw, the Benson kids had landed parents who not only loved them but could provide everything they needed and just about anything they would want for as far ahead as they could imagine.

Louisiana Diversion

The Bensons' middle child, Renee, may have been the first of their children to frustrate the plans her father had for her future.

After completing her elementary education at Mount Sacred Heart Catholic School and graduating high school at Ursuline Academy in San Antonio, Renee broke ranks and headed toward her South Louisiana birthplace.[6] Initially, she enrolled at Nicholls State University in Thibodaux, southwest of New Orleans. But college didn't hold her interest for long. She did not continue her classes or earn a degree.[7] What she apparently did find in the bayou country of South Louisiana was love.

Russell Anthony LeBlanc, a native of Lafourche Parish an hour south of New Orleans, was six years older than Renee and different in other ways from boys she had come across in San Antonio. He had a vaguely wild air and colorful sense of humor that are common among the people who live and work along Bayou Lafourche. The waterway lined with fishing vessels, barges, and workboats lies at the eastern edge of Louisiana's Cajun country and meanders southward through alligator-filled wetlands on its way to the Gulf of Mexico.

Many of the residents in bayou communities such as Larose, Cut Off, Golden Meadow, and Galliano are commercial fishermen or work in businesses that service the offshore oil industry. They work on fishing boats that leave docks long before the sun rises to cast their nets on open waters. Or they work in area plants that build and repair oil-drilling equipment or provide supplies, labor, and transportation to the companies that mine oil and gas in the Gulf of Mexico. Residents of Lafourche Parish are a hardy lot who for many years have withstood the economic ups and downs of the state's biggest business, the oil and gas industry, and endured the ravages of storms that have repeatedly battered the Louisiana coast.

It takes a certain stubbornness and defiant spirit to thrive in the wetlands of South Louisiana, and acquaintances say that the rough-around-the-edges Russell LeBlanc fit the bill. Certainly, he captured the interest of a quiet young woman who had spent most of her life in all-girls schools.

A year after graduating from high school, Renee Benson married Russell LeBlanc. By some assessments, he was not the husband Tom Benson envisioned for her. "Tom told his daughter not to come home with a longhaired hippie, and Renee's husband was both," says a person who was close to the family.

The couple initially settled into a home in the tiny community of Cut Off, but Tom Benson pressed the pair to relocate to Texas. After the birth in 1977 of Renee and Russell's daughter, Rita Mae LeBlanc, the pressure rose, and soon they were on their way to San Antonio.

Renee began planning a house to be built on a portion of Tom Benson's 2,300 acres outside of Johnson City.[8] And by the time the LeBlancs' second child, Ryan Joseph, came along a few years later, the family was firmly rooted in Texas. In the decades to come, Renee would own homes in San Antonio and New Orleans, but for the most part, she would remain a denizen of the Texas Hill Country.

Tom and Shirley Benson's oldest child, Robert, who was born in Louisiana, also spent most of his life in the San Antonio area and remained close to the family. After graduating from Central Catholic High School in San Antonio, he entered the U.S. Navy during the latter years of the Vietnam War and served on an aircraft carrier.

Upon his safe return home, Robert married his eighteen-year-old sweetheart, Karen Wiemers. In 1970, they became the parents of a baby girl, Dawn Marie Benson.[9]

A year later, Robert and Karen were divorced. Robert Benson would remarry, divorce, and wed once more, before his life ended.[10]

By most accounts, he remained close to his father, and he was excited to see Tom Benson become the owner of the New Orleans Saints. Robert stood at Tom's side during the press conference announcing that the sale was complete.

Robert Carter Benson, Tom Benson's oldest child, died in 1986. (Courtesy of the Benson family)

But Robert would not enjoy the thrill of NFL ownership for long. He succumbed to lung cancer just a few months after the family celebrated Tom Benson's purchase of the team.[11] Robert Benson was thirty-seven.

Tootsie

The Bensons' youngest child, Tootsie, was the only one of Tom Benson's children to put significant distance between herself and the tightly knit Benson family in adulthood. Described by some as a free spirit who loved her family and adored her older brother but often clashed with her father, Tootsie seemed determined to plot a course that led away from Tom Benson's power and influence. She embraced the rebelliousness of the 1970s and early '80s, including the fashions and incipient trend among young adults of body piercings and tattoos.[12]

Having spent much of her childhood on the Benson ranch, Tootsie was an avid horsewoman who made a name for herself in equestrian competitions around central Texas and beyond. She loved horses and caring for the thoroughbreds housed at the ranch, but she had no interest in her father's other businesses. Tootsie was more inclined to cerebral pursuits and eventually would gravitate toward the study of mystical religions.[13]

After graduating from high school at Ursuline Academy in San Antonio, Tootsie enrolled at the all-female Stephens College in Columbia, Missouri.[14] But she stayed in Missouri for only a year before returning to Texas, perhaps out of concern for her mother, who was in declining health.

Not long after the death of Shirley Benson, in 1980, Tootsie, then twenty-one, married twenty-seven-year-old Harry Vowell, Jr. At some point during their marriage, Tootsie enrolled at Texas A&M University, but after she and Vowell divorced in 1986, she returned to Stephens College for one semester.

A short time later, Tootsie married Missouri native Peter Nebergall, whom she had met years earlier and who was a graduate student in archaeology at the University of Missouri at Columbia. Tootsie shared his love of photography and music, and they both valued intellectual pursuits above the quest for money.

Tom Benson was not happy about Tootsie's choice of a mate.

In fact, by Nebergall's account, Benson intensely disliked his daughter's husband.

Anxious to bring Tootsie back home, Benson tried to get the couple to come to Texas and take up residence at the ranch, but the effort failed.

Tootsie, who had frequently defied her father as she was growing up, maintained her rebellious stance throughout her twenties. Her relationship with Tom Benson became more complicated after her mother died and as Tootsie experienced the onset of a debilitating condition similar to multiple sclerosis. As the disease progressed, attacking her muscular system, she sometimes struggled to walk and at times had to use a wheelchair.

Todd Gold, who was about the same age as Tootsie and whose father worked closely with Tom Benson in his auto dealerships, remembers his family spending time at the Benson ranch when Todd and Tootsie were children. "I knew Tootsie well, and I remember that she had just about anything a child could want at that age, including horses galore," he says.

As they both grew up, Gold saw Tootsie less frequently but had heard that she had contracted a difficult illness. "One of the last times I saw her she was in a wheelchair, and I remember thinking how sad it was," he says.

By the time she reached age thirty, Tootsie was making occasional trips between Columbia and San Antonio. Her deteriorating health forced her to seek the comforts of home and the care of her stand-in mother, Viola Searcy, the Benson family's beloved housekeeper.

It was shortly after she returned to Columbia from one of these visits that Tootsie decided to end her life.[15] On April 15, 1991, her husband found Tootsie in her

Jeanne Marie "Tootsie" Benson, Tom Benson's youngest child, died in 1991. (Courtesy of the Benson family)

bed, with a bullet wound to her head and a Colt .38 revolver in her hand. Poetry she had written and left nearby suggested she had wanted to end her life. State Police investigators ruled the death a suicide.[16]

Her sister, Renee, was the first to receive the news on that fateful morning, and she relayed the terrible message to their father. He immediately traveled to Missouri and met with the investigators.[17] But when a funeral service was held for Tootsie in Columbia several days later, Tom Benson was not on hand.

By the time Tom Benson was sixty-five years old, his first wife and two of his children had died. He had achieved huge success in business and amassed assets worth hundreds of millions of dollars. But he had repeatedly had to muster resilience in the face of personal tragedy.

Benson had remarried in 1982 and found happiness a second time. He was devoted to his wife, Grace Trudeau Benson, and he embraced her four adult children.

But now only one of his own children remained alive, and he had three grandchildren. He became more consumed with estate planning and finding ways to ensure that his fortune and many assets would remain in those individuals' hands after his death.

Complicating his succession planning at this stage was Benson's ownership of a professional football team. Though he took early steps to gives his heirs ownership interests in the team, the idea of leaving them in charge of running the New Orleans Saints presented bigger challenges than planning for the transfer of, say, a car dealership or a bank.

Who would take over?

Hill Country Denizen

Tom Benson's remaining daughter, Renee Benson LeBlanc, was not the stereotypical child of wealth. By most accounts, the quiet teenager had grown into a shy woman who lived a relatively modest lifestyle. She never wanted for anything, but her tastes did not run toward expensive clothes or lavish living. The trendy clothes, jewelry, and makeup that are consuming interests for many young women held no interest for Renee Benson. If anything, she had become a person who could easily be overlooked in a crowded room, and she seemed to like it that way. "She doesn't seem to feel the need for any pretense," a friend told a reporter in 2015.[18]

Renee also liked living on her father's ranch, though she did not take to riding horses, as both her brother and sister had enjoyed. From the time her father bought the ranch, in fact, Renee kept her distance from the animals. "I got stepped on right away, so that made me not like the horses too much," she said.[19] She did, however, learn to manage the breeding schedules for the thoroughbreds that Tom Benson kept on the farm in the 1980s.[20]

The relative remoteness of the ranch allowed her a comfortable degree of isolation from local society, and like her siblings, Renee was also free of worry over how she would support herself in the future.

Through the 1970s and '80s, she lived with her husband, Russell LeBlanc, and their two children, on the ranch. When she and Russell divorced after twenty years of marriage, she faced none of the financial worries common for working-class single mothers. Her father's wealth sustained her and her family. In fact, beginning a few years before her divorce from LeBlanc, Renee began receiving payments of $10,000 a month from the trust her father had set up for her in her mother's name.[21]

Renee Benson would marry again, two years after her divorce. She and her new husband, Roy McNett, Jr., who was the publisher of the *Blanco County News,* would live at the ranch home, among other spots, until they divorced three years later.[22]

In 2006, at the age of fifty, Renee would tie the knot for a third time, marrying John Daniel Benham II,[23] a longtime resident of the San Antonio area who loved airplanes and was a commercial airline pilot. The couple settled into a home just outside of Blanco.

Renee and her husband shared a love of big recreational vehicles, the luxury-type rides favored by celebrities and touring musicians. Each of them, at the time of their marriage, owned a high-end, thirty-foot motor home known as a Wanderlodge Bluebird. Their ownership of the vehicles put them into the company of other owners of fancy RVs around the country, many of whom cruised the highways toward San Antonio in June 2006 to join hundreds of other people celebrating the Benson-Benham wedding.[24]

Community Project

When she was in her mid-forties, with her two children, Rita and Ryan, now grown, Renee began widening her community interests. Already a supporter of the performing arts and member of a local choir in Blanco, Texas, a town of about 1,800 residents that lies ten miles south of the Benson ranch on Highway 281, she decided to tackle a community restoration project.

Her idea was to create an "arts and entertainment" district that would generate revenue and support the arts by providing exhibit and performance spaces in renovated, aging buildings. The area she targeted was a square block of Blanco that lies along Main Street, where cars and eighteen-wheel trucks streak through town on their way to and from San Antonio. Perhaps in a nod to the genteel Uptown section of New Orleans, the city where she was born, Renee dubbed her project Uptown Blanco.

In 1999, Renee Benson began buying up all the buildings in the block, which included an old-time movie theater and a couple of properties considered historically significant. By 2004, she had purchased a dozen properties valued at around $3 million.[25]

She spent several years renovating the properties, and in late 2008 she opened the project's first new business, the Uptown Blanco Restaurant.[26] "Renovating buildings is one of my joys in life," Benson said following a ribbon cutting for the project.[27]

Several years later, an exhibition and studio space for artists opened in the block, followed by a textile store offering colorful fabrics and sewing supplies. Benson also planned to open an upscale tavern next to the restaurant and a community theater that would provide performance space for area artists. She envisioned the courtyard space in the interior of the block as a spot for community gatherings and a setting for weddings, and she renovated a ballroom in a second-floor space of a former Masonic lodge to accommodate small concerts.[28]

She even landscaped the open area behind the Uptown Blanco buildings to give it the look of a long-established courtyard.

In 2011, she had three mature, thirty-foot-tall live oak trees transplanted onto the property. The job required a heavy crane to lift the trees off a flatbed truck and a crew to replant them.[29] The trees stand near a gazebo that Benson envisioned as a setting for weddings and other outdoor events.

On a Friday in November 2015, several customers browsed the colorful fabrics and quilting supplies in the textile shop at one end of Uptown Blanco, but the rest of the block was quiet. Renee Benson had closed her restaurant in February 2015.[30] Though the upstairs ballroom that overlooks Main Street still hosts the occasional musical performance, and works by local artists remain on display in another nearby building, Uptown Blanco is largely dark.

The project that Renee Benson had focused much of her attention on in recent years likely suffered somewhat from the family discord that erupted early in 2015, when Tom Benson cut ties with Renee and her two children and they responded with a legal filing seeking to have him declared mentally incompetent. As the legal battle expanded into several courts in Louisiana and Texas, Renee's management of the Uptown Blanco project came into question.

In testimony she gave in a probate court in San Antonio, Renee described Uptown Blanco in response to questions by Tom Benson's attorney. "It's an art entertainment district. It's a historical building that was my idea . . . and it really enhances the community of Blanco," she said during the early 2015 court appearance.[31]

Asked whether her father viewed the project as "a favorable investment," she replied: "We had a discussion about it. And we both agreed that the trust would buy the property and he would not [expect] to get paid back until at such time that we would sell it. . . . He was not expecting the business that I created to rent the property to pay him back or pay the estate back. It was like a long-term investment."[32]

In later testimony, Renee acknowledged that Uptown Blanco had been losing about $200,000 a year.[33]

Her father, meanwhile, complained in a court filing that the trust he had established in Renee's mother's name had invested more than $20 million in Renee's "pet project" and that Uptown Blanco owed him $17 million. In the filing, his lawyers described Uptown Blanco as "a perennial drain" on the trust, noting that payments from the fund had covered the project's annual insurance and property tax bills.[34]

Renee Benson's attorneys denied that the project owed Tom Benson $17 million.

Meanwhile, receivers whom a judge had temporarily put in charge of the trust asked the court to OK payments to cover expenses at Uptown Blanco and a $100,000 renovation of the Benson family's Lake Tahoe vacation house, to include "remodeling the master bedroom and bathroom, construction of a steam room, craft room and lower deck, an electric service upgrade and miscellaneous general work."[35]

Renee as Businesswoman

Though Renee said neither she nor her father had expected a return on Uptown Blanco until it might be sold at a profit "many, many years" down the line,[36] the family's legal fight invited questions about her capabilities as a businesswoman, as when she was asked in court to describe the operations of Renson Enterprises, a company she said she founded.

She explained that it was her idea to start the firm, because her father in 1996 had decided to scale back on his car dealerships in Louisiana and Texas. Renee Benson said that she suggested creating a small management company in San Antonio to serve the local dealerships, mimicking the operation of a larger New Orleans-based company that had for years provided support services to all the dealerships in both states. "That's how Renson was born," she stated.[37]

Describing how Renson Enterprises functioned during its nearly twenty years of existence, Renee said: "We'd take care of all the things that are cost savings, more or less. Like something that's in common with all the franchisees. Like IT or human resource, those kinds of things . . . I think we went as far as to see about janitorial service and maintenance of the property, you know, like the yard—not yard but, what do you call it, landscaper."[38]

She said that Renson Enterprises, LLC was in charge of hiring and firing at Benson's San Antonio dealerships. Her lawyers stated in a court filing that Renee "was responsible for reviewing and critiquing financial statements and month-end packages," in addition to overseeing staff and managing dealership rents and leases, and that the dealerships paid Renson for the work.[39] Court documents showed that the three Texas dealerships paid Renson $75,000 a month for the services.

Renee Benson said she went to several industry meetings a year with other dealers around the country to keep up on best practices in the business and how to improve dealership profits.

By some indications, it was Tom Roddy who actually ran Renson Enterprises. Roddy became a trusted business associate of Tom Benson through decades of heading up Benson's banking operations in Texas. He helped take Benson Financial Corporation through a public stock offering in 1995, and shortly thereafter he helped sell the firm to Norwest. He left the banking business after completing that transaction, and Tom Benson named him president of Benson Motors Corporation, replacing Benson's brother Jerome in that position as Jerome took over ownership and operation of several of Benson's New Orleans dealerships.[40]

Roddy's step into Tom Benson's automobile business coincided with the startup of Renson Enterprises, and though Renee claimed credit for the company's founding and is shown as its president in a Texas business record,[41] in other documents Roddy lists himself as president of the entity and provides Renson's phone number and address as his contact information.[42]

In some of the other Benson businesses in which Renee Benson became involved, Roddy also appeared to have a leading role. When Tom Benson returned to the banking business in 2003 with the purchase of Clear Lake National Bank, he named his daughter a director of the company but tapped Roddy as chairman of the board. His closest legal adviser, Stanley Rosenberg, also sat on the bank's board.[43]

Renee Benson and her children became directors in the five dealerships still owned by her father, and she was president of his Texas dealerships while Tom Benson remained chairman, according to business filings from 2014.

As for Renson Enterprises, a lawyer for Renee Benson said in

February 2015 that the company had shut down, and payments from the three San Antonio auto dealerships to the company had stopped.⁴⁴ It appeared that monthly payments to Renee from the trust her father had set up for her in her mother's name also had ceased. Along with compensation and dividends Renee received over the years from her participation as a director or owner in her father's various businesses, she had received $10,000 from the trust every month for more than twenty years.

Chapter 11
Born Rich, Part Two

Technology billionaire Mark Cuban once confessed to losing sleep over how to keep his three young children from becoming complacent adults with no sense of social or personal responsibility. Cuban, who owns the National Basketball Association team the Dallas Mavericks, said he wanted to be sure his kids eventually could "stand on their own two feet" rather than relying on their inherited assets. "I don't want them to be entitled jerks," he said.[1]

But parents who were, themselves, born to great wealth may have a different perspective on the issue that Cuban raised. They may not be particularly concerned about whether their children understand what it means to face financial worries, since they never encountered such anxieties themselves.

If Tom Benson's three children lacked an understanding of how their father and mother grew up and came to be some of the wealthiest people in their community, Benson's grandchildren were even further removed from the financial realities of his early life.

Rita Mae LeBlanc and Ryan Joseph LeBlanc, the children of Renee and Russell LeBlanc, were financially secure from the moment of their birth. Still, Rita, born in 1977, and Ryan, who came along three years later, were not products of a particularly lavish or society-centered upbringing.

Their mother, known as a quiet, shy person who largely kept to herself, had maintained a low profile throughout her life. In adulthood, she seemed to enjoy the relative isolation of her home on the Benson family's Texas ranch.

Rita LeBlanc and her grandfather, Tom Benson, receive an award from the United Way of Greater New Orleans in 2007. (Cheryl Gerber Photo)

Ryan LeBlanc, the son of Renee Benson, is the youngest of Tom Benson's three grandchildren. (Cheryl Gerber Photo)

The children's father, meanwhile, had come from working-class roots in the bayou country of South Louisiana. Perhaps it was a nod to Russell LeBlanc's upbringing that—despite their mother's having attended private schools in San Antonio as a child—both of the LeBlanc children received a public-school education, graduating from Lyndon B. Johnson High School in Johnson City. Choosing the nearby public school allowed the family to live year round on the ranch, located about an hour away from San Antonio.

Renee Benson, while in her twenties, had conceived the design of their home, a plainly styled, low-slung structure that stretches along the crest of a hill near the western edge of the ranch.[2] The cream-hued house derives its color from caliche, a type of rock that forms in arid soils and was used in the home's construction.

As he grew up in that house, Ryan LeBlanc came to know the 2,300 acres of the Benson ranch intimately. He liked the ranch life, and he liked learning how to manage the livestock, and later wild game, that Tom Benson brought there.

After graduating from high school, Ryan briefly enrolled at Blinn College,[3] a two-year Texas institution that offers workforce training and continuing education.

He remained closely attached to the Johnson City ranch and became manager of the business around 2002. He oversaw the cattle raising and later served as a guide for hunters who scheduled visits during the November-January season.[4] He claimed that under his management the ranch in 2004 turned its first profit, as it developed a following among recreational hunters who came to shoot doves or deer or stalk wild game with bow and arrow.[5]

LeBlanc began spending less time at the ranch when, in line with Tom Benson's practice of involving family members in his businesses, Benson in 2010 named his grandson chief operating officer of Benson Automotive Group,[6] whose holdings included Mercedes-Benz, Chevrolet, and Honda franchises. The dealerships would better position him to eventually own and perhaps control the Benson automotive business.

Two years after taking charge of operations, LeBlanc seemed proud of having participated in a meeting at the then-U.S. headquarters of Mercedes-Benz, in Montvale, New Jersey. When he posted to his

LinkedIn social-media profile a photo of himself in the company's lobby, he captioned the picture: *"Thirty-two years old, going to meet with Steve Cannon, President of Mercedes-Benz USA."*[7]

Ryan LeBlanc married central Texas native Tracy Baird in 2006,[8] and the couple had two children. The family today lives in a gated community in north San Antonio.

It was also in 2006 that Tom Benson named LeBlanc and his sister, Rita LeBlanc, to the board of directors of his Lone Star Capital Bank.[9] Later he placed both on the boards of his auto dealerships[10] and named them directors of WVUE-TV,[11] the New Orleans television station he bought in 2008. In 2012, Benson would also grant Ryan and Rita LeBlanc nonvoting ownership shares in the New Orleans Saints and New Orleans Pelicans.[12]

Small-Town Millionaires

The remote setting of the ranch where the LeBlanc children grew up ensured that Rita and Ryan would know a certain feeling of isolation during childhood and develop a resourcefulness that rural kids tend to learn. "When you grow up like that—in big, wide-open spaces, with only small towns around—you pretty much have to rely on yourself," Rita LeBlanc told a reporter in 2009. "You're surrounded by pasture land, so if something goes wrong, if you get hurt, you're stuck out there. If you do something silly, you're going to have to walk back to the house. You have to be slightly more responsible."[13]

For Rita, who once said she "was born loving books," the best thing about heading off to elementary school was that it introduced her to reading. "I was always told when I was young that I would learn to read in the first grade. So the first day of the first grade, I came home from school furious because I hadn't learned to read yet," she joked.[14] She later described the nineteenth-century adventure classic *The Count of Monte Cristo*, by Alexandre Dumas, as her favorite book.

By her own account, Rita was not an exceptional student and did not participate in team sports, though she became manager of a girls' volleyball team. She took a few theater classes but said that the dramatic arts didn't hold her interest "because I didn't want to be around weird people with colored hair."[15]

Her small-town upbringing and her family's quiet lifestyle kept Rita mostly anchored in the Texas hills, at least until her grandfather sent her and a friend on a trip to New York City during their freshman year in high school. Rita loved it. "My mother will say that I came back and I realized there was a really big world out there," she said in 2012.[16]

After high school, Rita headed for College Station, Texas, the home of Texas A&M University, about 150 miles northeast of Johnson City. At A&M she majored in agribusiness—a common field for students attending any of the country's "land grant" educational institutions, which were established to focus on agriculture, science, engineering, and other traditionally practical curricula. She studied in Italy during the final semester of her sixth year at A&M.[17]

Rita LeBlanc claimed a long-running fascination with football. She was eight years old when her grandfather bought the New Orleans Saints, and she loved visiting the team's headquarters and hearing the football conversations at family gatherings. She said she became increasingly interested in becoming involved with the team as she got older, and she began to picture herself owning the team. "I always knew that I wanted to," she told a reporter.[18]

But even though she attended one of the most football-oriented universities in the country and soon after college would get her grandfather's nod as his heir to an NFL team, Rita LeBlanc apparently did not consider studying sport management at Texas A&M. The university's program is arguably among the top five in the United States and has sent hundreds of its graduates into professional management and sports-marketing careers. But Rita leaned toward on-the-job training for her future career, reportedly doing odd jobs at the Saints' training camp during summers of her college years and short internships at NFL offices such as the league's community relations department in New York, its publishing group in Los Angeles, and its film division in New Jersey.[19]

She was barely a year out of college when Tom Benson began hinting publicly that she would one day own the New Orleans Saints.[20] "Of everybody in my family . . . Rita is the only one that showed a real interest," he said later. "We have a very good relationship. She's intelligent. I hope it works out for her."[21]

Eventually, Rita LeBlanc, who began using "Benson" as a middle name when she started working with the Saints, participated in a new, one-week educational program designed for NFL executives at Stanford University.

Out of the Limelight

Of Tom Benson's three grandchildren, the firstborn is the least widely known, and that is likely by her own design. Dawn Marie Benson Jones, who is the daughter of Tom Benson's deceased son, Robert, grew up in a different environment from her cousins, which may partially explain why she developed attitudes that set her apart from them in adulthood.

Dawn would have no memory of living under the same roof with her mother and father, as her parents divorced when she was barely a year old.[22]

Her mother, Karen Wiemers Benson, remarried several years later, and Dawn Benson grew up living mainly with her mother and stepfather in Hondo, Texas, forty miles west of San Antonio. She did, however, maintain relationships with her Benson kin and spent some time at Tom Benson's ranch.

When her father died of cancer in 1986, Dawn Benson was sixteen years old. Twelve years later, she would marry Christopher Jones.[23]

While she is an heir to the Benson fortune, Dawn chose not to become involved in her grandfather's businesses. Instead, she focused on building a career and life outside of the Benson family's sphere of influence.

After graduating from Baylor University with a master's degree in education, she taught middle school for several years and later worked as a consultant for an educational software company in San Antonio. Eventually, she launched a similar business on her own and, in time, started her own learning center, providing various educational services for children. She ran the business until her family began to grow. She and Chris had a son in 2007, followed by twins two years later.

Today Dawn and her husband, who is a product manager for Dell, Inc., live with the three youngest of their four children in the Austin area. Chris's oldest son, who graduated from Baylor University, now works in banking.[24]

In early 2015, after her aunt Renee and cousins Rita and Ryan

The family of Tom Benson's oldest grandchild, Dawn Benson Jones, pictured at a gathering in Kennebunkport, Maine. From left: Chris Jones, Dawn Benson Jones, Gayle Benson, Tom Benson, Tyler Jones; front row: Sawyer, Sierra, and Seth Jones. (Courtesy of the Benson family)

asked a court to declare Tom Benson mentally incompetent, Dawn Benson Jones released a statement to San Antonio and New Orleans news media, decrying the family's actions. Referring to the "ugly conflict" that had unfolded publicly, she said she had hoped for a quick resolution "once other family members saw the irreparable damage that was being done by their actions." But because it had become clear "that they have no intention of stopping their relentless attacks, . . . I would like to publicly state my support for my grandfather, Tom Benson."[25] Noting that she remains close to her grandfather and his wife, Dawn added that she was "brokenhearted that other family members have chosen to publicly harass and humiliate the patriarch of our family—the very person who is responsible for giving them everything they have."

As her aunt and cousins continued their legal efforts to remove Tom Benson as trustee of their estate, Dawn Benson Jones, who also is named as an heir, sought to separate herself from their actions. In October 2015, she asked the court to let her remove her share of the trust and place the assets in a separate trust exclusively for her benefit.[26]

Chapter 12

The Grace Years

Almost anyone who becomes a "second spouse" in an established family can find it tricky to strike the right emotional chords with stepsons and stepdaughters they barely know. So it was for Grace Marie Trudeau Walker after she married Tom Benson in 1982.

Benson's thirty-five-year marriage to his first wife, Shirley, had been an exciting saga that took them through the adoptions of three children, the start of his career in auto retailing, the family's move from New Orleans to San Antonio, and years of wealth-building that had produced a fortune valued in the tens of millions of dollars. Shirley Benson was a beloved matriarch during those years as she raised the children and became a fixture at her husband's side. Many who knew her seemed to speak of her in the same terms—a "sweet lady" who loved her husband and children and was adored in return.

When Shirley Benson died in November 1980, it had been only about a year since doctors had diagnosed her with lupus, a condition that had steadily weakened her body. She passed away at the age of fifty-three. Tom and Shirley's children at the time ranged in age from twenty-one to thirty-two, and the couple had three grandchildren.

For Tom Benson, Shirley's death would bring on the worst of times. Though making money had become the fuel that drove him through every day of his working life, sharing his wealth and showering attention on his family gave him purpose. He loved coming home from the office to people who worshipped him. When Shirley died, he was as close as he has ever come to being inconsolable. "I'm going crazy. I just can't stand being alone," he confided to the family's longtime housekeeper, Viola Searcy, during the weeks after Shirley's death.[1]

Benson's daughter Renee later said in court testimony that her father called her every morning after Shirley died "because he would wake up and know he was alone."[2] The awful solitude moved Tom Benson quickly to a new relationship.

"I Just Want to Be Sure You're Here"

He had met Grace Trudeau in his high-school days, when he attended St. Aloysius in New Orleans and she was at St. Joseph's Academy, a private Catholic school for girls. The two had mutual friends and attended some of the same roller-skating parties.[3] Later, as Tom struck up a romance with his future wife, Shirley Landry, Grace was getting to know her future husband, Melvin Walker.

After Grace and Melvin married, she worked at Whitney National Bank in New Orleans, while her husband went to work at a Chevrolet dealership—the same company where Tom Benson began his career.[4] Melvin Walker eventually would work for Benson and would move the Walker family to San Antonio, where Benson was growing his dealership business. As Melvin and Grace Walker raised their five children in Texas, they sometimes socialized with Tom and Shirley Benson at auto industry conventions and other events that brought them all together.

Twenty-five years into the Walkers' marriage, tragedy struck, changing their relationship forever. The youngest of their children, Tim, was killed in an automobile accident in San Antonio. He was sixteen.

The death of a child can put a marriage under extreme stress, and Grace's sister, Marillyn Barbot, says Tim's death was hard on the Walkers' marriage. "Grace and Melvin split up a few years after Tim died. I just don't think Melvin knew how to handle Tim's death."

It was several years after her divorce from Melvin that Grace Walker reconnected with Tom Benson. She called on him to express her sympathies after Shirley Benson passed away, and Tom later telephoned her. Their first dinner date was on Valentine's Day.

In 1982, about eighteen months after Shirley Benson's death, Tom married Grace Trudeau Walker in San Antonio. It was the beginning of an enduring relationship between two people who had experienced deep personal loss. But at least two of Tom's children did not take well to the change.

People who were close to the family say that both of Tom Benson's daughters, Renee and Tootsie, appeared uneasy about the new woman in their father's life, and Renee was particularly offended by the marriage. "I think Renee wanted her father to herself," notes a relative who witnessed the family interactions. Anyone who tried to get close to Tom got a cold shoulder from Renee, says the relative, who adds: "She didn't want to share her father with anybody. That's my opinion."

Grace, whose inclination was to try to get along with everyone no matter what, at first showed few outward signs that the testy relationship with Benson's daughters bothered her, and for a long time she didn't discuss with her own children the difficulties she was up against in Tom's family. Tom Benson, too, tried to gloss over the awkward moments that would sometimes surface, a family member said.

Grace's two sons and two daughters, some of whom were starting families of their own at the time, had little occasion to interact directly with the Benson children as they saw them only rarely, such as at an occasional Saints game. Tom, who had purchased the team three years after marrying Grace, embraced her children as part of his family when it came to providing them with tickets and hosting them in his suite at home games.

But over the twenty-one years of her marriage to Tom, strained relations with his kids took a toll on Grace. Family members speculate that late in her life, after Grace was diagnosed with Parkinson's disease, the emotional pressures brought on by family friction may have speeded the progress of the malady.

Grace's daughter Mimi Peake told a reporter in 2015 that Grace had tried to remain active up until the end, but Peake wondered if her mother "would have lived longer" had she not been so upset by the friction. "It definitely took a toll on her," Peake said.[5]

Peake's sister, Susan Walker, agrees. She says that Grace endured "a constant belittling" by Tom Benson's kids during their marriage. "They were not happy that she married him."

Nevertheless, Walker and others say that Grace and Tom Benson had a happy marriage. Grace was able to feel joyful once again after the tragic death of her son and the failure of her first marriage. For Tom, it was a revival of a lifestyle that he had lost when Shirley Benson passed away.

"He was constantly holding Grace's hand and touching her, and he'd say, 'I just want to be sure you're here,'" Marillyn Barbot recalls.

After marrying, Tom sold the sprawling house on Pontiac Lane in San Antonio where he and Shirley had lived when they weren't spending time at the Johnson City ranch.[6] In its place, he bought a waterfront home in Rockport, Texas, situated along Aransas Bay about thirty minutes north of Corpus Christi. It became their favorite destination when they were in the Lone Star State. Grace loved being near the water, her family says, and she was crazy about fishing. "Their home was right on the water, and they had a long pier out into the water, and I'm telling you she fished until midnight," Barbot recalls.

Tom bought a two-way radio for Grace to use when she would stay on the pier after dark. "He would keep calling her to make sure she was all right," Barbot says.

In New Orleans, Tom and Grace Benson had a number of homes, all of which allowed easy access to Saints headquarters on Airline Drive in Metairie. For some years they lived in a large home on Brockenbraugh Court in the high-demand area called Old Metairie. Later they bought a condominium in Lake Marina Tower, overlooking Lake Pontchartrain. And after a few years they moved downtown to the One River Place condominiums, located in a high-rise along the Mississippi River. Tom Benson purchased a double unit in the elegant tower in 1991, and it became a hub for their local entertaining.

When Grace's health began to deteriorate in the late 1990s, the couple returned to their home in Old Metairie, where Benson owned a number of properties and several other relatives resided. "Tom took very good care of Grace," says Barbot. "She had 24/7 help."

Suited to Her Role

After her husband bought the New Orleans Saints, Grace

Benson adapted well to the changes in their lives. While Tom Benson had generally ducked media attention and maintained a low public profile throughout his business career, his purchase of an NFL team thrust him into a spotlight.

Benson adjusted grudgingly to increased demands for press interviews and the growing public interest in his businesses and personal life, while Grace embraced the couple's rising profile. An attractive and gracious woman who loved meeting people, Grace moved easily in social circles and seemed to enjoy being in the public eye. She took on volunteer responsibilities in various organizations and lent her name to a host of charitable fundraising efforts. Grace was well suited to her role as the wife of an NFL owner, friends said.

The couple enjoyed traveling, and Grace loved to shop for clothes and diamond jewelry during their occasional trips to Europe and Asia, including their 1993 visit to Japan where the Saints prevailed in an exhibition game against the Philadelphia Eagles in Tokyo. But many of the couple's favorite vacations were journeys in which they packed into a luxury recreational vehicle and joined fellow RV travelers for road trips that took them across several states.

After a number of years of owning the Saints, Tom Benson would indulge in the splashier "toys" typically held by professional sports team owners. He bought his first yacht in the early 1990s and dubbed the eighty-eight-footer the *Lady Grace Marie*.

In 1998, he transferred Grace's name to his new yacht, a 107-foot vessel that Burger Boat Company delivered to him in the Bahamas. Grace Benson consulted closely with designers on the vessel's interior, which included hand-painted furnishings, wood inlays, and Asian-themed decor. The couple frequently hosted family and other guests for parties and outdoor barbecues aboard the yacht, and they enjoyed cruising from Palm Beach, Florida, northward along the East Coast as far as Maine and Canada during summer vacations. They home-ported the vessel in New Orleans during football season.

"Tom loved family, and he enjoyed giving parties," Marillyn Barbot says. "Many times on a Saturday afternoon he'd invite some of the family over and go around Lake Pontchartrain in the yacht. That was Grace's thrill."

Blending Family

Along with the heady times surrounding the couple's involvement with the NFL, the years of Grace's marriage to Tom Benson brought heartbreaks. Less than a year after his purchase of the Saints, his son, Robert, passed away from lung cancer. Just five years later, his daughter Tootsie took her own life.

His ongoing work and responsibilities, and the support of Grace Benson and other family members, kept Tom Benson from sinking into despair in the wake of these losses. And as he absorbed their impact and turned for comfort to his remaining daughter, Renee, he also continued to embrace Grace's adult children, who were building their own lives in Texas and Louisiana.

As Benson looked to reduce his automobile holdings in the 1990s in order to concentrate on his football team, he turned, as always, to family members to see whether he might be able to draw them into the business. Mimi Walker had worked for some time in human resources for Benson's New Orleans dealerships, and she had eventually married another Benson employee, Martin Peake. As Tom Benson looked to downsize, he offered to sell his BMW dealership to Mimi and Martin Peake, and they jumped at the chance. Peake BMW has operated at Benson's original dealership location in Kenner ever since.

A year or so after launching the Peakes into their business, Benson offered to do the same for Susan Walker. Walker, who had a nursing degree from the University of Texas and had worked as an administrator for an insurance company, says she was surprised when her stepfather approached her one day and asked if she would like to be in the car business. The mother of two was intrigued by the prospect and soon agreed to the career change. Today Walker is the owner of Walker Volkswagen and Walker Acura in Metairie and Northshore Volkswagen in Mandeville. Her two grown children now work in management in her dealerships.

"Tom is an extremely generous person," Walker says. "He took care of everybody in his family. My two kids went to college on a trust fund he gave them. And he gave me the opportunity to buy these dealerships, as he did with my sister and brother-in-law."

Walker says Tom Benson's generosity to Grace Benson's

children did not end after her mother died. She and her siblings still get a call from Benson's office before Saints home games. "We still get tickets and parking passes to sit in the suite with him," she says.

Members of the family were part of Tom Benson's entourage at the Super Bowl in Miami in 2010 and had seats on the fifty-yard line, Walker notes. "He flew us all over there as part of the team. We had hotel rooms and were invited to the pregame party and picnic, and we had pictures taken with him—we were included in all of that."

When Grace Benson died in November 2003, then-NFL commissioner Paul Tagliabue was among those who weighed in with praise for her life. Calling her a "warm and gentle person" of great courage, he said in a statement released after her death: "She had the ability—at league meetings, at Super Bowls or in the Benson suite at Saints games—to make others feel that they were gracing her with their presence when the direct opposite was nearly always the case."[7]

Not everyone remembers Grace Benson with such warmth. In testimony she gave during court proceedings in San Antonio, in connection with her efforts to have her father removed as head of her trust funds, Renee Benson did not hide her ambivalence toward her stepmother.

"Did you have a good relationship with Grace?" a lawyer asked Renee in court.

"Good? Hmmmm. It varied. In the very beginning it was—she was very insecure and she wanted no one around except for her and my dad. Not her kids, not us, you know, not anybody," Renee said.[8]

Renee Benson went on to say that her relationship with Grace Benson improved somewhat as time went on. But most of Renee's complaints in her court testimony focused not on Grace but rather on Tom Benson's third spouse, Gayle.

With the death of Grace, Tom Benson had plunged once again into the loneliness that had haunted him after his first wife died twenty-three years earlier, and he had even less tolerance of it this time than before. Eleven months after Grace died, Benson made another trip to the altar with his new love, Gayle Marie LaJaunie Bird.

Like Grace, Gayle Benson would prove to be a good partner in the demanding and highly visible world of major league sports. She was attractive, poised, gracious, and well received by the people she met.

But also like Grace, Gayle Benson would not hit it off with Tom Benson's close relatives. Through more than a decade of marriage to Benson, the tension between Gayle and Tom's daughter Renee, as well as his grandchildren Rita and Ryan LeBlanc, simmered below the surface.

CHAPTER 13
Making Money in the NFL

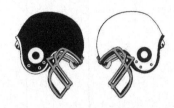

It takes a steep ante to enter the game of NFL ownership. While some of the thirty-two members of this exclusive club inherited either a team or the money to buy one, the rest amassed the required millions through their own businesses, which ranged from oil drilling to technology innovation to the sale of auto parts.

New England Patriots owner Robert Kraft got his start in a relative's packaging materials company, which he parlayed into an international business that fueled his $172 million purchase of the team. For Minnesota Vikings owner Zygi Wilf, his family's home-building business provided his share of the team's $600 million price.

Stephen Biscotti, one of the youngest NFL owners and the founder of staffing companies that served the engineering and technology sectors, earned his way to the fortune that enabled his purchase of the Baltimore Ravens for $325 million. Shahid Khan made a fortune in car bumpers and pumped $770 million of it into the startup of the Jacksonville Jaguars.

The NFL owners are a motley collection of individuals, or their successors, who built wealth mostly in traditional business and then catapulted themselves toward much greater fortunes through their ownership of a professional football team.

Tom Benson's foray into NFL ownership came after twenty-five years of building an automobile retailing business in Texas and Louisiana and buying and selling community banks. The deal he put together to buy the New Orleans Saints in 1985 likely could not be repeated today because of its complexity and the number of other investors involved. Benson bought a 31 percent controlling share in the team, which included 5 percent held by a family trust.

The NFL approved the cash-and-debt deal, in which small groups owned portions ranging from 5 to 10 percent of the team, but neither the league nor Benson was in love with the idea of having so many fractional owners involved. "I like 51 [percent ownership] because you don't have disputes among partners," then-NFL commissioner Pete Rozelle said shortly after Benson announced his purchase.[1] So within just a few years of acquiring the team, Benson bought out a few of his investors and raised his stake to 51 percent, concentrating his power and reducing the chance of dissent over team business.

After Benson bought the Saints, his business life became vastly more complicated. On one hand, he felt pumped up and proud as he became a center of attention in New Orleans and beyond.

"I want everybody to know who I am," he told one of his lawyers. "Everybody is saying, 'He's just a used car dealer.' Well, let them see me now."[2]

But having huge new responsibilities associated with the Saints meant that he needed more help to manage his original businesses. Benson began relying more heavily on family members, including his brothers and a cousin, along with longtime associates including San Antonio banker Tom Roddy, to ride herd on his extensive automobile dealerships and expanding banking operations in Louisiana and Texas.

He not only faced a slew of strategic decisions related to his sports team, but in contrast to the world of traditional private business, many of his decisions now would undergo intense scrutiny by local and national sports media. He had acquired a professional football team, an asset that routinely captured the attention of millions of people around the world.

It was not a particularly comfortable position for the car dealer from New Orleans' Seventh Ward who had kept his business matters and family life largely under wraps for a half-century. But for the sake of the soaring wealth that the sports team would bring him, Benson would adjust.

Easy Money

Owners of NFL teams have Pete Rozelle to thank for creating an extraordinarily favorable investing environment that makes would-be team owners' eyes light up. The longtime commissioner who headed the league during the 1960s, '70s, and '80s made it his mission to optimize revenue that came to the NFL from the rights it sold to television networks to air the weekly games throughout the football season.

In 1961, Rozelle persuaded the league's owners to back a revenue-sharing plan that let the NFL sell the TV broadcasting rights as a single package and split the revenue from the contracts equally among all the teams. That, he said, would ensure that such small-city teams as the Green Bay Packers could be financially competitive with teams in bigger media markets, and they would have more resources to improve their on-field performance as well.[3]

The commissioner also had to convince Congress of the wisdom of his proposal, as lawmakers had to grant an exemption from antitrust law in order to allow sports leagues to negotiate collective television contracts. Congress backed Rozelle, and he signed a contract with the CBS network worth about $4.6 million annually to carry the NFL games for a couple of seasons. In those first years of revenue sharing, each team received about $330,000.[4]

Over time, the value of the TV contracts has skyrocketed, with multiyear deals and a fatter schedule of air dates pushing total annual TV revenue into the billions of dollars. The league's shared-revenue pool eventually has come to include revenue from cable TV networks; collective merchandising, licensing, and sponsorships; and video and digital products. In recent years, the pool has included such deals as a $400 million, five-year contract with Microsoft for all teams to use Surface tablets and other Microsoft technologies on the sidelines during games. The league also inked a four-year, $4 billion deal with DirecTV that allows viewers to watch every football broadcast on several channels.

The results of all this self-promotion have been eye-popping. Including locally generated revenue such as ticket sales that is also subject to a split, the league's shared-revenue pool topped $7 billion for the 2014 football season. That meant that each team received a $226 million check from the NFL that had nothing to do with their performance on the field.[5]

Many people give credit for the league's wild revenue growth to Roger Goodell, now the league's commissioner. He wins praise for his understanding of the business and the league's branding potential, and the NFL has rewarded him richly. Goodell's salary topped $44 million in 2013,[6] making him the highest-paid employee—including players—in the NFL.[7]

Tapping Taxpayers

In 1985, the NFL's shared-revenue numbers were much smaller, but they were hardly inconsequential, and Tom Benson was much too savvy to overlook the risk-reducing power of guaranteed annual payments that were likely to increase over time. He had been eyeing the potential of NFL team ownership for some time, and when an opportunity arose, he would not let it slip away.

In his early days as an owner, Benson, whom many saw as a plain-vanilla businessman who understood cars and banks but not football, may have seemed a fish out of water in the NFL. But his colleagues in the league quickly came to respect his financial skills as they saw how he negotiated favorable lease terms for the Saints in the taxpayer-owned Superdome in New Orleans. Benson, they discovered, was a tough-as-nails bargainer and extraordinarily skillful in turning the terms of a deal in his favor.

His initial arrangement with the state of Louisiana in 1985 landed the Saints a twenty-one-year lease on the Superdome and nearly $3 million in annual inducements, including exemptions from paying state and city sales taxes on game ticket sales. He also finagled a promise of free land from the state for a team training facility.

Benson's deal to buy the team became a springboard for future negotiations that would pit him against some lawmakers and critics over ever-sweeter deals. His tactics shaped a theme that would become familiar over time.

In 1986, just a year after buying the team, Benson said he planned to fund $20 million in improvements to the Superdome to increase the number of luxury suites and concessions services and boost team revenue. But when lawmakers, facing tight budget constraints, threatened to remove $3 million that was set aside for the Saints under terms of the team's lease, Benson raised the possibility that he would sell the team if the state cut his subsidy.

"There's no way for the Saints to operate if they take the $3 million out of the budget," he told a reporter. "There's a lot of interest in other cities," he said, though when asked to elaborate, he had no comment.[8]

Lawmakers relented and the subsidy stayed in place, and Benson proceeded to search for more opportunities to juice up revenue from the Superdome. While season ticket sales were one avenue, Benson focused heavily on the stadium to boost his growth potential.

As part of his deal to buy the Saints, management of the box suites in the Superdome came under the team's control. With suites then priced between $15,000 and $38,000 per year, expanding the lucrative luxury seating used by wealthy individuals or companies to entertain clients became his priority.[9] Benson more than doubled the number of suites in the Dome to about 130 within the first few years of owning the team, and the additions appeared to have the desired effect.

Asked in 1989 about the Saints' profitability relative to other teams in the league, Benson answered: "I can tell you we're in the top five."[10] Financial records introduced in a court case later brought by NFL players against the league bore him out. The records indicated that the Saints in 1990 were the most profitable team in the NFL, with operating profit—income from operations before payment of taxes and debt service—of $14 million.[11] Just behind the Saints were the Cincinnati Bengals, Pittsburgh Steelers, Seattle Seahawks, and Tampa Bay Buccaneers. Records in the court case brought later by Peter Glaser and Wendell Gauthier pegged the Saints' actual 1990 profit—after taxes and debt service—at $7.1 million and showed the profit rose to $9.5 million in the following year.[12]

After increasing his stake in the team from 31 to 51 percent in the early 1990s, Benson felt more empowered to act unilaterally in seeking subsidies from the state in connection with the Superdome. His next big push came in 1993, when Dome renovations became part of a larger "sports complex" bill offered up in the legislature. The $215 million proposal included seven separate projects and would pay off some $50 million in old bonds.

The measure authorized the Louisiana Stadium and Exposition

District, or Superdome Commission, to sell new bonds to fund projects that included $21 million in Dome renovations. Terms of the deal also included a lease extension on the Dome, securing the stadium for the Saints through 2018.[13]

Other pieces of the sports complex bill funded the construction next to the Dome of a new arena that eventually would house a National Basketball Association team (which Benson years later would own) and a new baseball field adjacent to the Saints practice field for the city's AAA baseball team, the New Orleans Zephyrs. Rising public interest in the Saints had inspired lawmakers to build New Orleans into a much bigger "sports town" than ever before, and the foundation they laid with taxpayer money would open more opportunities for Benson to grow his profits down the road.

Stadium Game

Benson's success in negotiating increasingly favorable terms for his team in Louisiana's stadium raised his stature among his fellow NFL owners. Soon the league named him to one of its most important posts—chairman of the Finance Committee. The assignment put the Saints owner at the heart of crucial financial decisions made by the money-obsessed league. Members of the Finance Committee plot NFL strategies related to matters ranging from the review of individual stadium leases to revenue sources such as television rights and the licensing of league merchandise worn, used, or displayed by football fans worldwide.

Benson would serve three separate stints as chairman of the influential committee during more than twenty years as a member of the group. Midway through his tenure on the committee, he began an effort that nearly every NFL owner undertakes at some point—the push for a new stadium.

Benson began talking up the idea publicly early in 2001, complaining that the aging Superdome did not have enough space or up-to-date features that would help boost the Saints' revenue. He sprinkled his comments with hints that some other cities might make more profitable homes for the Saints in the event the team had to leave. Following a February meeting with then-governor Mike Foster, Benson told reporters that while he and the governor didn't lay out an action plan, "the first step is to make sure the Saints stay in New Orleans."[14]

Just a few months later, Benson rolled out plans for a forty-acre downtown complex anchored by a $450 million retractable-roof stadium, the building of which would require the dismantling of a public housing complex and the relocation of a few thousand residents from the historic Treme neighborhood of New Orleans. The announcement of the plan stunned then-mayor Marc Morial, who said Benson had not so much as mentioned the idea to him.

"It won't happen," Morial declared. "I think Benson is insensitive to his fan base when he talks about eliminating a neighborhood."[15]

Shaking off the criticism, Benson continued his push for a new stadium—somewhere in the city—for which he said the state should pay about $350 million and the NFL could throw in about $100 million more. The governor, unwilling to cross Benson but reluctant to dive into stadium discussions, appointed a fifty-member commission to undertake a two-year study of Benson's proposals and also explore the alternative of reengineering the Superdome to accommodate more high-priced seats and suites in order to jack up revenue for the team.

Benson agreed to back off from the new-stadium plan temporarily. But he was not about to cool his heels for two years without some kind of reward, so he launched a demand for a new contract with the state that would bolster profits of the team as it made do with the Superdome.

He shifted his talks with Foster to focus on incentives that would make it worth the Saints' while to remain in New Orleans. Among other things, he sought a guarantee of $25 million in annual revenue as the study of stadium options proceeded. Keeping the threat of relocating the team alive, he also pressed for a clause in the contract that would allow the Saints to leave Louisiana before its lease expired by paying a penalty to the state.

The deal Benson walked away with a few months later would leave any sports-team owner weak with envy. The state agreed to pay the Saints annual inducements that would start at $12.5 million and rise incrementally to $23.5 million if the team would just promise to stay in New Orleans, potentially for another ten years. The payments would total $186 million, as long as the team simply stayed put. The deal also included $6.75 million to cover three-fourths of the cost to build an indoor practice center at Saints headquarters, with the team paying the remainder of the tab.

Published reports at the time said some of the toughest negotiations centered on the terms of an exit clause. "Saints officials wanted the ability to break the lease two years ahead of schedule if they rejected the state's decision on the stadium or decided New Orleans can't financially support a National Football League team," reporter Jeff Duncan wrote in a September 2001 article in the *Times-Picayune*.[16]

In the end, Benson agreed he would owe an $81 million fee to the state if he should decide to cart the team off before 2010, which he suggested he might be willing to do. He termed the $81 million penalty "an awful lot of money," then added, "but that's better than, I don't know, having an empty ballpark."[17]

Other NFL team owners, who also had to weigh in on the new lease, gave it a quick thumbs up. But even then, the league was not content to let matters ride in New Orleans. Days after the owners voted their unanimous approval of Benson's deal with the state, NFL commissioner Paul Tagliabue made it known that he wanted local businesses to make a commitment to the Saints as well.

The theory that teams in smaller markets such as New Orleans need extra support to turn the kind of profits that big-city owners enjoy had been a recurring theme in the NFL, and Tagliabue cited Buffalo, New York, as an example. In an agreement that the Buffalo Bills reached with the state, New York agreed to fund $60 million worth of new luxury suites and club concessions to keep the team in its existing stadium. But the Bills insisted on a clause stating that the agreement would be void if the team did not sell at least $11 million a year in suites and seats. To that end, a civic booster group came together to lobby local businesses to commit to ticket and sponsorship purchases.

"The critical thing for me was to get the private sector to commit to some long-term financial—not just goals—but obligations," Tagliabue said during a 2001 visit to New Orleans.[18]

Journalist Neil deMause, who has written extensively about

the politics and financing of sports, says that putting the power of the league behind an individual owner's local lobbying effort has become commonplace. "The NFL obviously takes an interest in these deals. Commissioners will fly in and make threats for an owner if the owner needs to scare the local officials. It really is a well-oiled machine."

Coauthor of the book *Field of Schemes: How the Great Stadium Swindle Turns Public Money into Private Profits,* deMause says that taxpayer assistance has provided "a huge revenue boost" for many team owners as subsidies have skyrocketed during the last several decades. Owners have come to expect some kind of public funding, whether in the form of a new stadium or annual direct payments, he notes. "It has really become part of the business model."

In his book, co-written with Joanna Cagan, deMause wrote that the drive for new arenas and stadiums drains billions of dollars annually from public treasuries for the sake of private owners.

He says that while Tom Benson's quest for a new stadium was typical of owner behavior, the 2001 deal with the state, which sent big annual payments to the Saints with no expectation other than that the team would stay put, broke new ground. "Benson really pioneered the concept of being paid to play in your own stadium. The state agreed to pay him $186 million over ten years to play at the Superdome. That's something that was not done at the time." In effect, the state said, "We don't want to build a new stadium but we'll pay you to play in the old one," deMause says.

In some respects, maybe the deal made sense. Rather than funnel money to the team through construction of a new stadium, "the state decided it was cheaper just to hand over the money straight up," he says.

Other sports-team owners were so impressed with this "gift that kept on giving" that some copied Benson's effort in their own cities, deMause says. National Basketball Association team the Indiana Pacers, for instance, finagled a similar deal to play in its arena and, like Benson, negotiated an out clause allowing it to cancel its lease in the event of sluggish revenues.

National Hockey League team the Arizona Coyotes "completely copied off the Benson model" in a subsidy deal with that state, deMause adds. "Benson certainly earned a place in sports history for coming up with a creative way" to get taxpayer money, he says.

"Helpful" NFL

Along with increasingly lucrative revenue sharing from national television rights, sponsorships, and merchandising, an ever-greater reliance on taxpayer support has nearly eliminated ordinary financial risk from the business of NFL team ownership. Though teams that are weighed down with debt may still struggle, most cruise from year to year on a cushion of easy revenue and subsidies that over the long run more than offset dollars the owners agree to invest into their own properties.

Still, some owners continue to bemoan thin profits, and because nearly all NFL teams are privately owned, their owners do not have to open their books to prove their purported financial pain. But occasionally, closely held information slips into public view.

Carolina Panthers owner Jerry Richardson, for instance, in 2010 and 2011 complained loudly of a difficult financial environment as the NFL prepared to tangle with its players over their collective-bargaining agreement. Richardson urged fellow owners to "take back our league" with a management-friendly contract.

But a later analysis of the Panthers' financial statements that was leaked to the press revealed that the team's operating profit for those years totaled more than $100 million. And as the team went 2-14 on the field in the 2010 season, Richardson and his partners paid themselves $12 million.[19]

Records of the Green Bay Packers provide a basis for estimating financial performance across the NFL because, as a publicly owned enterprise, the club's records are open to public view. It is through the records of the Packers, a corporation that since 1923 has been owned by thousands of fans who purchased shares in the club, that details of the NFL's national revenue-sharing with teams become clear.

In 2014, for example, the Packers received $226.4 million in revenue from the NFL's national TV contracts, sponsorships, and merchandise licensing, which shows that the NFL divided $7.24 billion among its thirty-two teams in that year. That total was a 21 percent jump from the previous year.

The Packers, which regularly releases public statements about its financial condition, set a revenue record in 2014, topping $375 million in a 15 percent revenue rise from the previous year "due mostly to the new national broadcast contracts that boosted the revenue of all the teams in the league," according to a team statement in July 2015.[20]

National revenue comprises about 60 percent of the Packers' total revenue, and the team said it also boosted its local revenue by $13 million with help from a new Pro Shop it opened at Lambeau Field.

Though the Packers' expenses also rose in 2014, due to stadium improvements paid for by the club, the team's operating income jumped 30 percent. After paying debt costs and other expenses, the Packers netted a $29 million profit.[21]

In other words, even as the team depreciates the $300 million it has poured into stadium improvements and continues to fund mega-contracts for star players, the Packers' bottom line remains strong. Team president Mark Murphy credited the rosy financial picture to factors including the rising popularity of professional football and the Packers, as well as a collective-bargaining agreement that gives owners greater predictability in player costs. "Plus, the league financing is really helpful," he said.[22]

Any thoughts that Benson's vision of a new stadium might fade into the background after he wrapped up terms of his 2001 subsidy deal with the state were misplaced. As the clock ticked toward what had become a three-year deadline for Louisiana's stadium commission to weigh in with the results of its study—and as the Saints received annual subsidies that climbed from $12.5 million to $15 million during that period—Benson remained focused on the shortcomings of the aging Superdome.

Why continue to push for a new stadium when the state and the NFL's national TV deals were sending the Saints "free money" in the form of annual subsidies and shared revenue? Longtime New Orleans sports columnist Pete Finney summed it up.

"It always amuses me to hear one owner after another say, 'I need a new stadium to remain competitive and compete for a championship,'" Finney wrote in a *Times-Picayune* column in November 2004. "What those owners should be saying is: 'I need a new stadium to increase the value of my franchise.'"[23]

Splashy new venues were boosting valuations of some teams, and owners whose teams played on older fields were anxious to jump into the game.

But events soon would converge to frustrate Tom Benson's stadium hopes in New Orleans. For one thing, a statewide election had put a new governor in office.

Kathleen Blanco had moved into the governor's mansion in January 2004, and one of her first challenges was to figure out how to address looming budget shortfalls. The likelihood that she would support a big taxpayer-financed stadium was slim.

In fact, Governor Blanco early on began to cast a skeptical eye on the 2001 deal the state had concluded with Benson. The state was slated to fork over $15 million to Benson in 2004 under that agreement and couldn't afford it, Blanco said, and Louisiana would have to "borrow" money from an economic-development

Louisiana governor Kathleen Blanco and Tom Benson answer questions in 2004 about $15 million the state owed the New Orleans Saints under an agreement signed by the previous governor. (AP Photo)

fund to cover the payment.[24] Blanco made it known that she would like to renegotiate the 2001 deal.

Not surprisingly, the panel appointed to study new-stadium feasibility also weighed in on the side of fiscal conservatism. A new stadium was unnecessary, a consulting group concluded, recommending instead a search for the money to do a $175 million renovation of the Superdome.

Blanco, meanwhile, invited Benson to open the Saints' financial records so that taxpayers could have a look at the team's books before making decisions about providing more financial support.[25]

The governor knew that a public review of the Saints' financials would not occur. But by the time the state officially nixed construction of a new venue, Benson had seen the writing on the wall anyway and revised his stadium stance. He would settle for an extensive renovation, preferably on the state's dime, and the state should not only continue its payment of annual subsidies to the team but extend the arrangement through 2020.

Benson followed his familiar pattern of reiterating that he was "totally committed" to keeping the team in New Orleans, while at the same time dangling the possibility of going elsewhere. He said time was of the essence in concluding a new, long-term agreement between the state and the Saints because the NFL wanted stability in New Orleans.

"I don't want to move. I don't want to sell," Benson stated. "We have three choices: we can build a new stadium, extend and enhance our current agreement, or tell us to leave. And we have to do this by early next year."[26]

NFL commissioner Tagliabue soon piped in with perspective from the league. The Saints' situation in New Orleans "doesn't look like it's any better today than it was a year ago," he told a reporter. "If anything, it looks worse."

He also hinted that the 2001 arrival of a professional basketball team, the New Orleans Hornets, was siphoning some local attention away from the Saints.[27] Then the league announced that New Orleans had been eliminated from consideration to host the 2009 Super Bowl because the Saints' lease with the state was set to expire in 2010.

Throughout the talks that occurred in 2004, the Saints,

through their then-director of administration Arnold Fielkow, emphasized the positive effect of the team on the economy of New Orleans and Louisiana. Team officials cited a 1999 study by a local economist who estimated the Saints generated $250 million a year in spending at other local businesses, and taxes paid as a result.

Meanwhile, Fielkow said that the Saints would need ongoing state subsidies in order to keep the team in the "middle of the pack" in terms of revenue among NFL franchises. The statement was accurate, within limits, based on the annual analysis done by *Forbes* magazine, which placed the Saints at number twenty in the NFL with $175 million in revenue in 2004.

But Fielkow stopped short of mentioning a more important measure. The *Forbes* analysis pegged the Saints' operating income—revenue minus most expenses—at $42.6 million in that year, putting the team in eighth place in operating profits among the thirty-two members of the league.[28]

As the Saints racked up that profit in 2004, the team had received a $15 million cash payment from the state of Louisiana and roughly $100 million from the NFL's pool of national revenue that is shared among the teams.

Chapter 14

Walloped by Katrina

Once the state of Louisiana officially took the matter of a new stadium for the New Orleans Saints off the table, at least temporarily, an uneasy relationship continued between Tom Benson and Gov. Kathleen Blanco.[1] Immediately after taking office, the governor had taken a tougher stance on subsidies for the team than had her easygoing predecessor, Mike Foster.

Armed with a consultant's report suggesting that about $175 million worth of improvements to the Superdome should keep the Saints competitive with peers, in terms of enhanced revenue and attracting upcoming Super Bowls, Blanco met with Benson a few times in early 2005.[2] She proposed that the state could undertake the recommended renovations, including adding luxury suites and pricey sideline seats, and could also continue paying annual subsidies to the team until renovations were complete. Thereafter, Louisiana would pay inducements at a lower rate, starting at $9.5 million per year.

She asked Benson to shoulder $40 million of the renovation costs. According to Superdome officials, Benson countered with a $17.5 million offer, representing 10 percent of the expected total.[3]

The two did not iron out their differences because Benson broke off talks in the spring, saying that he planned to focus on the upcoming football season and that he would resume discussions with Blanco after the season ended. During the summer, the governor tried to get Benson back to the negotiating table and even visited Saints headquarters in Metairie to ask him to resume talks. But by mid-August, the chasm between the Saints owner and the governor appeared as wide as ever.[4]

What neither knew at the time was that things were about to get a lot worse.

In late August 2005, residents of New Orleans were becoming fixated on reports of a tropical depression that had developed in the southeastern Bahamas and was moving slowly toward the northwest.

Locals were accustomed to tracking weather systems through the tropics during hurricane season and following forecasts of when and where the storms might make landfall. The development of a storm in late August was not unusual.

But some New Orleans residents had a bad feeling about this one. The system was large, and meteorologists said that atmospheric conditions were nearly ideal for it to grow and gain strength. The chances were high that it would enter the Gulf of Mexico, they cautioned.

Locals know that once a big storm makes its way into the Gulf, no one who lives on or near the coast can feel safe. They became more focused on the weather reports. The National Weather Service named the storm Katrina.

By August 26, Katrina was a major hurricane. It had, indeed, entered the Gulf—on weather maps the system almost completely obscured the water—and it had taken a northward turn, as forecasters predicted it might.

The graphical "cone" of potential landfall locations that forecasters showed on their maps had people in the Florida panhandle scrambling to get ready, as the storm appeared bound for the Pensacola area. New Orleans at that point was at the far western edge of the cone of possibilities.

The local threat appeared mild on that Friday as the Saints prepared to play their third preseason game, against the Baltimore Ravens, in the Superdome. But by the time the teams took the field, the picture had changed.

In a late-afternoon weather update, forecasters had shifted the entire landfall-prediction swath almost 175 miles to the west. Suddenly, New Orleans lay not at the edge of the cone but almost exactly at its center. And the massive hurricane was gaining strength. Governor Blanco declared a state of emergency, as did her Mississippi counterpart, Gov. Haley Barbour.

If there is anything good about a hurricane, it is that people who are in its path generally have time to prepare for its arrival and, if the threat is strong enough, get out of the way. Katrina was moving northward slowly enough that if people took heed, they would be safe. But the slow pace of the storm also meant it would have time to gain power as it swirled above the warm waters of the Gulf. In fact, the hurricane was building toward peak winds of about 170 miles per hour.

On Saturday morning, like residents throughout New Orleans, people at Saints headquarters went into a serious decision-making mode. The employees all had their own personal households to worry about, but managers in charge of both team and business operations had to keep Tom Benson's assets uppermost in their minds. As they prepared to leave the city, they knew that first they must batten down the hatches at the team's Airline Drive training camp and offices.

New Orleans mayor Ray Nagin issued a mandatory evacuation order for all residents in the city proper, and officials in surrounding areas were following suit.

It was a bad time for the football team to be distracted. The Saints were slated to play a fourth preseason game against the Oakland Raiders on Thursday as they neared their regular-season opener against the Carolina Panthers on September 11. Under then-head coach Jim Haslett, and led by quarterback Aaron Brooks, the team hoped to improve on its 8-8 record from 2004.

On Sunday, August 28, the Saints boarded a plane for San Jose, California, where they would practice at San Jose State University for the Raiders game. From there, they would watch and worry as news of the events in New Orleans splashed across television screens worldwide.

Tragedy on a Massive Scale

The days that followed would become the stuff of horrific legend as Hurricane Katrina slammed ashore in southeastern Louisiana and one of the biggest disasters in U.S. history began to unfold, seemingly in slow motion.

In many respects, the city actually dodged a deadly bullet when the eye of the storm, in a late course change, crossed the coast slightly to the east of New Orleans, with its winds weakened to about 125 miles per hour. Though downed trees and debris littered the city, and many homes and businesses had sustained serious wind and rain damage, the vast destruction many feared had not materialized.

But hours after the storm had passed, a new threat emerged. People started noticing standing water in streets. More alarming, the water was rising.

It would take hours more for the reality of what was occurring to become clear: surging waters driven by Katrina's winds had forced their way into local canals. Overwhelmed by the pressure, man-made levees and floodwalls on several of the waterways had burst open, releasing gushing saltwater from the Gulf and nearby lakes into New Orleans. Within a few hours, 80 percent of the city was under water, as deep as fifteen feet in some areas.

The toll on New Orleans was unimaginable. Some 1,500 people who were trapped by fast-rising waters had drowned. Tens of thousands of homes and businesses were wrecked; whole neighborhoods were left in shambles. Hundreds of people who had sought safety on rooftops would huddle there for days until rescuers in boats or helicopters could find and save them.

As the water rose throughout the city on the first day, a separate tragedy became apparent in the heart of downtown.

In an emergency decision on the day before Katrina made landfall, Mayor Nagin and Louisiana Superdome officials designated the Dome as a shelter of last resort, meaning that people who were unable to leave the city or had nowhere safe to go would be allowed to enter the Dome and stay until the danger had passed. What no one had foreseen was that the Dome itself would become a casualty. Katrina's winds ripped a hole in the roof, allowing drenching rains to pour in as some sixteen thousand people who had gone there seeking safety scrambled to get out of the way. To make matters worse, the subsequent flooding of the city pushed water into the basement of the Dome and all the way around the structure, creating an island prison of human anguish and misery that New Orleans would never forget.

New Orleans in the days to come would see a massive if halting mobilization of local, state, and federal resources aimed at restoring order and safety in the city. As military personnel carrying rifles and semiautomatic weapons patrolled city streets in Humvees, heavy trucks plowed through standing water bringing supplies into some areas and debris out of others. The drone of helicopters overhead was nearly constant.

As the emergency response continued over a period of weeks, a cadre of stunned business and civic leaders, putting one foot in front of the other in the wake of an unprecedented disaster, called citywide planning meetings to figure out what they could possibly do to keep their 300-year-old city alive. It was a struggle that would go on for years.

Chaos Engulfs Saints

As their city rubbed its eyes in disbelief following the events of August 29, 2005, the New Orleans Saints fretted from afar. Players and staff who had fled to California ahead of the storm dealt with problems in their own households at home as best they could, while also preparing for the Oakland preseason game on September 1.

After losing that game, the team boarded a plane bound for San Antonio, which Saints spokesman Greg Bensel announced would become their homebase for the immediate future. For Tom Benson, San Antonio seemed the natural place to flee with his team, given his history in the city. He still had auto and banking businesses in the area and his ranch nearby, and he knew that local officials, who had long wanted the city to have its own football team, would welcome the Saints in a time of need.

Two days after the storm, some Saints staffers who had evacuated New Orleans with their families to other cities and states received orders via text message—the only mode of mass communication that worked reliably after the hurricane—to get to San Antonio as soon as possible. Others were told to head for Baton Rouge and join a police-escorted convoy to the team's headquarters in Metairie, where they would help load trucks with desks, files, and football equipment to be taken to San Antonio.

The plan for the Saints' 2005 season came together fairly quickly. They would play most of their season on the road, dividing their "home" games between their temporary headquarters at San Antonio's Alamodome and LSU's Tiger Stadium in Baton Rouge, after playing the first one at Giants Stadium in New Jersey.

Shortly after the team took up temporary residence in Texas, rumors began to swirl that the Saints had left New Orleans for good. It was a difficult story for Louisiana officials to counter given that the Saints' "home," the Superdome, had suffered serious damage from the hurricane, the subsequent flood, and several days of housing thousands of people without electrical power, water, or working sewage systems.

The Saints training camp was not immediately available either. Though the hurricane had not done extensive damage to the buildings, and while the camp is located in a suburban area that did not see serious flooding, emergency management personnel, including the Federal Emergency Management Agency, had taken over the Saints facilities and surrounding grounds as a staging area for equipment and personnel brought in to tackle the city's cleanup.

Clearly, the team would not be able to return to New Orleans quickly.

Benson and Saints spokesmen later would deny vehemently that the owner had ever given serious consideration to permanently relocating the team to San Antonio or anywhere else. Obviously in the wake of the storm, they said, the team could not operate from its headquarters. And as much as the team and its owner might want to show support for the city during its time of need, Benson had to concern himself with the stability and ongoing viability of his NFL property.

No other NFL team had ever faced the challenges that the Saints found themselves up against in 2005. A disruption in the team's ability to fulfill its game schedule and live up to other league-wide obligations could have serious repercussions not only for the team and its owner but for the NFL.

What Tom Benson saw in front of him was a major-league

sports team that had a value somewhere around $800 million and a payroll well above $100 million. The team had been forced out of its home, but its expenses continued and were growing daily, with the added costs of dislocation and housing the team and staff in another city.

As the organization operated from makeshift offices in the basement of the Alamodome in downtown San Antonio, Benson and his senior staff not only had to figure out how to keep the operation going through the crisis but also how to respond to criticism from people in New Orleans who were getting jittery about the possibility that the team would not return. By some accounts, that concern led to the departure of a key executive soon after the Saints' regular season began.

Executive Vice President of Administration Arnold Fielkow had been with the Saints executive staff since 2000, after working in Major League Baseball's player development system. His primary mission was to expand the Saints' fan base to encompass a wider geographic area.

As one of the smaller cities in the NFL family, New Orleans presented challenges in terms of selling game tickets. In a time when home games did not air on television in the home market if the stadium seats did not sell out, an inability to fill the Superdome could have costly repercussions.

Fielkow's job was to reach throughout Louisiana and into neighboring markets along the Gulf Coast that did not have an NFL team nearby, and generate excitement and loyalty around the New Orleans Saints. By most measures, the effort succeeded. Ticket sales grew, with a substantial number of buyers located fifty miles or more away from New Orleans. Box suite and corporate sponsorship sales also increased.

But in the weeks after Katrina, serious conflicts developed between Fielkow and his boss. Suddenly, in mid-October 2005, the day after the Saints lost a heartbreaker to archrival the Atlanta Falcons in the Alamodome, the organization released a statement saying that Fielkow "is no longer associated with the team."[5]

Fielkow would not comment on the reason for his departure and still declines to discuss the matter.

But after leaving the team, the Wisconsin native whose family had come to love New Orleans, decided to run for a seat on the City Council. He prevailed in his campaign against a longtime incumbent to win an at-large position on the seven-member body, and many political observers believed that the public's perception that he had fought to keep the Saints in New Orleans helped swing votes his way. "He lost his job with the Saints because he had the guts to tell his boss that the team needed to do more to demonstrate its commitment to the city," editors at New Orleans newspaper *Gambit Weekly* said of Fielkow in a pre-election endorsement statement.[6]

Three other Saints execs would part ways with the team soon after Fielkow's departure. Marketing director Connie Kowal resigned at Benson's request the day after Fielkow left. Mike Feder, general manager of Benson's Arena Football League team and manager of business operations in Baton Rouge, resigned several weeks later, as did corporate sales director Chris Kenyon.[7]

"Stealing a Dead Man's Wallet"

If people in New Orleans saw Tom Benson's firing of Arnie Fielkow as a bad sign for the future of the team in their city, observers in Texas saw the flip side of the coin. "The New Orleans Saints may have one less advocate for keeping the team in New Orleans," the *San Antonio Business Journal* said in reporting Fielkow's departure.[8] While the paper noted that Benson had said he would not comment on the future of the team until the season ended, the article postulated: "The move may make it a little easier for San Antonio mayor Phil Hardberger to convince Benson to keep the Saints in San Antonio permanently."[9]

The possibility of the Saints taking up full-time residence in San Antonio was not an idea that had hatched overnight, nor was it born out of the disaster in New Orleans. In fact, the potential relocation of the team to San Antonio had been a hot topic in the local press for some time.

Lawyer Phil Hardberger had made Tom Benson's perceived interest in moving to Texas part of his campaign pitch as he began his run for mayor early in 2005. Vowing to bring the Saints to San Antonio, Hardberger won the election in a runoff and took office in June 2005.

Months later, after the Saints sought refuge in his city, the mayor seized the moment to reinvigorate his campaign promise. "I think Tom Benson would like to stay here permanently and I, as mayor of San Antonio, would like to have the team stay here permanently,"[10] he told a reporter in mid-October 2005.

Hardberger claimed that Benson had agreed to participate in discussions aimed at making the team the "San Antonio Saints" before the start of the 2006 season. "I'm pretty comfortable in saying he wants to be here," Hardberger said.[11]

Though Benson was careful after Katrina to avoid a suggestion that he was considering a permanent relocation of the team, few people were buying it. And no wonder: Mayor Hardberger was hardly the only person in San Antonio to talk up the possibility of a Saints move before tragedy struck New Orleans.

More than three months before Katrina came ashore, an article published by *USA Today* reported comments made by Benson's longtime lawyer and close friend, Stanley Rosenberg. Speaking to a San Antonio reporter in May 2005, Rosenberg, who had been closely associated with Benson for nearly forty years, said that Benson was interested in moving the Saints to San Antonio, Albuquerque, or Los Angeles and that the team owner was considering invoking an exit clause in his lease at the Louisiana Superdome after the 2005 season.

"Tom has a house in San Antonio, a ranch in San Antonio and business interests in San Antonio," Rosenberg was quoted as telling a local paper. "He likes San Antonio very much."[12]

Rosenberg went on to say that, as Benson's lawyer, he had received several offers from parties interested in buying the Saints or persuading Benson to move the team. One offer exceeded $1 billion, he stated.[13]

"Tom has many alternatives when it comes to the Saints and he has received many different offers, including one from Los Angeles," Rosenberg said. He added that he had met during the previous week with a representative of New Mexico governor Bill Richardson about the possibility of the Saints moving to Albuquerque.[14]

Other newspapers around the country picked up on Rosenberg's comments, and as the story found a wider following, a reporter finally got Benson to respond. "My plan right now is to stay in New Orleans and let my granddaughter take this club over," he told the reporter while attending a spring NFL meeting in Washington, D.C. Benson's granddaughter Rita LeBlanc was then in her third year as an executive with the club.

"Lawyers sometimes talk too much," Benson said, trying to downplay Rosenberg's comments. "I'm not looking at any markets."[15]

But those words carried little weight in New Orleans after Katrina. Critics there said San Antonio's overt attempt to grab the Saints at such a time was "like stealing a dead man's wallet."

As speculation about his intentions with the team revved up post-Katrina, Benson and company were adamant that he, personally, had not specifically threatened to take the team to another city and that he did not intend to discuss the team's future until the current season ended. "No decision has been made about the future of the team, because no decision has been made about the future of New Orleans," Benson wrote in a lengthy open letter to Saints fans that appeared as a full-page ad published in several Louisiana newspapers in October 2005.[16]

Pointing out that in the wake of the devastation, the Saints were no different from many other local businesses whose future in New Orleans was thrown into question by the circumstances, he said the team's potential return to the city was made even more difficult by the fact that FEMA had taken over the Saints training camp without so much as asking permission.

Benson reminded readers that New Orleans is his hometown and that he had contributed millions of dollars to charities in the area. And he said he had refused numerous "lucrative offers to sell the Saints in order to maintain their presence in New Orleans."

Despite the fact that anguish and stress still blanketed the city, Benson could not resist including in his statement a thinly veiled mention of the team's need for a new stadium. "It must be made very clear that the future of our team in New Orleans will be determined by factors that are yet unresolved, such as economics and facilities, the very issues that we have struggled with prior to Hurricane Katrina," the letter said.[17]

Benson's letter did little to quell either the speculation about a team relocation or fans' anger over that possibility. Residents of the battered city were tired and depressed and had only begun trying to pick up the pieces of their broken lives. But they still had it in them to get riled up at the prospect of no longer having Saints football to rally around.

People in New Orleans had always felt deep personal ties to "their" football team. For nearly forty years, fans had stuck with the team, often in spite of its performance. There was something about having a team named "Saints" and going to games in the big domed stadium on Poydras Street that was quintessentially New Orleans. Tailgating parties in this city were more like backyard crawfish boils, and some fans donned Mardi Gras-style costumes for the games. The music that echoed through the streets on game days had an unmistakably local beat, and fans couldn't get enough of it.

Football games in New Orleans are all-out parties, and even when fans were so disgusted with the Saints' performance on the field that they wore bags over their heads and called the team Aints, the city, down deep, loved its team. Which is why all the talk of the Saints' possible departure in the weeks after Katrina got under people's skin.

"Is Tom Benson proud of himself? Does he not have a shred of human decency?" a man asked in an op-ed letter that termed Benson "a ruthless, uncaring, mean and greedy man."[18]

"Wanted: New Owner"

If Benson was taking any of the criticism to heart, it did not show. Several weeks after the hurricane, he tried to break the Saints' lease on the Metairie training facility, citing damage he said it had received at the hands of federal agencies that used it following the storm. Benson's lawyer Phil Wittmann sent a letter to Superdome management and several federal agencies complaining that, because of the damage, the team was unable to return to its headquarters and had to relocate its operations to San Antonio "at a very substantial cost" to the organization.[19] "The Saints will not be in a position to reoccupy the training facility for some time (if ever) and they intend to hold the agency/agencies responsible for the damage," the letter stated.[20]

But when a group of state and federal officials toured the training camp to assess damages, they found almost none. The administrative building, practice facility, and cafeteria received "very minimal damage" and there was no reason that the team could not move back in immediately, Superdome Commission chairman Tim Coulon declared. "I certainly would challenge the fact the facility is not usable," he said.[21]

Later, NFL commissioner Paul Tagliabue and NFL Players Association executive director Gene Upshaw also visited Saints headquarters to check conditions for themselves, and they, too, deemed it ready for occupancy.

A fan made his feelings about the matter known on an online message board. "Tom Benson is a liar. Period," he wrote in a posting that included photos of the training camp buildings.[22]

Nevertheless, Benson kept his team in San Antonio during the months when the Saints had arranged to play four "home" games in Baton Rouge. He did so despite the fact that no NFL-level training quarters were available in San Antonio, and the team had to practice in venues ranging from the Alamodome to a high-school field to a vacant building. Saints players complained about having to fly to every game in their schedule, except for the three they played at the Alamodome, when they could have been working out at their headquarters in New Orleans and traveling no farther than Baton Rouge for half of their games.[23]

Meanwhile, the public Benson bashing continued in letters, online message boards, and radio call-in shows. A local newspaper published a photo of a fan standing in front of Saints headquarters holding up a handmade sign. *Wanted: new owner. Caring, not greedy. PR experience a must,* the sign said.[24]

Chapter 15

Bad Day in Baton Rouge

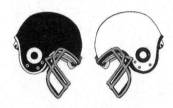

Five months after Tom Benson tried to distance himself from his lawyer's declaration that Benson planned to move the Saints out of New Orleans, and weeks after the city's near-death experience with the flood, Benson found himself in a changed world. The disaster had displaced his team just before the start of its regular season. Its upcoming game schedule was a mishmash of contests to be played in other clubs' stadiums, and the Saints organization was operating from the basement of San Antonio's Alamodome, where hastily hung curtains separated "offices," and floors were a jumble of electrical and phone wires that formed a communication network of sorts.

Benson had just booted Arnie Fielkow from the executive office, and news sources were pointing to Fielkow's strong support of having the Saints play their home games in Baton Rouge rather than San Antonio as a big reason why he lost his job. If Benson did have a distaste for playing in Baton Rouge, it would soon grow more bitter.

In the team's emergency scheduling efforts after Hurricane Katrina, the Saints had struck an arrangement with Louisiana State University officials to play four home games at Tiger Stadium on the LSU campus. The first Baton Rouge game would occur on October 30, between the Saints and the Miami Dolphins.

Ten days earlier, as Louisiana governor Kathleen Blanco weighed the state's budget priorities in light of potential spending needed for New Orleans' recovery, she had called NFL commissioner Paul Tagliabue to get his read on the future of the Saints. The commissioner had been circumspect, saying it was too early to gauge the city's economic comeback or its ongoing ability to support an NFL team.

But speculation that Tom Benson wanted to shop the Saints to other cities had become a hot topic inside the NFL. As questions arose about how the league might respond, Tagliabue formed a committee of eight team owners to consider the Saints' situation. The group included Pat Bowlen (Denver), Lamar Hunt (Kansas City), Robert Kraft (New England), Jeff Lurie (Philadelphia), Mike McCaskey (Chicago), Jerry Richardson (Carolina), Dan Rooney (Pittsburgh), and Wayne Weaver (Jacksonville).

When Tagliabue spoke to Blanco in mid-October, he assured her that a decision about whether the Saints would return to New Orleans would be made not by Benson but the league.[1]

Tagliabue traveled to Louisiana on October 30, accompanied by then-NFL executive vice president Roger Goodell, to attend the Saints' first game in Tiger Stadium, but earlier in the day he joined Blanco and other state officials for lunch at the governor's mansion. Also on hand were U.S. Sen. David Vitter, R-La., and Mitch Landrieu, a Democrat who was then Louisiana's lieutenant governor and later would become mayor of New Orleans.[2] The governor's spokesman said that the purpose of Tagliabue's visit was to show support for the storm-battered area and discuss options for the Saints' 2006 season.

That afternoon, the NFL execs also met with LSU chancellor Sean O'Keefe and a group of Baton Rouge business leaders.[3]

Tagliabue had met alone with Tom Benson earlier that week, while Benson was in New York to attend the funeral of a colleague. The commissioner was well acquainted with the rancor that the Saints' presence in San Antonio had stirred up around Louisiana and in other regions. Increasingly, it appeared that one of his greatest concerns was the impact the controversy could have on the image of the National Football League. While Tagliabue could sympathize with the financial squeeze that the team's forced relocation placed on Benson, he was worried about the fallout if the NFL were to be seen as abandoning New Orleans in its darkest hour.

All these concerns formed a fretful backdrop for the football matchup between the Saints and the Miami Dolphins that was set to begin at four o'clock on October 30.

It didn't help matters that the head coach of the Dolphins at that point was none other than Nick Saban, who had coached the LSU Tigers for five seasons and led the team to a BCS championship before leaving at the end of the 2004 season for a new career with the pros. Many LSU fans had not forgiven Saban for jumping ship, and they hoped to see the Saints bash the Dolphins and send a humbled Saban slouching out of the stadium.

Some 61,000 fans gathered for the game—not a bad turnout for a rescheduled pro game, but not nearly enough to fill the 90,000-seat Tiger Stadium—and those who saw Tom Benson on the sidelines said he didn't look happy. At one point, Benson and Tagliabue stood together and appeared to engage in a tense verbal exchange. One observer speculated that it might have been the moment when the NFL commissioner told Benson the league would not back him if he tried to take the Saints out of New Orleans permanently.

"You could just see Benson's reaction," the observer says. "He was so bitter and pissed off. It was after that that he got into it with a reporter and cameraman."[4]

After the Dolphins pounded the Saints 21-6, frustrated fans taunted Benson as he walked past the stands with his wife, Gayle, granddaughter Rita, and grandson, Ryan LeBlanc. Accounts differ as to whether Benson was itching for a fight or just caught off-guard as he navigated through unfamiliar territory, but Benson had a verbal exchange with a fan and then focused his attention on a nearby television reporter and cameraman who were covering the postgame activity. According to some reports, Benson lunged at the cameraman, slapped his hand at the camera, and knocked down a microphone.[5]

That night, Benson sent an e-mail to Tagliabue, saying that he would not return to Tiger Stadium because of inadequate security and that Benson and his family "could have all been severely injured or killed" in the stadium incident. New Orleans television station WWL-TV, whose reporter had covered the incident and claimed that Benson had not been in any danger, obtained a copy of the e-mail and publicized it.[6]

Saints spokesman Greg Bensel acknowledged that Benson had written an e-mail. "It was an emotional and distressing situation and very unfortunate for him and his family," Bensel said.[7]

When word of the stadium incident and Benson's letter to the commissioner got out, Saints fans became more worried than ever that Benson was about to cart off their team, and they were indignant at his suggestion that fans posed a threat of physical harm to Benson or his family.

If anything good came out of the events of October 30, it may have been the temporary truce that Benson struck with the state a week later, after tempers had cooled slightly. Tagliabue reportedly was behind a letter that Benson sent to Blanco suggesting a postponement of deadlines in the Saints lease on the Superdome that would have allowed the team to break the contract because the Dome was not usable. The delay, which Blanco agreed to immediately, bought both the state and the team more time to consider decisions that would have a long-range impact.[8]

Dome Decision

From the standpoint of Kathleen Blanco, Louisiana's fear of losing the Saints arose out of emotions, not economic concerns.

Quantifying the financial benefits to the state of having the team fill the Superdome eight times a year and helping to draw the occasional Super Bowl to New Orleans had always been tough. The crowds and the excitement the team stirred were clear, but the dollar impact, not so much, especially given that nearly all money generated in the Dome on game days went to the team, which had received an exemption from paying sales taxes on tickets, concessions, and the like.

Meanwhile, the outflow from the state to the team had been substantial, particularly in the wake of what Blanco saw as the ill-advised agreement that her predecessor, Mike Foster, had signed with Tom Benson in 2001. When concerns bubbled up in 2005 that Benson might take the team to San Antonio, Blanco couldn't help pointing to the $186 million in no-strings-attached inducements that Louisiana, under Foster, had agreed to pay the Saints over a ten-year period in return for the team doing little more than showing up for games.

"The Saints actually had been a huge economic burden to the state," she says. "I used to joke that San Antonio can't afford Tom Benson."

Blanco notes that ordinarily when the state invests in a business by granting some type of incentive, it expects to be rewarded as that business pays taxes, which the state can reinvest in education and other needs. But Benson always had a take-no-prisoners approach to negotiating, she says. "Tom believes that every penny generated by the Saints, including the taxes the players pay to the state, should go back to the Saints."

Nevertheless, Blanco understood the importance of the team to the people of Louisiana both before and after the hurricane. "People had an emotional stake in the team and the Superdome, and after Katrina, the people in and around New Orleans were working so hard to put their world back together," she says. "It was exhausting, depressing, and they were suffering because there was always one more hurdle, one more thing that they had to do in order to get their lives back."

Blanco was facing budget pressures that included the usual funding challenges, such as paying for public education and healthcare for the uninsured, along with the extraordinary costs of hurricane recovery across south Louisiana. The entire region had been hammered not only by Katrina but also by Hurricane Rita, which came along just a few weeks later and did substantial damage in south-central and southwestern Louisiana.

The state was projecting a billion-dollar budget shortfall. Still, Blanco had come to feel that putting the Superdome back in order should be a priority. "We had to do something with the Dome whether the Saints stayed or left," she says. "We couldn't predict what Tom Benson was going to eventually do, but we knew if we did not do anything, our chances of losing the Saints were heightened, and if we did do something, there was a possibility that we could keep the team."

Whether any amount of refurbishing on the Dome would be enough to hold the Saints was an open question. Blanco says that only one thing could have decisively "stopped the noise" about the team leaving. "Tom Benson really wanted us to build him a new stadium, and when the storm came along, he even talked about it again."

A new stadium was out of the question in Louisiana in 2005, but Blanco launched first steps toward a rehab of the existing one. She ordered engineering studies to determine whether the Dome had been destabilized or fundamentally compromised by the storm. After learning that it was structurally sound, "we started trying to figure the cost of renovation and where the money would come from," she says.

As a state-owned property, the Superdome was eligible to receive FEMA assistance for a restoration, and the state expected a substantial insurance payment. The question was, should the state spend more to upgrade the Dome rather than merely return it to its pre-Katrina condition?

"That's when Paul Tagliabue called," Blanco says. Tagliabue was pleased to hear that Louisiana would move forward with Superdome repairs and said he understood the difficulty that uncertainty about the Saints presented.

At that point, the state had laid out a two-year timetable for repairing and making renovations to the Dome. But Tagliabue presented a new challenge to Louisiana. As Blanco recalls it, Tagliabue said:

"You know, Tom has been very upset, and his business is at stake. But if you can get that Dome game-ready for the first regular game next year in September, I will guarantee you that Tom Benson will not leave New Orleans. I will take care of Tom if you think you can get the building ready."

The challenge of meeting that timetable was almost unimaginable. The Dome had a hole in the roof, water had blown in, and weeks after the storm, mold and mildew permeated every inch of the place. All the seats, equipment, and flooring were ruined. The 1.8 million-square-foot Dome would have to be completely gutted before anything else could happen. And construction teams were increasingly hard to find with much of the city in need of repair.

Blanco made a leap of faith. "I said yes, not knowing if we really could do it."

Oversight of the construction project fell to Doug Thornton, local head of Philadelphia-based SMG, which manages the Superdome. Thornton would be the one to ride herd on the job start to finish, often working nearly around the clock to monitor work that now included not just repairs but a substantial upgrade that planners said would enable the return of the Saints and provide Tom Benson with new suites, concession space, and

Gov. Kathleen Blanco and NFL commissioner Paul Tagliabue discuss progress on post-Hurricane Katrina Superdome repairs with Rita LeBlanc and Tom Benson in 2006. (Cheryl Gerber Photo)

other opportunities to squeeze more revenue out of the facility.

By the time the rehabilitation project wrapped up several years later, the state and Superdome commission had put in $165 million, FEMA paid $156 million, and the NFL contributed $15 million to the effort.[9] The payoff for the people of Louisiana was that New Orleans was able to win its bid to host the 2013 Super Bowl, marking its tenth time serving as a host city.

Fretful Owner, Few Allies

Blanco says that during meetings she had with Benson during the first few months after Katrina, the Saints owner had struck her as being depressed. "He was upset on many levels," she says. "He was worried, searching, trying to figure it out."

She said the reception his team received at games in Baton Rouge disappointed him. After the ugly incident that occurred after the first game in Tiger Stadium, the Saints had drawn far fewer people to their subsequent matchups there, and the big LSU stadium made the crowds seem even skimpier.

"I think Tom felt unappreciated and wanted more attention," Blanco says.

Paul Tagliabue may have made a similar assessment. He was dealing with an owner who was distraught over what his team's dislocation might mean to the Saints' financial future. The uncertainty that hung over New Orleans and the team was driving Benson crazy.

But Tagliabue was deeply concerned about ensuring that the NFL show compassion and sensitivity to New Orleans. The idea of the team running for the exits while the city was flat on its back was simply unacceptable to the image-conscious league, and Tagliabue was determined not to let it happen.

He wanted to line up some powerful local voices to talk about the team's future in the city, and for help he turned to an NFL friend, Houston Texans owner Bob McNair. Through his long history in the oil and gas business, McNair had made many friends in New Orleans, and he had shown his support for the city quickly after the Katrina crisis, launching a telethon to raise recovery money and pledging $1 million from his own pocket.

Tagliabue asked McNair to help identify key New Orleans individuals who could talk with him and Benson about the city's future.[10] The list they came up with included a handful of the city's wealthiest and most powerful men, one of whom, Thomas Coleman, offered to host a gathering of the group in early December 2005.

Coleman's father, James Coleman, Sr., in the 1930s founded a bulk liquid storage company called International Matex Tank Terminals, which grew into one of the largest such businesses in the country. After selling a portion of the company several years earlier, the Colemans in 2014 sold the remainder of the business for more than $1 billion.[11] Several Coleman family members are longtime residents of the tony Uptown New Orleans boulevard called Audubon Place, which is also home to Tom Benson and his wife, Gayle.

But when Tom Coleman hosted the group of eight or so businessmen for the first of what would become several meetings in late 2005 and early 2006, they did not gather at his Audubon Place residence but at a house his family owns on the batture along the Mississippi River, a location hidden from city streets by the twenty-five-foot levee that parallels the river. Among the businesspeople Coleman and Tagliabue tapped for these meetings were Gary Solomon, founder of Crescent City Bank & Trust; John Koerner, owner of Koerner Capital, LLC; John Georges, owner of Georges Enterprises, who would later buy the daily newspaper the *Advocate*; First Bank and Trust founder and chairman Joe Canizaro; shipyard owner Donald "Boysie" Bollinger; Audubon Nature Institute president Ron Forman; and real-estate developer Darryl Berger. Tom Benson attended some, but not all, of the meetings.

One businessman says the purpose of the sessions attended by Benson seemed to be to let the team owner "vent" about problems that had beset him after the hurricane and convince him not to take the Saints out of New Orleans permanently. The businessmen listened to Benson's concerns and spoke candidly about what they were doing in their own businesses and the city at large to try to build momentum behind a recovery. They told Benson why they felt that the Saints were important to the city's comeback.

Some said later that they found it hard to believe any owner would think of relocating a team at such a time. But one says that there was no question Benson was intent on putting New Orleans in his rearview mirror.

"He was leaving," Koerner says. "There was no BS about it. He was leaving, and we did everything we could" to change his mind.

Koerner says it was clear that Tagliabue feared that Benson's eagerness to move the team would become an embarrassment to the NFL, which is why the commissioner made multiple visits to the city during the first few months after the flood.

The commissioner was not present, however, at a meeting held in early 2006 that brought about thirty business leaders together with Benson, Saints senior vice president Dennis Lauscha, and general manager Mickey Loomis. One prominent New Orleans business owner who attended the meeting says he won't forget it.

Held in a room at the New Orleans Convention and Visitors Bureau, the meeting included many people who were longtime members of the city's largest business organizations, such as the New Orleans Business Council, and a handful of local tourism-industry leaders. People who attended the meeting were expecting it might be something of a call to action, an entreaty to the business community to join in finding ways to help the NFL team stay and succeed in New Orleans despite the tragedy that had befallen the city. But that's not how it went down.

"The meeting was nothing like: 'Thank you all so much for rallying and supporting the team by buying suites and tickets; now let's try and work this out,'" says the business owner. "I was shocked. Benson, Loomis, and Lauscha had all teamed up to tell us, basically, to go jump in the lake. Benson was absolutely committed to leaving the city. I mean he had absolutely no qualms about picking up and leaving here. That was the tone of that meeting."[12]

The Saints executives made clear that they wanted the team to play in a larger city with a bigger fan base, the business owner says. "Their attitude was: how does little New Orleans have the gall to be telling us we should stay here?"[13]

Lauscha and Loomis, who sat on either side of Benson at a table in the front of the room during the meeting, did most of the talking, and they stated in no uncertain terms that staying in New Orleans was neither the team's preference nor their intention.

"I really felt insulted, and I think everybody there did. Benson wanted to move the team," the individual says. "I came away thinking that they called the meeting to give us the bad news, that they were leaving. That was the takeaway."[14]

For some who had attended, the meeting had the effect of kicking them into action. They were more motivated than ever to find some way to hold on to the team, and soon they began to realize that they had an ally in Paul Tagliabue. A few of the individuals met privately with him for dinner a few weeks later.

"Mr. Tagliabue made it very clear that the Saints were staying in New Orleans whether Benson wanted it or not, and he was going to see to it," recalls one who attended the dinner. "Based on what Tagliabue said, it was other NFL owners who were telling Benson, 'You're not moving that team.'"[15]

Feeling more empowered by Tagliabue's support, business owners came up with a new approach to helping the Saints. Coleman, with assistance from Convention and Visitors Bureau president Stephen Perry, took the lead in forming the Saints Business Council, a group of twenty-seven individuals who would work to boost future revenue for the Saints by promoting the sale of tickets, Superdome suites, and high-dollar sponsorships. Members of the group made multiyear suite commitments and asked other local businesspeople to do the same.

"Our group will work closely with the Saints to provide support at all levels . . . working as hard as we can to help them succeed here," a joint statement by Coleman and Perry said.[16]

NFL "Part of the Recovery"

Chances are that Tom Benson did not enjoy being yanked into line by the heavy hand of the NFL. But Paul Tagliabue had decided at an early stage in New Orleans' crisis that he would not allow the NFL to be seen as insensitive to one of its member cities, particularly when that city was in distress. "We had to make it clear to the people of New Orleans that the Saints were their team. We had to be part of the recovery," he said.[17]

Tagliabue made clear that he would not hesitate to bring the weight of the NFL to bear on the situation, if necessary, in order to protect the brand and put an errant owner in sync with the broader interests of the league. The NFL, after all, was at that point doling out more than $100 million a year to each of its teams from television contracts and other national revenue sources. Owners were getting richer by the year from that revenue alone.

Tagliabue described the league's perspective on the Saints to reporters before the 2006 Super Bowl in Detroit. Referring to the annual revenue of the Saints, then estimated at about $175 million, he pointed out that the relocation of a team requires the approval of three-quarters of the thirty-two NFL team owners.

"The league is a $5.5 billion to $6 billion business," he said, explaining why the NFL, not Tom Benson, would determine where the Saints would play their next season. "I told the owners from the beginning that we needed to view this as a league responsibility," he said.[18]

So it was that Tagliabue instructed Benson that his team would play at least some of its post-Katrina games in Louisiana and that Benson would delay the early-out provision in his Superdome lease with the state, allowing everyone more time to plan the team's longer-term future. It was Tagliabue who decided that the NFL, through Roger Goodell, would deal directly with SMG's Doug

Thornton, rather than with the Saints, in monitoring progress on the Dome repairs. And when the last football weekend of 2005 came around, Tagliabue joined Benson to announce that the Saints would return to the Dome for the next season.[19]

Shortly before that, the state of Louisiana sent a letter to Tom Benson's attorneys formally requesting that the Saints return in January 2006 to their training facility, which was owned by the state and provided to the team at a rental cost of one dollar a year. The state would arrange to have the "minor storm-related damage" to the complex repaired, and the work would be minimal enough that it could be done while the team used the facility, the letter said.[20]

Speaking to a *New York Times* reporter in February 2006, Benson insisted that he had never intended to move the team to San Antonio permanently and that he, not the NFL, made the decision to return to New Orleans for the next season. "I was working real hard to do everything I could to make sure the Saints will be a viable part of New Orleans," he said.[21]

But there were also indications that he would keep one foot set solidly in San Antonio. In October 2006, Benson purchased a double unit in a high-rise condominium building in Alamo Heights, a high-demand neighborhood a short distance from downtown San Antonio. The condo had a value of $2.8 million in 2015.[22]

Officials at Saints headquarters remained adamant that Benson never specifically threatened to permanently move the team out of New Orleans, but critics say that's a statement steeped in semantics. Local fans by 2005 had grown used to hearing talk of losing the team to another city every time Benson began negotiating with state government over stadium issues. The dare he posed to state officials in 2004 when he delineated three choices regarding the team—provide a new stadium, offer more inducements, "or tell us to leave"—had stuck in local memories, and some people felt that if Benson did not want to be associated with such a threat, he could easily have put the matter to rest.[23]

Bad Day in Baton Rouge 157

After Saints staff visited their Metairie headquarters in late October 2005, not in preparation for moving back but to retrieve more items to take to their temporary digs in San Antonio, State Sen. Ken Hollis of Metairie threw up his hands in frustration. "I think what people want to hear [Benson] say is, 'It doesn't matter about the roofs or where we're going to play temporarily, we're coming back to New Orleans.' He's not said that," Hollis said.

The lawmaker added that he wished the state could force Benson's hand and make him declare his intentions. Referring to an $81 million penalty that the Saints would owe if they were to break their Superdome lease and leave the state-funded training camp before their contract expired, Hollis said he hoped Benson had not agreed to play four games in Baton Rouge simply as a delaying tactic. "If he's planning on leaving after using us to play at Tiger Stadium, and driving out in U-Haul trailers with our $81 million check, I guess I have some real problems with us accommodating him," Hollis stated.[24]

A month later, as talk of a Saints relocation continued to swirl, veteran sportswriter Peter Finney lambasted Benson for what he saw as a continuing lack of sensitivity to New Orleans. Finney said that Benson could have spared the city additional anguish in the aftermath of Katrina by stepping forward publicly to say that while he could not make promises during a time of so much uncertainty, he would do his best to keep their team in place.

In his column, Finney suggested a script that Benson could have used in addressing the people of New Orleans. It read, in part: "This season we're looking forward to playing some of our home games in Baton Rouge, close to the loyal fans. . . . We're planning to return to our training camp in New Orleans . . . as soon as the season ends. . . . It's my hope the Saints will always be part of my hometown."

If Benson had just said something along those lines, Finney wrote, "he'd be a hero in his hometown."[25]

On the tenth anniversary of the Katrina disaster, Paul Tagliabue joined in a charity event in New Orleans honoring SMG executive Doug Thornton, who led the daunting effort to return the Superdome to service quickly after the storm. The evening brought together many of the key players from 2005, and seated around the head table with Thornton, Tagliabue, and their wives were Tom and Gayle Benson and former governor Kathleen Blanco and her husband.

In his comments during the event, Thornton said that "New Orleans has never had a better friend than Paul Tagliabue." He added that the NFL commissioner, Blanco, and Benson had worked in "total unity" to enable the return of professional sports to the Superdome.

Tagliabue, meanwhile, lauded the city's response to challenges in 2005 that "really tested who we are."

In reflecting today on events of that period, Tagliabue says he has no doubt that the NFL did the right thing in standing by New Orleans, and he credits the local business community with stepping up at a crucial time to support the team. "They understood the economic importance of the Saints and the Superdome as well as their intangible importance—inspirational and symbolic," he says. "The business community was a major positive force" in helping New Orleans hold on to the team.

Tagliabue also makes a glancing reference to efforts by San Antonio leaders to yank the Saints away after the storm. New Orleans business leaders, he says, "provided a strong counterbalance to the business communities elsewhere that were pitching the Saints to relocate."

Chapter 16

Big Easy Business

When NFL commissioner Paul Tagliabue in 2005 wanted to talk with New Orleans business leaders to get their take on the city's future and the Saints' potential role in a recovery, it was ironic that he did not seek Tom Benson's advice about whom to call. Benson had grown up in New Orleans. He had married and become a father there, and he started his automobile retailing career in the city. He had owned a local bank, and area residents had bought tens of thousands of cars from his dealerships. His sports team had received hundreds of millions of dollars from Louisiana taxpayers. But when the NFL commissioner wanted the names of people who had their finger on the pulse of New Orleans business, he consulted a friend in Texas.

Robert McNair, owner of NFL team the Houston Texans, had many contacts in New Orleans from his years in the oil and gas business. Industry links between Houston and New Orleans had been strong for decades, and people frequently traveled between the two cities on both business and pleasure trips.

It was McNair who suggested that Tagliabue get in touch with Thomas Coleman.[1] Coleman agreed to help and suggested others who could speak thoughtfully about the issues facing the city and the relative importance of the NFL team in its future.

The individuals who agreed to meet with Tagliabue were not only among the most successful business owners in the region, they were also prominent civic activists and corporate citizens. Each of them for years had invested time and money into efforts to improve the New Orleans business climate and diversify the local economy. They did this work while continuing to build their own businesses, and in doing so, they seldom came across Tom Benson. "That isn't what Tom Benson likes to do," says a business owner who has chaired several of the city's largest business organizations.[2]

The men and women in these organizations contributed money to fund studies of the local economy. They worked on projects aimed at improving fundamentals, ranging from higher education to the criminal justice system. They mentored young people and supported business startups. In short, they devoted a substantial amount of time away from their own businesses to efforts they hoped would produce a better future for the city at large.

When Hurricane Katrina and the resulting flood left New Orleans in shambles, scores of these same individuals—all of them dealing with the adverse impacts of the disaster on their own companies and employees—joined in a citywide recovery initiative called Bring New Orleans Back. It was a sprawling effort that encompassed urban planning, federal government lobbying, neighborhood rehabilitation, and decision-making on a scale few cities had ever faced.

The Bring Back initiative and many spinoff efforts would tap the time and talents of local citizens for years as New Orleans clawed its way back to viability. But Tom Benson was seldom on hand.

An individual who recalls seeing Benson at a New Orleans Business Council meeting years ago notes that Benson never showed up after that. "I've had almost no interplay with him," the business owner says of Benson. "He works hard apparently, but that's all he does."[3]

Yet, after Katrina—and for years leading up to it—the Saints had no trouble tracking down many of these same business owners to pitch them on buying Superdome suites or blocks of tickets.

In 2006, after the Saints had made a firmer commitment to staying in the city, the business community, at Tagliabue's urging, got on board to support the team. "We were all calling each other about buying or sharing suites and reaching out to others to get them to buy—we were all making three- and five-year commitments for suites," says one business owner. "Everyone really rallied after the NFL said they were staying, so we wanted to show our appreciation."[4]

Barriers to Entry

In earlier times in New Orleans, the local business community had a reputation as a closed society. Many of its stalwart companies were closely held businesses owned by a single family for generations, and much of the business networking that occurred in the city happened in private clubs.

The exclusionary nature of the networking stemmed in part from the city's deeply rooted Carnival tradition, in which tightly knit groups formed "krewes" that staged elaborate parades and masked balls in celebration of the annual New Orleans Mardi Gras. Over time, these groups contributed to a stratification of local society that extended into the business community. Each Carnival krewe crowned "royalty" who generally represented the city's wealthiest families, and some of the krewes were so secretive that they would not reveal members' names. Becoming a member of the oldest Carnival krewes required a level of acceptance and financial wherewithal that was out of reach for many people in New Orleans, and those on the "outside" sometimes complained privately that the city's blueblood power structure cut them off from business opportunities.

Growing up in a part of town miles away from Uptown New Orleans, Tom Benson had no thoughts of cracking into that circle. He knew that if he were to become successful in business, his path would not run along St. Charles Avenue.

That realization may have been one reason why, after he and his family made the move from New Orleans to San Antonio in 1956, Benson came to embrace life in the Texas Hill Country. Particularly after buying his ranch near Johnson City, he felt comfortable and at ease in his adopted home.

But twenty years later, Benson's hometown drew him back, as he saw opportunity in an economy that was bustling, largely due to strength in the oil and gas industry. As he returned and began to expand his auto business in the city—and after he bought the New Orleans Saints—his life once again became more focused on New Orleans. Tom and Grace Benson traveled often between New

Orleans and San Antonio and to their waterfront home in Rockport, Texas. But through the 1980s and '90s, they were increasingly at home in their downtown New Orleans condominium or their house on Brockenbraugh Court in Old Metairie.

Changing Faces

During those decades, the New Orleans business community was starting to see changes that over time would alter its character. A younger generation of business owners and entrepreneurs was beginning to exert more influence in the city by joining existing business organizations and founding new groups such as the Young Leadership Council, which would become a mainstay of the rising professional class.

This period would also see the formation of the Greater New Orleans Sports Foundation, whose aim was to further the agenda of turning the city into a big-name sports town. A young man named Doug Thornton would become an early director of the foundation, and when he moved on to become regional vice president of SMG, the company that manages the Superdome and New Orleans Arena, another energetic businessman named Jay Cicero would take his place.

Both men went on to play leading roles in the growth of local sports, and the Sports Foundation drew support from hundreds of local individuals and companies to bring a host of high-profile sporting events to the city. Suddenly, New Orleans was hosting NCAA playoffs and Final Fours, national track-and-field championships and Olympic trials, golf tourneys—even sport-fishing championships.

The benefits of these efforts would accrue in a big way to Tom Benson, whose NFL team had become the primary tenant of the Superdome and who eventually would own the NBA team that played in the New Orleans Arena.

The Sports Foundation and SMG would team up to bid on scores of sporting events on the city's behalf, and in the years before Katrina they would land two Super Bowls, NCAA Men's and Women's Final Fours, SEC basketball tournaments, and smaller events ranging from wrestling, boxing, and volleyball championships to soccer and gymnastics competitions. Their success in this bidding, of course, required the availability of excellent sports venues, and that demand made the nonprofit Sports Foundation and SMG powerful allies of Tom Benson in keeping the Superdome and New Orleans Arena in top condition. When he needed assistance in lobbying the state legislature and other entities for help to upgrade the venues, a cadre of local businesspeople went to bat for the cause.

The growing importance of the Sports Foundation in New Orleans paralleled a trend toward increasing activism among other business organizations and local business generally. Many company owners and managers were investing more money and volunteer time into efforts aimed at improving the local economic outlook and, in doing so, were changing the face of New Orleans business.

After 2005, when a wealth of outside assistance began flowing into the city to aid in disaster recovery, the business community would evolve even faster, taking on a more progressive character that over the next decade would bring New Orleans a national reputation for nurturing entrepreneurial activity and supporting the growth of new companies. But even before Katrina, the business community had begun evolving away from the closed and exclusionary style that had characterized it in the 1950s, when Tom Benson had first left the city for San Antonio.

So when Paul Tagliabue in late 2005 sought input from local businesses about the future of New Orleans and the Saints, the people he met with were a mix of individuals from blueblood and middle-class backgrounds who had been collaborating with one another in various organizations for years.

In the aftermath of Katrina, cooperation among these businesspeople took on a new urgency as they worked in groups such as the Bring New Orleans Back Commission and Louisiana Recovery Association. It was in the midst of this work that some of them also answered the call for help to hold on to the New Orleans Saints.

Some who did so remain critical of Tom Benson's behavior in the aftermath of the Katrina disaster but hesitate to voice their feelings publicly because they are happy that the Saints have remained in New Orleans and developed a larger-than-ever following. They also point out that in recent years, Tom Benson has become a more benevolent owner. His philanthropic commitments during the years since Hurricane Katrina likely total close to $100 million.

In addition, some say, Benson deserves credit for keeping a National Basketball Association team in the city. The New Orleans Hornets—now the Pelicans—could easily have been plucked off by another city a few years after Katrina when then-owner George Shinn decided he wanted out. But after the NBA took the unusual step of buying the team while searching for an owner who would commit to keeping it in New Orleans, it was Benson who stepped up and acquired the team in 2012.

"I give him full credit for keeping the Pelicans here," says a local business owner. "Once the NFL told him, 'You're staying in New Orleans,' he has been wonderful for the community."[5]

Chapter 17

Rough Going for Rita

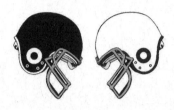

As Tom Benson's net worth climbed past $1 billion and his public profile rose through his ownership of an NFL team, a concern he harbored privately was that people would not understand that he had earned his fortune through his own efforts and had not inherited wealth or stumbled across an easy path to riches. "A lot of people don't realize that I worked for everything I have," he confided to a friend.[1]

Benson did not necessarily resent individuals who had been born rich, but he had little use for people who had come by money easily and arrogantly wielded the power and influence that came along with it.

Thayer Willis, author of *Navigating the Dark Side of Wealth*, says that such arrogance, which she loosely terms "spoiled brat behavior," can afflict individuals who are born to wealth if they don't take charge of their future at a young age and find work that gives them a sense of purpose and an identity beyond being rich. She says it is common for individuals who grow up rich to struggle with identity problems later in life. A wealthy young person who succumbs to complacency and attitudes of entitlement can end up feeling useless and lost, she says.

"Young adults need to get out in the world and make something of themselves. I tell parents not to give their kids financial wealth. Instead give them encouragement, education, and all kinds of support except money," she says.

Two generations removed from Tom Benson, Rita LeBlanc's experience in business was sharply different from that of the family patriarch.

Particularly after she finished college and her grandfather began hinting publicly that he might designate her as his heir to the Saints, LeBlanc enjoyed the attention and elevated social status that came with the territory. She had worked at Saints headquarters between college semesters and completed internships in the NFL's film, publications, and community-relations divisions. But when she began working full-time for the Saints, as the owner's granddaughter, she found herself plopped into the middle of highly experienced executive staff.

Some observers believe that tossing a woman in her early twenties into a male-dominated organization that was part of a sports league ruled by powerful men was simply too much too soon.

By some indications, Rita over time developed a tendency to flaunt her position and wield power over underlings, a type of behavior that Tom Benson—despite his inherent toughness and lack of patience with people who don't measure up to his expectations—seldom showed.

To outside observers, when Rita began showing up regularly at her grandfather's side at the Saints training camp and games, and later at NFL owners meetings, she was a fresh face in a business where middle-aged men predominate. People who met her found her to be enthusiastic and engaged in the business. They said she was anxious to learn the ropes. "She's an outstanding executive and is working hard to become familiar in all areas of the operation of the team," NFL public relations chief Greg Aiello stated in 2004, after Tom Benson had officially added his granddaughter's name to the list of team owners in the Saints media guide.[2]

Dennis Lauscha, who was an executive in the finance department before rising through the ranks to become president of the Saints, shouldered some tutoring responsibilities when LeBlanc first began working full-time at Saints headquarters, and he noted that she absorbed the education quickly. "She wasn't just a college kid. She had lots of experience, a willingness to learn, and she wanted to be involved. It was very refreshing," Lauscha told a reporter in 2009. He added that over a period of several years, LeBlanc had become skilled at handling weekly business meetings attended by Saints vice presidents and legal counsel.[3]

Her grandfather, too, chimed in about how eagerly LeBlanc had embraced her role as a corporate citizen, representing him and the Saints in a number of community organizations. "She sits on all these boards—just one thing after another," Tom Benson said. "You couldn't pay me enough to do that."[4]

But not everyone who worked with LeBlanc saw her in the same light. While she seemed to represent her grandfather's interests well in public settings where she appeared on behalf of the Saints organization, she increasingly became known behind the scenes for disdainful behavior toward individuals whom she felt no need to impress.

Sports executive Mike Feder, who spent five seasons with the Saints, was director of regional sales and marketing at the time the organization launched an Arena Football League franchise called the VooDoo in 2003. Benson had named Feder general manager of the VooDoo and put his granddaughter in charge of marketing and special events for the team.

Feder, who resigned from the organization in late 2005, later said that working with Rita LeBlanc was less than a pleasure. "I know she's intelligent," he told a reporter. "I just think she hadn't figured out how to deal with people."[5]

Feder, whose previous experience was in minor league baseball and who later became a special project manager with the Arizona Diamondbacks, worked closely during his first years at Saints headquarters with then-Executive Vice President of Administration Arnie Fielkow. Their primary job was to grow the Saints' fan base to a size that would help solidify the team's position within the NFL.

New Orleans, by population, was among the three smallest cities in the league, and ensuring that each home game was a sellout—and therefore eligible under an NFL rule to be shown on network television in the team's home market—was no slam dunk. But with millions of dollars in television rights at stake, Tom Benson demanded action. "I sometimes dreaded Thursdays, when we had a home game on Sunday, because of the intense pressure to achieve a sellout," Feder recalls.

Fielkow's plan to expand the base involved building support for the Saints in neighboring regions that had no close connection with other teams. He opened nine regional offices to cover the territory from the Florida panhandle through southern Alabama, the Mississippi Gulf Coast, and the entire state of Louisiana, and Feder took over business operations in Baton Rouge. In time, buyers who lived more than fifty miles away from New Orleans came to represent a substantial chunk of Saints season ticket sales.

Feder was in the thick of this effort when Tom Benson also put him in charge of the VooDoo and named Rita LeBlanc to the number-two spot behind him. It became a classic nightmarish workplace scenario where an upstart, who happens to be the boss's granddaughter, gets under the skin of a veteran.

The working relationship between Feder, who had nearly three decades of sports-management experience, and the twenty-six-year-old newly minted football executive was rocky from the start, as the young woman showed no interest in learning the ropes, Feder says. "She would just jump into things she knew nothing about," he says of LeBlanc. "She interfered with things all the time, even in other departments, and wanted to take the credit. It was all about ego."

The VooDoo in its first year became one of the top teams in the league in terms of on-field performance and game attendance. But Feder could not have been pleased when, in June 2004, the league named LeBlanc its Executive of the Year.

"I am overwhelmed by this great honor," she said in accepting the award during the annual ArenaBall event in Phoenix. "The process of building a first-year team was both arduous and exalting."[6]

Feder, who says he loved working for the organization, stuck with the VooDoo and continued working with Fielkow to build the Saints fan base, until a huge storm came rolling into New Orleans in August 2005.

After Hurricane Katrina, Arnie Fielkow lost his job; his marketing vice president, Connie Kowal, resigned; and corporate sales director Chris Kenyon quit. But the most momentous staff change that Tom Benson made late in 2005 may have been in naming Fielkow's replacement. He gave the title of executive vice president of administration to Rita LeBlanc.[7]

For Feder, it was the last straw. "I was at a fairly high level in the organization, and now Arnie [Fielkow], the guy who brought me into this job, is gone, and who am I reporting to? Rita. I knew it was going to be a disaster," he says.

Feder made it official a short time later, handing his letter of resignation to Saints vice president Dennis Lauscha.

When Tom Benson learned that Feder had opted to resign rather than deal with LeBlanc, he was characteristically loyal to LeBlanc. "If he can't work with my granddaughter, then let him leave," Benson was overheard saying of Feder.

Soon after that, Feder signed on as general manager of the Austin Wranglers, an Arena Football League team in Texas.

Reflecting years later on his departure from New Orleans, Feder says he understands that Benson, in promoting and supporting Rita LeBlanc, did what he believed was right for his family. And he thinks that Saints executives who praised LeBlanc's performance publicly along the way were simply doing their job.

"Everybody who still worked for the team had to maintain that attitude. They liked their jobs, and they had to be good soldiers," he says.

Feder insists his difficulties with LeBlanc did not stem merely from her youth. "Mr. Benson had a good business head, and Rita didn't," which made it hard for people at a high level to work with her, he says. "But I don't think anybody got along with Rita very well."

Disdain and Disrespect

Some who once were part of the rank and file at Saints headquarters agree. In 2015, after LeBlanc, her mother, Renee Benson, and brother, Ryan LeBlanc, became embroiled in a series of ugly court battles with Tom Benson, complaints began surfacing from individuals who had worked closely with Rita LeBlanc in the past and who either were fired or quit because they were unable to please her or just could not deal with her.

Those willing to comment on their experiences had varying complaints, but the problems largely stemmed from one factor: Rita LeBlanc showed them no respect. "Within two days after accepting the job, I realized I'd made a huge mistake," says one individual who worked as an executive assistant to LeBlanc for about eight months before bailing out. "She was rude, and she was dismissive."

The individual quickly began searching for another job and also consulted privately with others in the Saints organization, who offered sympathy and insights on the realities of working for LeBlanc. "Only then did I find out how many assistants she had gone through," the individual says.

By some accounts, LeBlanc hired more than two dozen assistants during a six-year period, with most of them resigning or being fired within a few months, or weeks, after starting work. In one or two cases, she hired individuals who had been her personal friends. A few were members of prominent New Orleans business families, and they sought to become LeBlanc's assistants simply because they thought working for the Saints organization would be fun. Insiders say that once these individuals were on the job they got a rude awakening, because LeBlanc was as disdainful of them as she was of other staffers.

Many complaints seemed to boil down to simple rudeness. "She'd walk in, and you'd say, 'Good morning,' and she wouldn't even respond," recalls one, adding that LeBlanc would freely bark orders at subordinates and become indignant if anyone asked her a question to clarify her instructions.

The former assistant notes that remarks other interviewers made during the job application process probably should have raised a red flag. An administrative staffer who conducted preliminary interviews with LeBlanc's assistant candidates posed a particularly pertinent question. The staffer "asked me how I would handle a situation where I am blamed for something I didn't do," the former assistant recalls.

In contrast to LeBlanc, her grandfather, when he would stop by her office, was described as being cordial to her staff. "Mr. Benson was always just a nice guy," the ex-employee says.

Rudeness in the workplace is not a rarity. Plenty of employees throughout corporate America can complain of insensitive bosses. But some observers say LeBlanc's pattern of disrespecting not only her assistants but also employees in other departments whom she did not directly supervise seemed to push the envelope.

She occasionally hired "personal" assistants, whose specified duties could include errands such as picking up her laundry or doing her grocery shopping. But LeBlanc by some reports did not hesitate to tap higher-level staff in other departments for similarly menial tasks.

In one instance, she was scheduled to attend an early-evening event and had planned to wear a dress that she had brought to the office. A few hours before leaving, she realized that the dress required a special undergarment that she had not brought from home. According to a former assistant, she picked up the phone and called a male manager in another department.

"She told him she needed this particular bra for her dress, and she sent him to her house to get it," the assistant says. "Her attitude was, if you worked for the Saints, you worked for her, and you had to do whatever she told you to do."

Former employees say LeBlanc is intolerant of perceived slights to her position. Once, after she and another Saints executive arrived at an out-of-town meeting and had checked into their respective hotel rooms at their destination, she called her assistant in New Orleans and complained that the hotel had upgraded the other executive to a room exactly like hers. She ordered the assistant to make sure it didn't happen again because, she said, no one in the organization, outside of her grandfather, should ever have a hotel room that equaled the room reserved for her.

Some Saints staff complained that LeBlanc had trouble making decisions, deliberating too long over basic matters, such as the design of game tickets, and endlessly seeking input from other executives. Employees who could not move ahead with their own work until getting an approval from her were frustrated, not only by delays but also by LeBlanc frequently insisting on last-minute changes after giving an OK.

Tom Benson reportedly was often miffed at not being able to locate his granddaughter because she had not arrived at the office or had stepped out.[8] A former assistant says that LeBlanc's staff looked forward to periods when the Saints owner traveled out of town, because when Tom Benson was not at Saints headquarters, LeBlanc wasn't there either.

Banished and Rewarded?

Troubles emanating from LeBlanc's second-floor office appeared to reach a peak around the time when Tom Benson made the decision to expand his sports holdings with the purchase of National Basketball Association team the New Orleans Hornets. The negotiations and final announcement of the purchase had sports reporters in a frenzy during the spring of 2012, and after the dust settled, a reporter took note of the conspicuous absence of Rita LeBlanc at the high-profile events.

Throughout the media hoopla surrounding the team's purchase, and most notably at the NBA press conference held in New York City and another in New Orleans to announce the sale, LeBlanc was nowhere to be seen, according to an April 2012 news article by *Times-Picayune* sports reporter Jeff Duncan. He cited sources who said LeBlanc had visited Saints headquarters only occasionally during the previous couple of months. "The woman widely viewed as Benson's heir to the burgeoning sports empire was MIA," Duncan wrote.[9]

Saints officials declined to comment on LeBlanc's absence, then raised more questions by citing a policy regarding personnel matters.

In his article, Duncan cited "multiple sources" as saying that Benson had placed his thirty-five-year-old granddaughter on a "form of unofficial paid administrative leave" because he saw "a pattern of behavior that needed to be corrected."[10]

"She's smart and has talent—but she's just all over the map," Duncan quoted an unidentified person who had worked with LeBlanc as stating. "I think she really enjoys the glitz and glamour of being the owner, but she doesn't really roll up her sleeves and get into the business side of it."

LeBlanc's apparent fall from grace occurred within a surprisingly short time after local and national press had showered her with praise as a rising star in the world of NFL business. Many of the accolades stemmed from her efforts in post-Hurricane Katrina New Orleans to get the Saints back to the Superdome after their forced exile in San Antonio. The extraordinary circumstances had put LeBlanc in a public spotlight at that moment in the city's history. Not only was the disaster itself unprecedented, but in its wake, Tom Benson had fast become a local pariah as rumors spread that he intended to move the Saints out of New Orleans.

It was that possibility, or rather the response to it by Saints administrative chief Arnie Fielkow, that got Fielkow fired from the Saints organization and resulted in LeBlanc taking his place, which gave her an opportunity to shine by showing grit and determination against the odds. "Just to survive and operate in several different locations and stadiums was an incredible challenge," she told a reporter, reflecting on the aftermath of Katrina. "We were in tents, basements, but folding an NFL club was not an alternative."[11]

Rita worked closely with people such as Superdome manager Doug Thornton and NFL commissioner Paul Tagliabue, among others, to garner the support needed to repair the Superdome and negotiate some flexibility in the Saints' lease. In this, LeBlanc had to walk a delicate line. Showing support for bringing the Saints back to the city while not appearing to cross or disrespect her grandfather was not easy.

LeBlanc concentrated on the season at hand rather than the more distant future, reportedly spearheading efforts to track down displaced season-ticket holders and lobby them to come back. She worked with NFL marketers to amass a host of national and international sponsors behind the Saints' return, and she helped form the Saints Business Council, a group of two dozen New Orleans business leaders who bought tickets, luxury suites, and sponsorships.[12] On LeBlanc's watch, all 137 luxury suites were fully leased during the Saints' first season back.

When the Saints organization announced its 2006 schedule, it was the twenty-nine-year-old LeBlanc, not Tom Benson, who stood with Tagliabue and addressed the news media.

She also received credit for helping to design a new ticket-pricing structure that made Saints tickets more affordable to a population whose economic demographics changed after Katrina. The system helped enable a sellout of every game once the team had returned to the Dome.

Saints general manager Mickey Loomis was among those who weighed in with praise for LeBlanc. "It was during [the Saints' displacement after Katrina] that she was able to really utilize all of those skills she had learned leading up to her new position with the team," Loomis said in 2007. "She understood the landscape there in Texas, and she knew our business here in New Orleans and was valuable in pulling things together quickly."

He went on to applaud LeBlanc for bringing a "fresh approach" to the team's business and marketing efforts. "From my perspective on the football side, that is very important to our success as well," he said.[13]

Her post-Katrina work on the team's behalf helped boost LeBlanc's profile. In the circle of team owners, she became a member of the NFL's International Committee and chaired the Employee Benefits Committee.

Once Tom Benson reached a deal with the state of Louisiana that secured the Saints in New Orleans through 2025, LeBlanc helped oversee a revitalization of the area surrounding the Superdome, including the Benson Tower office building and the pregame entertainment area called Champions Square. She also stepped up her participation in local civic and business groups and in programs to benefit local youth, and she was a key player in New Orleans' successful bid to host the 2013 Super Bowl, as well as NCAA basketball Final Fours.

National media made frequent note of LeBlanc's rise with glowing profiles of the young executive. *Street and Smith's Sports Business Journal* recognized her three times as one of the forty most influential sports executives under the age of forty, and the group Women in Sports and Events named her one of three "Women of the Year" in 2008. A year later, *Forbes* magazine heralded LeBlanc as one of their "Most Powerful Women in Sports."

In New Orleans, LeBlanc took seats on the boards of the influential New Orleans Business Council, economic development agency Greater New Orleans, Inc., and the New Orleans Business Alliance. And she represented the Saints at a host of charitable events. "Everything she does, six years since Katrina, is still geared toward promoting New Orleans," an ESPN.com reporter wrote in early 2012 about the then-thirty-five-year-old LeBlanc.[14]

But LeBlanc's role soon came into question as her temporary banishment from Saints headquarters by her grandfather came to light. While no specific offense that might have prompted his action ever surfaced publicly, rumors abounded that inappropriate public behavior on her part had gotten her into hot water with Tom Benson. Reports also cited sources who criticized her for a "lack of focus" and an "abrasive management style."[15]

Some individuals, outside the Saints organization, believe that LeBlanc has gotten a bad rap over her management style because people are jealous of her success, and they complain that reporters gave too much attention to the number of assistants who came and went through her office. "If she had been a guy, nobody would have had a second thought about that," says one acquaintance. Another, who characterizes LeBlanc as "super-intelligent and capable," notes: "When you're in a position to hire and fire people, you are going to make enemies."

Some individuals who have met and talked with LeBlanc describe her as attentive and engaging. And many mention that she is unusually well read.

"She is a voracious reader," said Chicago sports consultant Marc Ganis, who had once done work for the Saints. "She moves from business books to artsy books to history accounts," he noted in a 2007 interview about Rita.[16]

People outside of the Saints organization who have worked with LeBlanc in some capacity offer mixed impressions of her. A member of a business organization in which LeBlanc was a board member says that the group was pleased to have her there, as a representative of the Saints, and that she was an avid note-taker at meetings, but that was as far as her participation went. "The real work gets done in small groups that take on specific projects, and I don't think she's ever volunteered for any of that," the individual says.

A few others who have interacted with LeBlanc on projects involving the sports teams say that while she was congenial and seemed interested, she lacked focus when it came to executing specific tasks, and they had trouble getting clear answers from her that would have helped move the projects ahead.

Inside the Saints organization, some have suggested that achievements LeBlanc received credit for would not have come to fruition had other top executives, namely Dennis Lauscha, not ridden herd on the projects.[17]

Rita LeBlanc's official banishment lasted about three months before she suddenly returned to her office at Saints headquarters. Her reemergence coincided with an announcement by Benson that he had promoted the forty-three-year-old Lauscha to the newly created position of president of the Saints. Benson also announced an added title for his granddaughter: vice chairwoman of the Saints board of directors.

As to her extended absence from the organization, Benson gave a typically folksy explanation. "You know, Rita took a couple months vacation there, and people got the wrong impression," he said. "We're not reducing her in any kind of way. As we've taken on some of these outside activities, I told Rita I want her to get more involved in them, even if it took away some time here [with the Saints], and leaning on Dennis a little more."[18]

Though LeBlanc's return to Saints headquarters appeared to outside observers to go smoothly, an undercurrent of bad feeling seemed to have taken hold inside the organization. In addition to her mysterious temporary absence, employees at every level, even if they did not have direct contact with LeBlanc, had heard accounts of her treatment of her assistants, and the stories did not make her popular.[19]

In addition, her apparent continuing rise in the organization despite Tom Benson's obvious earlier concerns over her behavior planted worries in the minds of key people. Benson at this point seemed sturdy and tough, but he was eighty-five years old. What if something happened to him suddenly? Could the professional future of dozens of top people—from the front office to the playing field—fall into the hands of a person who had just completed a three-month forced exile?

While Benson tried to smooth over the flap about his granddaughter, the team's stars were developing a case of nerves. In time, rumors would surface that Saints head coach Sean Payton and quarterback Drew Brees had both voiced concern over the future of the team. And after the Benson family's internal conflicts erupted publicly at the end of 2014, it became more difficult for Saints insiders to ignore the goings-on.

By some reports, Payton requested a contract provision that gave him a way out of the organization in the event that someone other than Benson should come to control the team. In a video report in late 2015, NFL.com reporter Ian Rappaport said three sources had told him that Payton had a "change of control clause" written into his contract stating that if Tom Benson did not control the team in 2016, Payton could become a free agent.[20] Whether such a clause was part of the contract extension that Payton signed in the spring of 2016 was unknown, but Payton by that time had stated repeatedly his intention to remain with the Saints for the long term.

A person who is close to the Saints organization says there's no question that many Saints employees, on the field and in the front office, have serious concerns about what would happen if Rita LeBlanc were to come into control of the team. "They just can't believe what Rita is like. Nobody there wants to work with her," the individual says.

Publicly, the organization continued to present a unified front to show that it remained focused on delivering results to New Orleans fans. And whether growing concern inside Saints headquarters eventually contributed to conflicts that erupted within Tom Benson's family is hard to say. But within just a few years of welcoming his granddaughter back into the organization from her "vacation," Benson would find himself embroiled in a complex and bitter legal fight with LeBlanc, her mother, Renee, and her brother, Ryan.

Among those who were shocked to hear of the family turmoil was former Saints executive Mike Feder, who believes that, among other things, Tom Benson's dedication to his granddaughter finally came to no good. "Mr. Benson was loyal to a fault in defending her," Feder says. "He gave her chances, opportunity, and now it has come back to bite him."

Chapter 18

Gayle: Behind the Smile

As Tom Benson navigated the chaos and criticism that engulfed him after Hurricane Katrina, he found solace in his relationship with his new wife, Gayle, whom he had married in 2004. Benson had met New Orleans native Gayle Marie LaJaunie Bird several months after his second wife, Grace, passed away following her struggle with Parkinson's disease. His pursuit of a new relationship so soon after Grace's death may have raised a few eyebrows, but people close to him knew something important about his emotional makeup. Though Benson always musters resilience in times of crisis, the one thing he cannot tolerate is solitude.

After his first wife, Shirley, died in 1980, the loneliness haunted him until he remarried two years later. When Grace Benson passed away in 2003, he felt desolation blanketing him again.

Throughout his life, Benson has derived strength from two sources—work and his religion. He grew up in a devoutly Catholic family and, as an adult, counted a number of clergy among his closest friends. He contributed generously to the Church over the years and was close to several archbishops. Priests and nuns are regulars among the guests in Benson's suite at the Superdome and, of course, at the Mass that he holds at the Dome before every Saints home game.

Like Benson, Gayle LaJaunie Bird was devoted to her Catholic faith. She attended Catholic schools as a child and in adulthood became close to many members of the clergy. Regular churchgoers were accustomed to seeing her at the lectern reading Scriptures during services, and she was active in charitable efforts of the Church. She attended Mass every day.

Acquaintances take note that, when Gayle appears in public,

she is always perfectly coifed, dressed, and manicured. "She has always been very well put together," says a friend, who recalls noticing Gayle for the first time when she got up to do a reading during a Mass at St. Louis Cathedral. "She was dressed to the nines, and she looked beautiful."

So it was that as Tom Benson, then seventy-seven, sat in the cathedral early one morning in April 2004, he was struck by the attractive lady who rose from a pew in the front of the church and stepped up to read from the Book of Acts. He wanted to meet the soft-spoken brunette, and when the service ended, he asked the priest to introduce them.

"After Mass, back in the sacristy, Monsignor came up to me and said, 'Do you know Tom Benson?'" Gayle Benson recalled in 2013.[1] Moments later, Tom Benson entered the room.

He first walked toward the cleric and made a point of thanking him for the funeral service he had performed months earlier for Benson's wife, Grace. Then Benson stepped toward Gayle. "And who is this young lady?" he asked.

Gayle, then fifty-seven, said she was embarrassed by the attention and left the room shortly after shaking Benson's hand.

A day later, she received a call from the priest asking her permission to give Benson her phone number so that Benson could invite her to an arena football game. Gayle, who knew little about football, let alone arena football, said she wasn't interested.

But the priest reminded her that the cathedral was in need of some repairs. "You know, Gayle, we're working on that roof and we're trying to raise money, so you might want to go," the priest said.

"Reluctantly, I went," she recalled during a radio interview conducted by her close friend, radio talk show host and former New Orleans television news anchor Angela Hill. Gayle went on to say that Benson told her he would send his driver to pick her up. "I was totally against that," she said. "I told him I know how to drive."

But Benson sent the car anyway, and after she arrived at the New Orleans Arena, the driver escorted her to Benson's suite. She was initially uncomfortable when Benson invited her to take a seat right next to him. "I'm thinking, I'm really not interested in this, but maybe I could talk to him about giving me a check for the church," she said.

After the game, Benson asked her to have dinner with him, and when they got to his car, he sent his driver home and slid behind the wheel himself. Then, rather than driving to a restaurant ten minutes away, Benson headed out of downtown and toward Lake Pontchartrain.

"We're going to the lakefront," he told her. "I have a boat dock out there."

"So we drive out to the lakefront, and he opens the gate, and it was a boat dock with no boat," she recalled, laughing. "I said, 'Oh, that's pretty,' because what are you going to say?"

Benson proceeded to explain that his "boat," which was docked elsewhere at the time, was a 100-foot-long yacht.

On the way back downtown for dinner at Delmonico's, Benson asked her if she was married. When she answered no, he asked, "What are those rings you're wearing?"

She explained that she was wearing rosary rings, beaded rings meant to be used like a rosary while praying.

Despite her purported reservations, Gayle said the two "had a wonderful time" at dinner. As Benson walked back to his car after taking her home, he turned and blew her a kiss.

Tom Benson and Gayle Bird dated for four months before he invited her to dinner at his home one night, and when they sat down at the table, he pulled a small ring box out of his pocket and set it down.

"He opens it and says, 'Will you marry me?'" she recalled. "I was shocked."

When all she could manage was "Oh my goodness," Benson prompted her: "That's not the right answer. We need a better answer than that." And she said yes.

Benson even insisted on going to her parents' home to ask permission to wed their daughter.

The next two months became a frenzy of planning. The fall wedding would have to fit somehow into the football season, which meant it had to occur during a bye week for the Saints. They would be married on October 29, 2004, in San Antonio, where Benson still had many businesses and friends, and they would have a pre-wedding party two days earlier at the New Orleans Museum of Art. The guest list for the two events included some two thousand people, sweeping the ranks of family, friends, clergy, football notables, politicians, and NFL executives, including Commissioner Paul Tagliabue and his soon-to-be replacement, Roger Goodell.

The wedding took place at the Immaculate Conception Memorial Chapel on the grounds of the Oblate School of Theology in San Antonio. Hill served as matron of honor, and Tom Benson's youngest brother, San Antonio lawyer Larry Benson, was the best man. The bridesmaids and groomsmen came from the couple's respective families—Gayle's sister and brother, Brenda LaJaunie Ernst and Wayne LaJaunie; and Tom's daughter Renee Benson and her two children, Rita LeBlanc and Ryan LeBlanc.

The couple and their guests danced in the Sky Room at the nearby University of the Incarnate Word in San Antonio. They drank a toast in front of the bride's cake, an elaborate, rose-embellished affair, and guests admired the groom's cake, which was a replica of the Superdome.[2]

The pair honeymooned in San Francisco, which meant they would be just a hop away from the next Saints game, in San Diego.

Gayle, who said she knew nothing about football before she met Tom, would continue her education about the game, courtesy of Saints general manager Mickey Loomis. "When we first got engaged, Tom introduced me to Mickey, and he would sit in our suite for the first half of the games and explain what was going on," she recalled.[3] She said that as she got a better feel for the game, she became a fan.

Critics Take Aim

Days before the wedding, Gayle told a reporter that she was still in shock over the fact that she was getting married again. "I got divorced when I was 39, and I never thought it would happen again," she said. "I never planned to marry again. I was a confirmed bachelorette."[4]

That Gayle LaJaunie Bird, by the time she reached middle age, had been uninterested in taking another walk down the aisle was no surprise to friends. Two previous marriages had soured her on the idea of wedded bliss and left her doubtful that she would ever give a close relationship another try.

She had made her first trip down the aisle not long after graduating from Martin Behrman High School, marrying young Nace Salomone, who had finished at Martin Behrman several years before her. The union did not last long, and the two divorced in 1972.

Her second try at wedded bliss left deeper scars. Gayle had married Thomas Bird, or "T-Bird," as many people called him, in 1976. He was a good-looking young police officer who also ran his own contracting business.

T-Bird eventually quit police work and went full-time into contracting. He and Gayle lived on Laurel Street, and Gayle, who was drawn to interior design and would later take a correspondence course in the art, decorated their home.

Over time, both the contracting business and the marriage ran into trouble, and Gayle filed for divorce.[5] In what would later become an ironic coincidence, the lawyer who represented her in the matter was Randall Smith. In 2015, Smith would sue Tom Benson on behalf of Benson's daughter and grandchildren in their effort to have him declared mentally incompetent.

But in the late 1980s, Smith helped Gayle Bird divorce Thomas Bird and obtain an injunction restraining Bird from interfering with her or her businesses.[6]

Some say the financial difficulties that beset Gayle in subsequent years stemmed in part from money problems and debts that began in the marriage. In 2015, asked to comment on a string of lawsuits Gayle had been involved in during the years before she married Benson, his lawyer released a statement saying: "As someone that went through an unfortunate marriage, [Gayle Benson] overcame the issues that marriage presented to her as a single woman and business owner. . . . While she does not dispute her struggles, she should be saluted not vilified for her ability to deal with those issues that were brought upon her by others." Lawyer Phillip Wittmann also noted in the statement that Gayle had "built her business without the assistance of someone handing her anything."[7]

Rough Road in Business

Gayle Marie LaJaunie had grown up on the West Bank, as the

area on the opposite side of the Mississippi River from downtown New Orleans is known. She attended St. Anthony Catholic School and Holy Name of Mary High School before graduating from Martin Behrman Senior High School in 1966.[8] She, her parents, and her younger brother and sister lived in a small house in Algiers, a neighborhood that in the past few decades has undergone gentrification. "I grew up in Algiers before it was fashionable," she joked in later years.

Much like her future husband Tom Benson, she knew nothing of privilege. Friends say she worked hard and wanted to make something of herself.

Her early working life centered around the jewelry business. She became a sales representative for a custom jeweler, working from her home.

According to a 2013 magazine article,[9] her interest in interior design grew when she began buying and renovating houses in New Orleans in the 1970s. A few years after marrying T-Bird, she gave up the jewelry business and began working with him, adding her design services to his contracting business. Eventually she established Gayle Bird Interiors, Ltd., which had clients ranging from hotels and grocery stores to owners of historic homes.

Some of this work led her into litigation with clients. More than a dozen suits, most filed by clients against Bird in the 1980s and '90s, complained of delays in completing work or breach of contract relating to the work done. Most of the suits sought relatively small monetary damages.

In one instance, Consolidated Freightways sued Bird over unpaid shipping costs related to the company's delivery of 170 chairs to the Court of Two Sisters restaurant, where Bird had designed a room. The suit resulted in a judgment against Bird of $1,700. She contested the decision in the Fourth Circuit Court of Appeal, arguing that the shipping rate was misquoted to her. The appeals court affirmed the lower court's judgment, though it reversed an order that she pay $400 in attorney fees.[10]

In another case, Bird was arrested on suspicion of theft after a client claimed she did not return an expensive desk that she agreed to store after finding a new one for him.[11] But Bird was never prosecuted, and she subsequently filed a federal civil case seeking $1.2 million in damages over the incident.[12] A judge dismissed the case several months later.

In a few cases, Bird was the plaintiff, including a suit she brought against the Fairmont Hotel New Orleans in 1997, claiming that the hotel failed to pay her for $33,000 worth of design work. The hotel countered that it had no contract with Bird, and the judge dismissed the case.[13]

One of the more serious cases against her business claimed multiple failures on her part. James Arcara, who owned a condominium on St. Charles Avenue, said he paid Bird $238,000 to decorate it, and he sued her over work delays and what he said was poor workmanship. Bird countersued, claiming that Arcara did not allow her access to the condo so that she could finish the job.[14] They settled the case, and Arcara's lawyer later said his client took Bird's car in lieu of payment.[15]

Some court filings arose directly from her marriage to Thomas Bird, including a proceeding brought against his construction company before the couple divorced.

Other complaints filed against Bird included a suit in 1999 by her mortgage lender. While she and Thomas Bird had shared a house on Valence Street in Uptown New Orleans, she continued to live there after the divorce and only her name was on the $300,000 mortgage. When she had difficulty paying the note, Bird tried to hold on to the home by renting it out to a tenant, but the arrangement did not work out and eventually the lender foreclosed on the property.[16]

Angela Hill, who met Gayle Bird and T-Bird in the late 1980s when the couple sold a house to Hill and her then-husband, Garland Robinette, says the Birds' contentious divorce was hard on her friend. "It was a very difficult time for her. It wasn't just the end of a relationship; it was the end of her business with T-Bird—their work was often linked," Hill says.

Watching Gayle go through the ugly divorce "showed me what a strong person this woman is," Hill says. "Resilience is almost her middle name."

In 2015, after Tom Benson's daughter and two of his

grandchildren sought to block removal of their ownership stakes in his sports businesses and his naming of Gayle Benson in their place, the lawsuits from her past became fodder for speculation over whether she would have the business skills necessary to run the sports teams if her husband were no longer around. Before meeting him, Gayle Benson was in "significant debt and had limited credit," his daughter Renee Benson and her children, Rita LeBlanc and Ryan LeBlanc—commonly referred to in legal filings as the "Three *R*s"—said in seeking to have Tom Benson declared unfit to manage his businesses.[17]

Their filing stated that Gayle had "never owned, operated, or managed a substantial business enterprise and has not received any formal training on how to do so."[18] The document also claimed that Gayle "had no interest in football, basketball, or in sports in general, before marrying Tom Benson," and noted that Tom Benson had required her to execute a prenuptial agreement that "limited her right to community property during marriage, upon divorce, and upon his death."[19]

Benson's lawyers countered that Gayle Benson had stood by Tom Benson's side "and assisted him in his personal and business dealings for over a decade." They said that the Three *R*s were seeking to "disparage" Gayle Benson and "self-servingly blame" her for a family rift.[20]

Comfortable in Her Role

Ten years after they had wed, Tom and Gayle Benson celebrated their anniversary by renewing their vows. Following a ceremony in 2014 officiated by Archbishop Gregory Aymond at St. Louis Cathedral, they had a reception at the New Orleans Museum of Art that mimicked the pre-wedding party they had held there. The two were the picture of a happy couple, and it seemed Gayle had found her calling. Thrust into a public spotlight brought on by her marriage to the owner of a high-profile sports organization, she appeared comfortable in her role as Tom Benson's soulmate and confidante and had become known for the smile that never seemed to leave her face.

Observers credited Gayle with smoothing out Tom Benson's rough spots. Much like his second wife, Grace, Gayle Benson moved easily among Tom's friends and business associates.

But whereas Grace had tended to comply with whatever her husband wanted, Gayle Benson was more likely to speak her mind when she saw fit. During their decade of marriage, Gayle had come to exert an influence on her husband's life and some of his business decisions.

Though she likely had little say in Tom Benson's choices for the Saints immediately after Hurricane Katrina, having been his wife for less than a year at that point, as a lifelong resident of New Orleans she no doubt felt torn while spending several months in Texas and hearing the rampant talk that Benson's football team could become the San Antonio Saints.

But as she gained confidence in their relationship, it began to be clear that Tom Benson was hearing, and sometimes heeding, Gayle's advice.

After signing the 2009 agreement with the state of Louisiana, which allowed the Saints to sell naming rights for the Superdome, for instance, Saints staff and Dome officials tossed around numerous corporate names as possible buyers. But it was Gayle Benson who came up with the winning idea: why not approach Mercedes-Benz?

Tom Benson had a long history with the automaker, having owned Mercedes-Benz dealerships in New Orleans and San Antonio for many years. In early 2011, Gayle pointed out to him that top executives from the automaker had shown concern for New Orleans after Katrina and had made personal visits to tour the city.[21]

Benson liked her suggestion and contacted Mercedes-Benz management. In April 2011, he and Gayle flew to Germany to meet with the company's CEO, and six months later, they announced a deal. The stadium would become the Mercedes-Benz Superdome under a ten-year contract whose value outside sources estimated at $50 million to $60 million.[22]

Gayle Benson made her influence over her husband's sports businesses known again in the following year.

The future of the National Basketball Association team the New Orleans Hornets had been in question for some time. Formerly known as the Charlotte Hornets, the team had moved to New Orleans from North Carolina in 2002 and, under owner George Shinn, had struggled to meet attendance goals at the New Orleans Arena.

In the wake of Hurricane Katrina, the team had temporarily relocated to Oklahoma City and played two full seasons there. After the Hornets returned to New Orleans, Shinn made repeated failed attempts to sell the team. Finally, the NBA took the unusual step in 2010 of buying the team in an effort to keep it in New Orleans and find a suitable long-term owner.

NBA officials set the stage for a sale by negotiating a new lease for the team at the New Orleans Arena and launching a program to boost ticket sales. Soon thereafter, NBA commissioner David Stern and Louisiana governor Bobby Jindal approached Tom Benson about buying the Hornets, and Gayle Benson urged her husband to take the plunge. "I just thought, as Tom did, it's a great thing for the city and for the fans, and we just needed that," she said in a 2013 interview.[23]

The collaborative efforts worked, drawing Tom Benson into the game. In April 2012, he signed an agreement to buy the team for a reported $338 million. And while he noted that keeping the team in New Orleans was one motivation, he made clear that his intention was to see the team become successful.

"We expect this club to be one of the most outstanding clubs in the league, otherwise I don't want to get involved," he said during the formal announcement of the deal. "This is just a good thing and I'm just glad to be a part of it."[24]

Stern declared that the league had succeeded in its mission to keep the team in place. "We really have found the perfect owner," he said. "Our goal all along has been to get the Hornets bought by somebody whose commitment to New Orleans would be unrivaled."[25]

His purchase of the New Orleans Hornets provided Benson with some positive publicity on the heels of a scandal surrounding his football team. The flap arose from claims by other teams that the Saints had paid "bounties" to defensive team members to encourage hits that would injure opposing players. An NFL investigation led to the season-long suspension of head coach Sean Payton. Only a day before the Saints announced Benson's purchase of the Hornets, the NFL club announced that assistant coach Joe Vitt would be elevated to interim coach for the coming football season, despite his own six-game suspension in connection with the bounty probe.[26]

Benson promised at the time of his purchase that a rebranding lay ahead for the Hornets, including a name change to better reflect the team's hometown. Gayle Benson would be involved in renaming the team and developing its new look.

In 2013, the team announced a name change to the New Orleans Pelicans, in a nod to Louisiana's state bird, the brown pelican, which had become identified with efforts to restore Louisiana's coast following damage from major storms and the 2010 BP oil spill in the Gulf of Mexico. During a press conference, Gayle Benson unveiled a new color scheme—blue, gold, and red—for the Pelicans' uniforms, logo, and other branding.

In that same year, Gayle scored points with the NFL for an extravagant party she organized for team owners, spouses, and league VIPs in conjunction with New Orleans' hosting of Super

Dallas Cowboys owner Jerry Jones chats with Gayle and Tom Benson, Rita LeBlanc, and her mother, Renee Benson before a game in New Orleans in 2013. (AP Photo)

Bowl XLVII. She and Tom had attended a grand gala in Germany, during a visit to Mercedes-Benz headquarters, and she used that event as a model for designing a similarly spectacular party in New Orleans.[27]

Working with New York event designer Bronson Van Wyck, she planned a splashy outdoor affair to be held at New Orleans City Park that would include glass-enclosed dining areas with chandeliers and a view of the park's sprawling oak trees strung with thousands of tiny lights. Arabian Nights-style tents sheltered cocktail bars, and cherubs wearing NFL team caps passed drinks and hors d'oeuvres. "The flowers were all white . . . chef Susan Spicer prepared dinner, and during the meal the Louisiana Philharmonic Orchestra played against a wall created out of green foliage," a magazine writer said in describing the scene.[28]

Gayle Benson also hosted a lavish luncheon for NFL spouses at the New Orleans Museum of Art.

"The Bensons were unbelievable hosts for the Super Bowl," New Orleans mayor Mitch Landrieu later told a reporter. "They are a major reason why we got the Super Bowl in the first place, and their hospitality for the owners and team executives are a reason why I'm confident New Orleans will host another Super Bowl again soon."[29]

Branching Out

As Gayle Benson gained her husband's trust in some business matters, he guided her in others. In 2014, Tom Benson suggested she put her name on a new enterprise and get a feel for another sport—horse racing.

Years earlier, Tom Benson had owned thoroughbreds and kept them on his Texas ranch. His son, Robert, loved the animals and ran the racing operation. At one time, they owned close to fifty horses.

After Robert Benson's death from cancer in 1986, his father lost interest in carrying on the business. But in recent years Tom Benson once again felt the pull of the sport.

Gayle Benson incorporated GMB Racing in May 2014, and she and Tom set about finding talented trainers to develop a stable of horses. They engaged three New Orleans-born trainers—Tom

Amoss, Dallas Stewart, and Al Stall—who helped them scout for promising animals, and Benson put more than $1 million into the purchase of seven yearlings.

"We want to win the Kentucky Derby, the Louisiana Derby, the Classics and hopefully take a shot at the Breeders' Cup. Why not?" Gayle Benson said.[30]

Gayle and Tom Benson's entry into the racing business seemed a mark of resilience in the face of the family conflicts that had beset him. Launching a new enterprise shifted the couple's focus away from the ongoing trauma of court proceedings and bad feelings among family members.

Throughout his life, Tom Benson had shown toughness in the face of pain and relied on work to get him through difficult times. But his wealth afforded him plenty of leisure-time distractions, such as yachting.

Gayle Benson was delighted to learn that her husband enjoyed cruising vacations, and after they married, he changed the name of his 107-foot vessel. Formerly known as the *Lady Grace Marie*, named for his second wife, the yacht soon became the *Lady Gayle Marie*.

In 2007, when he replaced the vessel with a new tri-deck 122-footer, Gayle's name would go on that one as well. And three years later, when he upgraded to a 140-foot yacht, it too became the *Lady Gayle Marie*, with Gayle overseeing its interior design.

Benson had his newest yacht equipped with ample entertainment features, including an outdoor barbecue area, and the couple has often hosted guests, from family members to Saints coaches and players, aboard the vessel. Typically, after football season ends, the crew takes the yacht to South Florida, and from there the Bensons might spend weeks cruising northward along the East Coast, making stops in New York before heading toward Boston, Kennebunkport, Maine and on to Canada.

Between vacations, the Bensons reside mainly on New Orleans' most exclusive boulevard. Through most of his married life in New Orleans, Tom Benson had lived either in Old Metairie or a downtown condominium. But Gayle, who had lived most of her adult life in the Uptown area, had her eye on a home on Audubon Place, a gated, private street anchored by the majestic mansion that is home to the president of Tulane University.

Tom and Gayle Benson bought this $4 million home on Audubon Place in New Orleans in 2008. (Cheryl Gerber Photo)

Gayle Benson watches from the sideline before a Saints game in 2015. (AP Photo)

When a home on the street became available in 2008, the Bensons snagged it, and Gayle went about redecorating. The home, valued above $4 million,[31] became a favorite subject for local magazine feature articles.

Friends say that Gayle Benson's journey from her New Orleans' West Bank roots to Audubon Place and her role as first lady of local sports reflects her toughness. "She has tremendous faith, and I've seen it at work over many years," says Hill.

Another friend terms Gayle Benson a "self-made" woman. "She really kind of invented herself along the way," the friend says.

But Gayle's improving fortunes took a toll on some of her closest relationships. Her sister, Brenda LaJaunie Ernst, who is four years younger than Gayle, says the two were close through most of their lives. And Brenda and her husband spent considerable time with Gayle and Tom during the first year of their marriage. But the sisters became estranged after a falling out that had to do with their parents' living arrangements after Hurricane Katrina.

During the months after 2005 storm and flood, when the Saints took up temporary residence in San Antonio, Tom and Gayle Benson spent much of their time in Rockport, Texas, where Tom had long owned a home and other property along the Gulf of Mexico. Gayle also brought her aging parents, who had lived most of their lives in Algiers, Louisiana to Rockport. But after a time her mother, Marie LaJaunie, became homesick and decided to return to Louisiana to live with her younger daughter. Her husband, Francis, meanwhile, stayed on in Rockport.

Brenda LaJaunie says that as their mother's health declined, issues over her care and where she would live drove a wedge between Brenda and Gayle. Soon, Brenda's relationship with both Gayle and Tom came to an end. "I am isolated from them," Brenda says.

Brenda also no longer has contact with her brother, Wayne LaJaunie. "Gayle and my brother kind of teamed up and left me out," she says.

Though she won't disclose exactly how her conflicts with Gayle developed, Brenda terms their differences "petty." The conflicts became more serious, however, as their mother grew increasingly ill with Alzheimer's disease. And in 2010, both parents died within six weeks of one another, in separate states.

Brenda offers no comment on a report that Gayle became angry with both her mother and sister when Marie LaJaunie returned to Louisiana to live with Brenda and that Gayle refused to help pay for their mother's care in a New Orleans nursing home or for the subsequent funeral expenses.[32]

In May 2010, Marie LaJaunie was buried in New Orleans, and in July her husband was laid to rest in San Antonio. "I wanted to bring him back here, but she [Gayle] wanted to keep him there," Brenda says of their father's burial.

Brenda says she and Gayle never reconciled. She adds that she still does not know the cause of their father's death.

Chapter 19

San Antonio

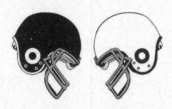

The city that Tom Benson adopted as his new home in the 1950s was a far different place than the San Antonio of today. The downtown Chevrolet dealership at the corner of St. Mary's and Navarro streets that became the first business to wear Benson's name no longer exists. Big-name hotels dominate the downtown landscape, towering above a scattering of restaurants, government offices, and empty storefronts that once housed businesses.

Most of the activity in the city's core now arises from tourist attractions that developed over several decades along a two-mile stretch of the San Antonio River, which loops through downtown. The stone pathways built along the river as part of a long-ago beautification project became the foundation for the Paseo del Rio, or River Walk, where millions of visitors each year stroll among restaurants, taverns, shops, and hotels.

The River Walk and the nearby Henry B. Gonzalez Convention Center are the primary drivers of downtown activity these days. Tourists also visit San Antonio to see historic sites, such as the Alamo Mission, where Col. James Bowie led a small company of men in a losing battle against Mexican general Antonio Lopez de Santa Anna in 1836.

Like many communities that had no natural barriers to contain their expansion, San Antonio has sprawled outward, with businesses and commercial developers gobbling up land along major thoroughfares, and residential growth following their lead.

When Tom Benson bought twenty-five acres of land along north San Pedro Avenue a half-century ago, it was because he foresaw some of what was to come in the next decades. He recognized that the business momentum would shift away from the city's core and that suburban areas were becoming more popular with shoppers. Plopping new car dealerships down in a largely rural area ten miles north of downtown could prove to be a good move, he thought.

Benson was right. His strategy panned out just as he hoped, as he not only moved the headquarters of his business to north San Pedro Avenue but proceeded to open five other dealerships there as well.

As he predicted, the area, which became known as North Park, grew into a bustling retail corridor filled with stores and services that catered to a growing suburban population. But even Benson probably did not foresee just how far San Antonio would one day stretch.

The little city named by seventeenth-century Spanish explorers for St. Anthony of Padua has become one of the largest and fastest-growing cities in the United States, with an economy centered around military bases and industries including healthcare, financial services, energy, and tourism. San Antonio's population doubled between 1970 and 2010, and demographers say it will continue to snowball past its 2014 total of 1.4 million people.[1]

Car shoppers heading for the North Park corridor, where three Tom Benson dealerships still operate, might travel there via Interstate 410, the first highway loop designed to skirt the inner city. But commercial and residential development now extends at least fifteen miles beyond that circle, with new subdivisions reaching far into the countryside.

Tom Benson has owned several homes in and around San Antonio over the years, and while he and his wife, Gayle, came to reside primarily in New Orleans, in 2006 he purchased a home in the wooded hills of San Antonio, five miles north of the city's downtown.[2] The $2.8 million luxury condominium is about ten miles from the home on Pontiac Lane[3] where he lived in the 1970s with his first wife, Shirley, and roughly fifteen miles from the gated community where his only grandson, Ryan LeBlanc, lives with his wife and two children.

In March 2016, in the heat of the family battle that erupted over Benson's estate, property records show that Benson turned his San Antonio condo over to his heirs,[4] possibly as part of an asset exchange aimed at ending the litigation.

Meanwhile, Benson's daughter Renee, who currently lives with her husband primarily in a ranch home just outside of Blanco, Texas, in April 2016 purchased another, small home five minutes away from her son's residence in San Antonio.

The changes have gradually drawn the Benson family members farther away from the Benson Farm and Ranch, which lies about an hour north of San Antonio. For many years, the ranch was part of the glue that held the family and extended family together, as they congregated frequently for weekend barbecues or holiday gatherings. Family gatherings these days are smaller and less frequent, with the family patriarch and benefactor notably absent.

Why Tom Benson—a child of the Seventh Ward of New Orleans and without an ounce of "cowboy" in his blood—came to own a ranch in Texas is a matter for conjecture. Perhaps the open spaces he saw in central Texas were an appealing contrast to densely populated New Orleans, where water nearly surrounds the city and thwarts urban growth at every turn.

Or maybe the national news media's focus on central Texas at the time snagged his attention. The rising profile of Texas Democrat Lyndon Baines Johnson, who served for twelve years in the U.S. House of Representatives followed by a dozen years in the U.S. Senate, had put on the map his hometown of Johnson City, a community founded in the early twentieth century by his cousin.

Johnson and his wife, Claudia "Lady Bird" Johnson, lived with their two daughters on their ranch just outside of Johnson City, and when LBJ became the vice-presidential running mate of John F. Kennedy in 1960, the area was put under a spotlight. After LBJ succeeded to the presidency for more than five years following President Kennedy's assassination in Dallas, he made dozens of trips to the ranch that lay along the Pedernales River, and it became known as the "Texas White House."

Tom Benson bought a 7,000-square-foot unit in this San Antonio condominium tower in 2006. Ten years later, he transferred the condo, valued at $2.8 million, to his heirs. (Kathy Finn Photo)

Tom Benson made his first purchase of ranchland around the time that LBJ became president, and the site he chose as the future home of the Benson Farm and Ranch lay just fifteen miles from the Texas White House. The Bensons and their children began spending weekends at their ranch, with Tom often commuting from San Antonio. As they embraced the country lifestyle, their circle grew to include other family members and friends. The kids, Robert, Renee, and Tootsie Benson, often invited their San Antonio schoolmates for weekends at the ranch.

The gatherings grew larger as more of the Benson family migrated from Louisiana to Texas. Benson's brothers Jerome and Augustin both followed Tom into the automobile business in San Antonio. Augustin moved there not long after Tom did and first went to work in one of Mike Persia's dealerships, becoming sales manager. Jerome would hold management positions in several of Tom's dealerships in San Antonio and New Orleans, before eventually becoming president of Benson Management Company and running the New Orleans operations.

Tom Benson's youngest brother, Larry, also settled in Texas after graduating from Louisiana State University. He attended law school at St. Mary's University in San Antonio, but even after obtaining a law degree he felt the pull of the car business. Larry not only became the chief legal adviser to his brother's auto empire but later became the owner of Ingram Park Auto Center in San Antonio.

In time, even Tom Benson's parents would relocate from New Orleans to a home in north San Antonio. Tom Benson, Sr., and his wife, Carmelite, would live there for the rest of their lives.

After Tom Benson, Jr., acquired a controlling interest in the New Orleans Saints, many of his San Antonio relatives traveled often to New Orleans to attend home games and enjoy his hospitality in the owner's suite at the Louisiana Superdome. And Benson himself strengthened his ties to the city where he was born. Over the years, particularly as he sold off some of his dealerships and exited the banking business, he spent increasing amounts of time in New Orleans and less time in San Antonio. But with his daughter, grandchildren, and many nieces, nephews, and cousins still rooted in the hills of central Texas, Benson remained close to the region, and the indications are that when the time comes, he will be laid to rest in the city that played a key role in his career.

Years ago, Sunset Memorial Cemetery, along Austin Highway northeast of downtown San Antonio, lay at the outer edges of the city, with a few miles of raw land separating it from the city center. But during decades of growth, the site was virtually engulfed by commercial and residential development.

Today, Sunset Funeral Home lies just yards away from a point where rush hours produce a knot of traffic at the intersection of Austin Highway and Eisenhauer Road. But despite the bustle, an air of calm hangs over the acres of graves that stretch into the woods behind the mortuary. A short distance inside Sunset Memorial Park stands the Benson family tomb.

A family plot can sometimes offer a glimpse into the lives of those therein, and the Benson tomb reflects diverse branches of Tom Benson's family tree. The stately twenty-five by twelve by ten foot white granite Benson mausoleum holds eighteen crypts, and the family name is etched into the space below the peak of its pitched roof. A twelve-by-twelve-foot concrete slab in front of the mausoleum holds two marble benches that give visitors a place to sit and reflect.

Only eight of the crypts, at the moment, hold the remains of Benson loved ones. The bodies of Tom Benson's parents, Thomas Milton Benson, Sr., and Carmelite "Carmen" Pintado Benson, lie in the vaults at the top of the tomb's center section, and in the bottom tier of the section lies Tom's son, Robert Carter Benson.

Above and to the left of Robert's grave is that of his mother, Shirley. And to the right of Robert's crypt is that of Tom's second wife, Grace. In two of the other vaults lie the remains of Shirley Benson's mother and sister. The mausoleum also has a link to Tom Benson's third wife, Gayle, as it holds the remains of her father, Francis LaJaunie.[5]

Two of Tom Benson's three brothers—Augustin, who died in 1983, and Larry, who passed away in 2013—are buried elsewhere in Sunset Memorial Park.

The Benson mausoleum, in Sunset Memorial Park in San Antonio, is the resting place of Tom Benson's parents, son, and first two wives. (Kathy Finn Photo)

Benson's youngest daughter, Jeanne Marie "Tootsie" Benson, is one of the few deceased members of the immediate family not buried in San Antonio. After her tragic death in 1991, her body was cremated and her remains placed in a cemetery in Columbia, Missouri, where she had been living with her husband. At the Benson mausoleum in San Antonio, Tootsie is commemorated with a tiny plaque, engraved with her name, that is attached to one of the benches facing the tomb.

The ten empty vaults in the Benson mausoleum leave a visitor to speculate as to which one will eventually become the final resting place of Tom Benson. A spot at the center of the grouping seems a good guess, with the chamber next to it perhaps reserved for his current wife, Gayle.

People in the "deathcare" business, as the funeral industry likes to call itself, say that decisions about who goes where in family plots can spark such intense emotions that they can tear a family apart. In the case of the Benson tomb, it's possible that decisions about who is buried there contributed to conflicts in Tom Benson's family, or that they at least aggravated a growing dissension.

Under ordinary circumstances, it would be a good bet that two of the mausoleum's chambers would be reserved for Tom's only remaining child, Renee Benson, and her husband. But the bitter feelings and lawsuits that have come between Tom Benson and his daughter make that an unlikely scenario.

Is it possible that the interment of Gayle Benson's father in the mausoleum, in 2010, contributed to a rift between Renee and Gayle? Outsiders likely will never know.

But it seems entirely possible that one day, maybe far in the future, the remains of Tom Benson, Jr., could lie in the Benson mausoleum, surrounded by the three women he loved and with whom he shared his life.

Chapter 20
Subsidized Billionaires

When Tom Benson in 1985 joined the elite fraternity of NFL owners, he didn't have to spend much time studying the ownership game. He understood it intuitively.

Owning a professional football team is like holding any other business asset. Its value increases with its ability to generate profit.

At the time he acquired the New Orleans Saints, Benson's largest holdings were his automobile and banking businesses. His twenty-three dealerships, including ten in San Antonio and thirteen in New Orleans, had combined sales of about $400 million, putting him in the ranks of the largest auto dealers in the country. He was the majority stockholder in six community banks whose assets totaled in the vicinity of $350 million, and he owned an estimated $50 million worth of real estate that included office buildings as well as dealership properties.[1]

Benson did not amass these assets simply by selling cars and making bank loans. He built his wealth by doing deals. He purchased more and more car dealerships to expand and diversify his product lines, and he acquired banks that brought him more depositors, whose cash enabled more lending and investment. He loved putting transactions together and prided himself on negotiating rock-bottom terms that helped offset whatever risk the deals might carry stemming from borrowed money or changing market conditions.

By most accounts, when Benson gathered up investors to help him buy the New Orleans Saints, risk was not a big concern to them. "I don't believe anyone thought there was a big downside risk," says Russ Herman, one of the lawyers who helped Benson put the purchase together and also became an investor. "The motivation was that I always wanted to be able to say I own part of a team."

If the safety of their investment was not the top priority for NFL team investors in 1985, its importance dwindled even more as time went on.

The lack of significant financial risk today distinguishes NFL team ownership from most traditional business. Though an owner who takes on too much debt could undercut the potential profits, most team owners don't bury themselves in debt. And though the fortunes of NFL owners could decline if the popularity of professional football should wane, that trend is unlikely to develop overnight.

"In major sports, there's not much risk, especially if you can subsidize your purchase and your operating cost. Then in essence you have socialized your private risk and have pushed it off onto the community," says Rick Eckstein, a Villanova University professor and expert on sports-stadium finance. He adds that team ownership has little risk these days because of the rapid appreciation in team value and because a lot of very rich people "are just dying to buy sports franchises."

Whenever word gets out that an owner may have an interest in selling, or that an expansion team could be in the works, buyers materialize out of nowhere, he says. "There are a lot of cities and owner groups who are fighting each other to get a piece of this pie."

The appreciation potential of a franchise on top of its ability to generate big revenue make the thirty-two ownership slots in the NFL nearly irresistible bait for the ultra-rich, Eckstein says. An owner who can finagle a fancy stadium and, for instance, pay for only part of it while receiving all the revenue from it not only boosts the team's profits but enhances the team's potential selling price in what has become, essentially, a seller's market.

Eckstein, who coauthored *Public Dollars, Private Stadiums: The Battle Over Building Sports Stadiums*,[2] believes that public subsidies for sports franchises are unnecessary because major sports teams are economically viable on their own. "But we've built this whole house of cards scenario and we, as a public, think the teams are so good for the community that we give them subsidies, as opposed to spending on schools, roads, or hospitals," he says.

Given the financial dynamics of team ownership, it was no wonder that Tom Benson, despite having no particular taste for the game of football, felt drawn to the National Football League. The NFL must have seemed an investor's paradise, with wide-open opportunity to grow revenue and value. This probably explains why, while showing off what ultimately snowballed into $330 million worth of post-Hurricane Katrina improvements to the Louisiana Superdome that were completed without financial help from him, Tom Benson finally sounded happy.

"This is a brand new stadium," he told reporters who had gathered for a stadium tour in 2011. "It's got all the things we wanted. I haven't seen a finer stadium in the country."[3]

A Real-Estate Deal

Toward the end of her term in office, Gov. Kathleen Blanco took heat from voters in North Louisiana and elsewhere for supporting upgrades to the Superdome to ensure the Saints would return to New Orleans after their forced departure in 2005. Blanco says she felt vindicated later as the Saints' fortunes on the field turned upward and fans across the Gulf Coast rallied behind the team.

But several years after Katrina, it became clear that the poststorm upgrades had cost even more than expected. The Louisiana Superdome Commission had issued $300 million worth of adjustable-rate bonds—securities that were subject to repricing in response to market conditions—in order to rehabilitate the Dome and pay off old debt. During the national financial downturn of 2008, the volatile bonds lost value, which sent their interest rates soaring to 12 percent.[4] The state rescued the commission by buying the bonds, and in the end Louisiana's cost to get out from under the complex deal topped $400 million, according to then-state treasurer John Kennedy.[5]

Though Blanco had supported the effort to bring the Dome back quickly after Katrina, she had railed against what she saw as the state's excessive support for the Saints in the agreement her predecessor had signed with the team in 2001. That pact promised the team $186 million in direct payments over ten years, and despite Blanco's attempts to renegotiate the deal, Louisiana continued to make annual, increasing payments to the team, even though it meant pulling funds away from other priorities.

Tom Benson and the state did eventually agree to drop the exit clauses in the deal that would have allowed either side to end the agreement early under certain conditions. That meant the team would stay in New Orleans for at least several years. But as that agreement wound toward its conclusion, Benson had his eye on new moneymaking possibilities.

His search for new revenue sources associated with the Superdome had Benson focusing on real estate, specifically a largely vacant office tower that stood next door to the Dome and had been damaged by Hurricane Katrina. His vision involved buying the office tower and a portion of a defunct shopping mall nearby. He would renovate the office building and lease it out, and he would demolish part of the mall to create an entertainment space adjacent to the Superdome, along the lines of the L.A. Live entertainment complex outside the Staples Center in Los Angeles. This "festival plaza" concept would enhance New Orleans' ability to bid on Super Bowls and other big events, he said.

The deal Benson envisioned would be complex and, not surprisingly, would require state assistance.

The Dominion Tower office building was one of the newest office buildings in downtown New Orleans, having been one of the last large structures erected at the height of the 1980s boom in the oil and gas industry. Directly behind the building was the New Orleans Centre mall, which had struggled to reach full occupancy from the time it opened in 1988.

Hurricane Katrina did substantial damage to both structures, and neither reopened after the storm, with the exception that the ground floor of the office tower housed a health clinic and a few offices for a time. The owner of the buildings, California real-estate investor Judah Hertz, put out word that he was interested in selling the properties.

Benson had the idea of putting the spaces back into commerce in ways that would support the Saints and enhance football fans' game-day experience, and he took his vision to the governor. Bobby Jindal had just moved into the governor's mansion and was already showing that he had few qualms about putting state money behind high-profile projects.

In its first go-round with the deal, the state looked at the possibility of having the Superdome Commission buy the office tower and then lease most of it to Louisiana for offices for state employees who at the time worked in various other spaces around New Orleans. But when the commission dropped that idea over concerns about having to find other tenants for 160,000 square feet of space not needed for the state workers, Benson came back with another option: he would buy the buildings and nearby parking garage and become landlord to both state workers and private tenants.

The multiple parts of his proposal, which included a new state commitment to upgrade the Superdome and a Saints agreement to stay in New Orleans through 2025, would not come together easily. It was tricky, for instance, to stipulate Superdome renovations as a condition of a private property deal involving the state and the Saints.

Benson got around the problem by proposing that a real-estate company owned by his family, separate from the Saints, would purchase the office tower. The family would rent about two-thirds of the twenty-six-floor building to various state agencies and would lease the mall to the Superdome Commission for development into a sports and entertainment district.

Pulling the pieces of the deal together kept Benson, the Dome commission, and key lawmakers scrambling during the next six months. Adding pressure was the fact that New Orleans was preparing to bid on the 2013 Super Bowl, and the NFL had said it would not consider the city for the game unless the Saints signed a long-term agreement with Louisiana.

Governor Jindal, who said he supported the proposal because it would secure the team without the more costly step of building a new stadium, talked up the deal with legislators while Benson negotiated with Hertz. Finally, in late summer 2009, all the pieces were in place. The Benson family, through its company Zelia, LLC (named for a favorite aunt of Tom Benson), would put $82 million into buying the office tower, mall, and parking garage and renovating the properties. The Bensons also pledged to put $10 million, which equaled the remaining payments due from the state under its old deal with the team, into the development of the outdoor entertainment space.

Louisiana would finally shed the onerous terms of its 2001 "pay to play" deal with the team and instead would pay the Saints no more than $6 million a year in inducements—or possibly nothing if the team surpassed certain revenue benchmarks. The state would move some nine hundred state workers into the renovated tower under a fifteen-year commitment that, along with rent on the outdoor entertainment area, would pay the Benson family more than $160 million.[6]

Tom Benson even found a way to ease the pain of shelling out cash to buy the office tower and renovate the former mall. With Jindal's help, he got the State Bond Commission to issue $60 million in bonds to cover the costs and use lease payments from the state and private tenants to repay the debt.[7] Meanwhile, the state agreed to put $85 million into renovations at the Superdome to widen concourses and add concession stands, club lounges, 3,100 seats, and sixteen luxury boxes, all of which would bring Benson more revenue.

Some lawmakers criticized the state's commitment to pay the Benson family office lease rates that were 30 percent above the market and guaranteed to rise in sync with the Consumer Price Index. One lawmaker who questioned signing such a deal at the same time the legislature was being asked to make cuts in higher education and healthcare programs said it made no sense. "It's a welfare check for one of the richest men in Louisiana and we're emptying our schools out," declared Sam Jones, a state representative from Louisiana's Cajun Country.[8]

But under pressure to give New Orleans a shot at another Super Bowl, the legislature relented. And the NFL owners responded by awarding the city the 2013 game. It would be New Orleans' tenth

Tom Benson bought this office tower, next to the Superdome, in a lucrative 2009 deal with Louisiana, which rents most of the building to house state employees. (Kathy Finn Photo)

time playing host to the league's premier event, and one of the team owners used the moment to express the league's solidarity with Benson.

"People have a lot of respect for Tom Benson, and Tom delivered for New Orleans," Miami Dolphins owner Stephen Ross told a reporter after the decision was announced. "Benson stayed steadfast behind New Orleans even in the worst of times," he said.[9]

An exuberant Benson, meanwhile, could barely contain himself. "We're just thrilled about what's going on. We're getting a new Superdome. Now we're going to get a Super Bowl on top of that. It couldn't be any more exciting than that," he said.[10]

Behind the Numbers

It would take a while for the full impact of that 2009 deal between Benson and the state to become clear. In September 2014, the state's legislative auditor released a report on the agreement that brought into focus just how generous Louisiana had been with the Saints owner.

The report showed that the total rent the state was paying for its space in the office building now called Benson Tower was 62 percent higher than the total previously paid to house the same employees in other buildings around New Orleans. The 2014 costs included an entire floor of office space that the state was not using but had committed to leasing.

On a price-per-square-foot basis, the state's leasing costs in New Orleans had nearly doubled, the auditor said.[11]

The Louisiana Office of Facility Planning was forced to search for private sublease tenants in an effort to cut the state's costs on its unused space. In 2016, after a new governor and attorney general took office, the state committed to moving the AG's office personnel in New Orleans into the vacant space.

Meanwhile, the combination of the office leasing terms, tax breaks granted by the state, and $85 million worth of additional seats, concessions space, luxury suites, and other amenities the state had provided at the Superdome would generate nearly $400 million in new revenue for the Saints over the life of the agreement.[12] That figure did not include an estimated $40 million that Benson could realize from fully renting several floors of office space that were not committed to the state.

Benson had also finagled a clause in the agreement requiring the state to pay the team $5 million for each Super Bowl played in New Orleans, including the 2013 game that the NFL awarded to the city just as the new agreement was coming together.

The 2009 agreement stipulated that the Saints would pay no rent to the state for the team's use of the Superdome. And under a particularly lucrative clause, Louisiana granted the team the right to sell naming rights for the Dome and keep all revenue associated with such a sale.[13]

In October 2011, Benson scored a big win with that clause when Mercedes-Benz signed a ten-year deal to put its name on the Superdome. Neither the team nor the company disclosed specific terms of the agreement, but most estimates placed its value at $50 million to $60 million.

Tom Benson's extraordinary deal-making skills enabled him to leverage business opportunities at nearly every turn in his career, and the rewards increased almost exponentially after he became an NFL owner. On top of all of the revenue that accrued to the New Orleans Saints from various sources during his ownership, he saw the team's value soar.

Fueled by shared revenue from the league and owners' ability to extract subsidies from the states and cities where their teams operate, the appreciation in some teams' value has been breathtaking, catapulting some millionaire owners into the billionaires' club. *Forbes* magazine, whose annual analyses of sports-team values and personal net worth have become widely known, says that Dallas Cowboys owner Jerry Jones, who made millions as an oilfield wildcatter before buying the team and its stadium for $140 million in 1989, today owns a team valued at $4 billion.[14]

Terming the Cowboys "the most valuable sports team in the world," *Forbes* stated that the team's value increased 25 percent just from 2015 to 2016. Jones' personal net worth hovers around $5 billion, according to *Forbes*.

The Mercedes-Benz Superdome was the site of Super Bowl XLVII in 2013. Louisiana paid Tom Benson $5 million for "hosting" the game in the state-owned Dome. (AP Photo)

NFL commissioner Roger Goodell talks with Rita LeBlanc and Tom and Gayle Benson before a Super Bowl XLVII news conference in New Orleans in 2013. (AP Photo)

Variations on Jones' story echo through the ranks of the other owners. Robert Kraft's estimated $4.3 billion net worth would be substantially less were it not for his ownership of the New England Patriots, which *Forbes* values at $3.2 billion.[15] Self-made billionaire Shahid Khan, who bought the Jacksonville Jaguars in 2012 for an estimated $760 million and so far has not seen his team log a winning season, watched the team's value balloon to $1.5 billion in just three years, according to *Forbes*, which pegs Khan's personal fortune at $4.9 billion.[16] Carolina Panthers owner Jerry Richardson, who in 1993 used profits from his fast-food restaurant chain to buy the expansion team for $206 million, today owns a $1.56 billion team, and *Forbes* estimates Richardson's personal net worth at the same level.[17]

Snowballing Wealth

In 1985, when Tom Benson began laying the groundwork to acquire the New Orleans Saints, his net worth likely totaled around $150 million, based on an analysis of the wealthiest Texans in the late eighties.[18] He told anyone who would listen that he could not swing the $72 million purchase by himself, and he relied on a score of limited partners and a bank loan to help him do the deal.

But thanks to the snowballing value of his team, just seven years later he was able to buy out his partners (to the chagrin of two of them who sued Benson for millions in damages). At the time of that buyout, Benson valued the Saints at $92 million,[19] and his own net worth had reportedly risen to $180 million.[20]

Fifteen years later, in 2007, though Benson had sold off all but five of his auto dealerships and reduced his bank holdings to a single institution, his wealth continued to burgeon, with Forbes valuing the Saints at a whopping $854 million.[21] Still, Benson's personal fortune had not yet reached the "big B."

The 2009 season would change that picture. Under the leadership of head coach Sean Payton and quarterback Drew Brees, the Saints went 13-3 in the regular season and sailed unscathed through the playoffs to contend in their first-ever Super Bowl. In 2010, the same year that the team brought home the Vince Lombardi Trophy, Louisiana began more than $300 million worth of upgrades at the Superdome.

All of this would accrue to the benefit of the team's owner. A *Forbes* analysis soon would show that the rising value of his team had pushed Benson's net worth to $1.1 billion.[22]

Benson celebrated the Saints' Super Bowl win as might be expected of a newly minted billionaire whose sports team had just brought home the league's biggest prize. He bought a new yacht.

The 140-foot three-decker, named *Lady Gayle Marie* for Benson's wife, replaced his 122-footer of the same name. Built to accommodate ten guests in five cabins and sporting a glass-enclosed circular elevator, the vessel's many other features include a formal salon and dining room, owner's office, butler's pantry, spa pool with sundeck, and all-glass exercise room.

The Saints owner, who already had a relatively new private jet, would wait a few more years before upgrading his Bombardier

Tom Benson anchors his 140-foot yacht, the Lady Gayle Marie, *in New Orleans during football season.* (Kathy Finn Photo)

Tom Benson's net worth soared into the billions after he became an NFL team owner. (AP Photo)

300. Finally, in 2014, he took delivery of a Bombardier Challenger 350, an eight-passenger aircraft classified as a "super midsize" jet and capable of transcontinental flight. The price on a new, fully equipped model runs upward of $25 million.

Benson could easily afford his purchases. By early 2016, *Forbes* estimated Benson's net worth at $2.2 billion,[23] and in September of that year, the magazine published a new estimate of the Saints' value, pegging it at $1.75 billion.

Chapter 21

Benson Gets a Makeover

Tom Benson's public image had suffered serious damage from his post-Katrina dithering over the future of the Saints, despite both his and Gayle's ongoing insistence that he had never intended to leave New Orleans. "We never were going to stay in San Antonio," Gayle said in 2013. "We had always made plans to come back here. We just needed to get things together."[1]

But Gayle could not miss the fact that her husband had lost a great deal of credibility and goodwill in New Orleans, as news articles and letters to the editor made clear. And she believed she could help turn public perceptions around.

Gayle Benson's reaction to her husband's image problem was intuitive. She knew that what local people needed to see from him was compassion and sensitivity—characteristics he did not muster easily—and she set about softening his persona.

She did this in part by injecting her own personality into his activities, at NFL gatherings, in public appearances with Tom, and throughout New Orleans society. In addition, she urged her husband to expand his charitable giving. Many people in New Orleans credit Gayle with engineering a makeover that in a relatively short period enabled Tom Benson to become as well known for generosity as for ruthless deal-making.

Though he had long been a financial supporter of the Catholic Church and a few local institutions, including Brother Martin High School, Benson dramatically expanded his giving during the years after Hurricane Katrina. In 2007, the couple established the Gayle and Tom Benson Charitable Foundation and began laying the groundwork for regular giving. Over the next several years, they made dozens of grants to a wide range of groups.

Along with a host of smaller gifts, the foundation pledged $10 million more to Brother Martin High School and $8 million to Loyola University of New Orleans for the Benson Jesuit Center, an existing center that underwent a renovation and gained a new chapel. The Benson foundation committed another $2 million to Loyola for the New Orleans Province of the Society of Jesus.

In 2010, the foundation donated $5 million to establish the five-story Gayle and Tom Benson Cancer Center at Ochsner Health System's Jefferson Highway campus. Several years later, they pledged $20 million more to add more cancer care services and fund clinical research.

The Bensons committed $7.5 million to Tulane University toward construction on the Tulane campus of Yulman Stadium, where the playing surface now is known as Benson Field. Ironically, Tom Benson's great-uncle, architect Herbert Benson, had designed the original Tulane stadium and was a president of the Sugar Bowl in the 1930s.[2]

Other major gifts by the Bensons' foundation included $5 million to Team Gleason, a charity founded by former New Orleans Saints player Steve Gleason, who was sidelined by ALS, a terminal neuromuscular disease.

In San Antonio, Tom Benson had years ago established an endowment fund at Central Catholic High School dedicated to the memory of his son, Robert Carter Benson, who graduated from the school. Tom Benson also established the Benson Memorial Library at the school and funded a library named for his son at St. Anthony Catholic School.

The Benson family had long supported the University of the Incarnate Word in San Antonio, but Tom and Gayle's foundation boosted their giving to the institution, and in 2008, the new Gayle and Tom Benson Stadium opened on the campus. "Can you believe someone who saw her first football game five years ago now has a field named after her?" Tom Benson later joked.[3]

Gayle Benson reinforced the foundation's giving with her own volunteer efforts. She chaired big fundraising events for Ochsner Health System and the Pro Bono Project of New Orleans. In 2014, Tulane University named her to its board of trustees. She has also been a board member of the NOCCA Institute, Audubon Nature Institute, and the New Orleans Museum of Art.

The Bensons have given millions of dollars to the Archdiocese of New Orleans, and Gayle Benson has been an active volunteer in the Church. Their support prompted Pope Benedict XVI in 2012 to bestow on the couple the Pro Ecclesia et Pontifice, the highest papal award given to a layperson. Gayle Benson also received the Order of St. Louis Medallion for her work.[4]

His increasing largesse helped show Tom Benson in a new light in a city previously critical of his actions. But some say Benson's image benefited just as much from steps he took at Saints headquarters.

While it was NFL commissioner Paul Tagliabue who engineered the team's recommitment to New Orleans after its forced absence from the city in 2005, Benson, once he was back in his office at the Airline Highway training camp, launched his own game plan—and began wielding an axe.

The team, perhaps understandably given its extraordinary post-Katrina circumstances, had gone 3-13 in the 2005 season. But during the two previous years, the Saints had been unable to break .500 and hadn't reached the playoffs since 2000. Benson decided that six seasons under head coach Jim Haslett were enough, and he gave the coach his walking papers.

That offseason saw a flurry of changes both on and off the field. With help from an NFL marketing official, hired by Tagliabue, the Saints instituted a new ticket-pricing structure and promoted season ticket sales aggressively.

Ticket sales soon had substantially outstripped totals of previous years. Helping to boost sales were changes occurring on the football-operations side of the organization.

After giving the go-ahead to sack Haslett, Tom Benson had entrusted his general manager, Mickey Loomis, with fixing what was wrong with the team. Hiring a new head coach was job one. Loomis homed in on an assistant head coach and quarterbacks coach for the Dallas Cowboys.

Sean Payton had worked with the best, including most notably Bill Parcells and Jon Gruden, and he was eager to start making his name in a top coaching spot. On January 20, 2006, he became the fourteenth head coach in the Saints' history.[5]

Sean Payton signed on as head coach of the New Orleans Saints in 2006. (Cheryl Gerber Photo)

The New Orleans Saints signed quarterback Drew Brees in 2006, marking his return to the game after injuring his shoulder while playing for the San Diego Chargers. (Cheryl Gerber Photo)

As he began fleshing out his coaching staff, Payton brought in Joe Vitt as linebackers coach and assistant head coach, Doug Marrone as offensive coordinator, and Pete Carmichael, Jr., as quarterbacks coach. Payton said his aim was to build an organization packed with "team players."[6]

As it turned out, that meant signing a twenty-seven-year-old quarterback who had recently undergone shoulder surgery following what some had thought was a career-ending injury while playing for the San Diego Chargers. Payton had had his eye on Drew Brees for months, and soon the Saints signed Brees to a six-year, $60 million contract.

"Sean brought Drew Brees' name up the very first day. And frankly, I think I heard Drew's name every single day thereafter," Loomis said during a press conference announcing the quarterback's signing.

Tom Benson chimed in on the momentous occasion. "I'm excited," he said. "I think both [Drew and his wife, Brittany Brees] are going to be outstanding citizens and help us rebuild this community."[7] Benson likely had no idea just how true his own statement would turn out to be.

As the rebuilding of the Saints continued, Payton and Loomis capped it off with another marquee name for the roster. In April 2006, they plucked Heisman Trophy-winning running back Reggie Bush from the draft. It was a coup that did much more than bring a high-value player with extraordinary athleticism to the team; it fired up the fan base.

Sportswriter Mike Detillier, an NFL draft expert and football analyst for WWL Radio in New Orleans, recalls a memorable moment that occurred during a public event the radio station held at Zephyr Field, next to Saints headquarters, on draft day. After the news broke that the Saints had snagged Bush, the crowd went crazy.

"We had a couple thousand people in the tents, with chairs set up on either side of an aisle," Detillier says. "As soon as Reggie Bush got picked, Tom Benson showed up and walked down that aisle, and his reception was almost as though he had just won an election."

Detillier, who says Bush at the time "was probably the biggest name to come out of college football since O. J. Simpson," says he had never seen a draft pick spark such a thrill among local fans. More astonishing, he adds, was that the cheering fans seemed—in a single moment—to forgive Benson for his past "sins" and put him on a pedestal.

"It was shocking," Detillier says. "This was the same guy people had vilified a few months earlier, and now all of a sudden, all that had changed in a heartbeat."

It was an indicator of how badly New Orleans football fans wanted, and needed, to see meaningful action on the field. Throughout the torturous back-and-forth with Benson that played out in news headlines after Katrina, even the most committed Saints fans sometimes had to wonder whether the anguish was worth it, given the team's disappointing record. But with promising new football talent coming into the picture, they had reasons to feel excited.

Their optimism found rewards as the 2006 season got under way. The Saints bagged wins in their first two regular-season games, which they played on the road, in Cleveland and Green Bay. New Orleans fans who watched the games on television were glued to the action as they sized up the prospects of the newly built team.

Then, on September 25, 2006, came one of the most important games the Saints would ever play. NFL commissioner Paul Tagliabue, in an effort to play up progress in New Orleans' recovery since Katrina, had made sure that the Saints' first home game of the season would be a nationally televised event on ESPN's "Monday Night Football." The Saints would meet their perennial archrival, the Atlanta Falcons, and millions of viewers would get a look inside the domed stadium that had become the stuff of horrific legend after the hurricane.

The Superdome had undergone an extensive renovation and upgrade in an extraordinarily short time under the supervision of its general manager, Doug Thornton. Now, the NFL would commemorate the Dome's return to action with a Super Bowl-like lineup of musical entertainment and festivities.

The national attention was hugely effective in showing the world that New Orleans was progressing toward a comeback. But

New Orleans Saints fans call themselves "Who Dats" in a nod to the team's unofficial chant, "Who dat say dey gonna beat dem Saints?" (Cheryl Gerber Photo)

none of the hoopla that the NFL had drummed up could top the impact of what happened on the field that night.

Less than two minutes into the game, Saints safety Steve Gleason charged through a hole in the Falcons' punt protection and took a flying leap to block the ball. Saints defensive back Curtis Deloatch scooped up the loose ball as he dived into the end zone for a touchdown.[8] The blocked punt would become famous.

"You could feel the Dome just rocking," Deloatch recalled a year later. "We must have celebrated for 20 minutes. They could have thrown all their flags on us, but I guess with it being such a special night . . . they let it slide."[9]

Many in the stadium said it appeared the Falcons were as happy for New Orleans at that moment as New Orleans was for itself, as tears streaked the faces of some seventy thousand people in the Dome.

Their early momentum carried the Saints to 23-3 victory.

"It was that type of magical day where everything just came together," NFL corporate communications chief Brian McCarthy later told a reporter. "It truly was Super Bowl-like—and much more important."[10]

As the Superdome erupted in roaring "Who dat!" chants after the game, Tom and Gayle Benson took to the field. Wielding the black-and-gold parasol that, in those years, he liked to hoist over his head after a win, Tom Benson held the parasol in one hand and Gayle's arm in the other, and he danced the little jig that had come to be known as the "Benson Boogie."

Chapter 22

Historic Climb, Hard Stumble

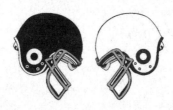

The almost surreal night in September 2006 that marked the Saints' return to the Superdome set the stage for an era in professional sports that many in New Orleans thought they would never witness.

The night had shown everyone that the city was on its feet and the Dome was game-ready once again. And for the Saints to score a big win at such a moment had a powerful effect on people across Louisiana. "Both physically and psychologically, that game provided a huge lift," former governor Kathleen Blanco says.

Some say it was also a night that launched the Saints on a historic climb.

The team had a 3-0 start on the season, and fans liked what they saw on the field. It was clear that the team had landed a talented quarterback, and the synergy between Drew Brees and coach Sean Payton was noticeable from the start.

That had to be gratifying to Benson, who had agreed to some big spending to reconstruct the team. By some accounts, Benson may have had some help in building the new dream team. In an analysis of the assistance the NFL provided to the Saints following Hurricane Katrina, economists Robert Baade and Victor Matheson wrote that in addition to the league kicking in $15 million toward Dome renovations and embedding outside marketing professionals to help boost ticket sales, individual team owners may have forked over some cash.

"Rumors have circulated . . . that the League passed the hat and owners provided $1 million each to help the Saints," the professors from College of the Holy Cross in Worcester, Massachusetts, wrote in 2007. "The rumored off-the-books $30 million may well have provided funds that enabled the signing of Drew Brees and Reggie Bush, two players that contributed substantially to reversing Saints fortunes on the field."[1]

The pricey new leadership did, indeed, energize the organization. The Saints went 10-6 in the 2006 season, finished first in the NFC South Division, and won a playoff game against the Philadelphia Eagles.

The season also brought a new buoyancy to the fan base. Many people were still struggling to repair homes and businesses damaged in 2005, and having a strong football team to cheer for boosted their morale.

It helped that Saints players and coaches embraced New Orleans in important ways off the field. Drew Brees over the next few years would become revered not only for his passing accuracy and leadership but for the way he and his wife involved themselves in a host of charitable and recovery efforts. In fact, the interest and compassion shown by Brees, Payton, and other members of the organization contributed to the ongoing rehabilitation of Tom Benson's image among local fans.

Benson had to be pretty happy with his investment.

All the Way

The next two seasons were bumpier ones for the Saints, with the team going 7-9, then 8-8, and getting shut out of the playoffs in both years. But fans still felt they were seeing higher-quality football on the field, particularly on the offensive side.

Brees continued to shine and was making stars out of such 2006 draft picks as wide receiver Marcus Colston, who quickly became one of the quarterback's favorite targets. While Reggie Bush delivered a spottier-than-hoped-for performance, other talented running backs, such as Pierre Thomas, emerged to pick up the slack.

As the team geared up for the 2009 season, coaches and players seemed to have a sense that it could be a big one. Through the spring, in fact, talk of a Super Bowl had been all the rage among local tourism promoters and state lawmakers, but that was because New Orleans was bidding to host the 2013 game, and the NFL had made clear that the city would have no shot at landing it unless the state could conclude a long-term agreement with the team.

Once the legislature approved Benson's package deal that included real estate near the Superdome and further upgrades to the stadium, and after the league awarded New Orleans the 2013 Super Bowl, it was time to focus on the current season. For fans, it was worth the wait.

Sometimes when a team looks strong in the preseason, its performance goes flat once regular-season games begin. Not so for the Saints in 2009. After bagging wins in three of four preseason games, the team went on to win one game after another in the fall lineup. The Saints kept winning through September, October, and November.

Criticism of Tom Benson had long since faded, if not from memory, at least from the streets of New Orleans. Talk these days was of the incredible performance the Saints were delivering and speculation about just how far they might go.

Benson had landed in somewhat unfamiliar territory. Everywhere he went in New Orleans, he was greeted with cheers and high-fives. Spontaneous bursts of applause were not unusual when he walked into a restaurant. It was clear that the good fortunes of the Saints were rubbing off on the city.

"It's just wonderful, what it's doing to the community," he said midway through the season. "I've never seen the excitement like this."[2]

Early in the season, quarterback Drew Brees seemed to feel in his bones that something big lay ahead. By mid-October, he was dropping words such as "destiny" and speaking of his own confidence that the team had it in them to go all the way.

"There's no doubt in my mind that we can win a championship together. Not only for the players and the organization, but for this city. Because no place deserves it more," he told a reporter.[3]

It was not until mid-December, with the team's record standing at 13-0, that the Saints' rising hopes of a perfect season took a tumble. The Dallas Cowboys did the deed, beating the Saints by a touchdown and setting the stage for two more Saints losses as the season wound to a close. Still, the Saints' performance overall had been impressive, and now the team was playoff bound. Players said the late-season losses simply gave them more to prove, and maybe they were right.

In the divisional playoff game in mid-January, the Saints trounced the Arizona Cardinals 45-14 and moved on to the conference championship. Then, in one of the most thrilling games of the season, the Saints bested the Minnesota Vikings, scoring a Garrett Hartley field goal in overtime and leaving the Superdome rocking with anticipation of the team's first-ever Super Bowl appearance.

People in New Orleans hardly dared to hope for a Super Bowl win. In fact, the thrill of having the team make it to the championship game was so energizing that, for many, the fairytale could just as easily have ended there.

But the team was not done. If the Saints' magical season had given New Orleans a lift, Super Bowl XLIV would leave locals walking on air. Few had dreamed that the Saints would upset the Indianapolis Colts, but there it was on the scoreboard: 31-17.

As ecstatic as they were over the championship, it would take time for locals to understand just how valuable a gift the team had delivered. New Orleans had not realized how much it needed a big win, until suddenly it had one.

Quarterback Drew Brees sets up a play in a game against the Arizona Cardinals. (Cheryl Gerber Photo)

Tom Benson hoists the Vince Lombardi Trophy after Super Bowl XLIV as Gayle Benson and Saints quarterback Drew Brees look on. (AP Photo)

The Saints' 2009 season had helped people put disaster in their rearview mirror and focus on the future. The team had not merely brought home the Vince Lombardi Trophy; it had helped save New Orleans from becoming a historical footnote.

Superdome manager Doug Thornton, who orchestrated the fast repair of the Superdome after the big storm, enabling the team's return to its home field, believes it is hard to overstate the role of the 2009 football season in the city's recovery. Reflecting in 2015 on how the team and the Dome have helped drive New Orleans' ongoing progress, he said: "I think it's got to be one of the greatest comeback stories in American history."[4]

Bounty Hunters?

The city's buoyancy and memories of Super Bowl XLIV lived on long after the game ended, tiding fans over during the next few seasons even though the Saints did not rise to the heights they had reached in 2009. But during the 2011 season, public grumblings about the Saints' on-field activities threatened to taint the team's success.

While the Drew Brees-led offense had become a model of savvy play-calling and execution, the reputation of the Saints defense around the NFL had never reached similar heights. It seemed that defensive coordinator Gregg Williams was becoming overly reliant on the blitz, in which defensive players charge toward the quarterback in unison, trying to disrupt an offensive play before it has a chance to develop into a yard-gaining pass or rush.

Complaints by opposing offensive players had begun to emerge, saying that the Saints' defense was becoming too aggressive and sometimes appeared to deliberately harm offensive linemen or even the quarterback. Critics grumbled that the behavior extended back to the Saints' 2009 Super Bowl-winning season, when the defense delivered a hard hit on Minnesota Vikings quarterback Brett Favre in a playoff game in the Superdome. The "high-low" blow, in which two defensive players tackled Favre simultaneously above the waist and below the knees, briefly sent the quarterback out of the game with an ankle injury. Though the officials did not call a penalty, ongoing complaints caught the league's attention.

Players and former players from various teams later would say that the practice of paying bonuses, or "bounties," to defensive players as rewards for effective hits had been an informal part of the game for years. Sometimes it was simply a matter of players trading bets among themselves in the locker room about who could hit hardest. In other cases, a team's defensive leader might be the one offering rewards.

Gradually, the complaints against the Saints snowballed into accusations that not only did Gregg Williams know of "bounties" being paid to players, but he might be directly involved, and that head coach Sean Payton could be aware of the practice too.

The fact that the NFL was increasingly coming under fire for not policing players' behavior strongly enough likely influenced how the league responded to the complaints. More and more former players who had suffered concussions during their careers, and who later developed physical maladies that they blamed on the head injuries, were filing lawsuits against the league, demanding compensation and stronger rules to protect players.

Perhaps feeling the pressure, NFL commissioner Roger Goodell launched an investigation into the defensive behavior of the Saints that involved the review of thousands of internal team documents and e-mails. In March 2012, the NFL released a report saying it had found evidence of the systematic payment of bounties to Saints players as rewards for harming opposing players. The report indicated that Gregg Williams had initiated the program in 2009, that two dozen players could be involved, and that Saints linebacker Jonathan Vilma had put up $10,000 before the Vikings matchup for anyone who could knock Brett Favre out of the game.[5]

"A combination of elements made this matter particularly unusual and egregious," Goodell said in releasing the report. "A strong and lasting message must be sent that such conduct is totally unacceptable and has no place in the game."[6]

Goodell fined the team $500,000 and said the Saints would forfeit their second-round selections in the 2012 and 2013 NFL drafts. The commissioner also took the jaw-dropping step of suspending Sean Payton without pay for the entire 2012 season, stating that Payton appeared to turn a blind eye on practices of the Saints defense. Goodell also suspended Saints general manager Mickey Loomis without pay for the first eight games of the season and suspended Gregg Williams indefinitely.

The investigative report noted that Saints owner Tom Benson had not been aware of the bounty program's existence and that, when he learned of the accusations, he told Loomis that if the behavior had occurred, it must stop.[7]

Goodell would also later announce suspensions of four players, including Vilma. Those players fought back, filing an appeal with help from the NFL Players Association. Goodell, who recused himself from the proceedings, appointed former NFL commissioner Paul Tagliabue to hear the matter.

Vilma also filed suit in federal court in New Orleans, contesting the league's authority to take such action against a player. In December 2012, Tagliabue vacated all the players' suspensions.

Gregg Williams, meanwhile, who had left the team soon after the scandal surfaced, suddenly became a witness in the NFL's investigation, providing accounts of harsh defensive play by the Saints and claiming that assistant coach Joe Vitt had urged the continuation of bounty payments when Williams wanted to end it. His cooperation with the investigation likely is why the league allowed Williams to return to coaching after sitting out for a year, working first for the Tennessee Titans and later the St. Louis Rams.

Whether, as some critics suggested, Goodell had overstepped his bounds, particularly in taking the unprecedented step of suspending Payton for a full season, will always be a thorny topic in New Orleans. Former Saints linebacker Scott Fujita, who by 2012 had moved on to the Cleveland Browns and was among the players vindicated by Tagliabue's ruling, said Goodell's "positions on player health and safety since a 2009 congressional hearing on concussions" were inconsistent. Among other things, he charged that Goodell had "failed to acknowledge a link between concussions and post-career brain disease" even as he pushed for a longer football season.[8]

Throughout the NFL's investigation into what became known

as the "bountygate" scandal, Tom Benson remained relatively quiet, though by some reports he was angry at Goodell. Whether or not Benson's resignation from a couple of NFL committees was intended as a message to the commissioner or simply a decision to cut back on work is hard to say.

It is possible that Benson felt it best to lie low in order to preserve a modicum of NFL goodwill, given that his most high-profile player had ripped into Goodell on several occasions.

"This process was kind of a sham from the start," Drew Brees told the NFL Network's Michael Irvin in a November 2012 interview. "We're being accused of things based on rhetoric, and based on the testimony of some very unreliable people, as opposed to real evidence and real facts."9

In any case, nobody at Saints headquarters could have been happy about the Saints 2012 season. Limping along under the management of assistant coaches, with Brees doing much of the play-calling on his own, the Saints went 7-9. While fans in New Orleans continued to support the team and fill the Superdome on game days, they could not deny that the air had gone out of the euphoric bubble that had engulfed the city after Super Bowl XLIV.

Meanwhile, in an ironic twist, as the ugly 2012 regular season drew to a close, New Orleans was in the throes of preparing to host Super Bowl XLVII, which in February 2013 would pit the Baltimore Ravens against the San Francisco 49ers in the Mercedes-Benz Superdome. As the hosting club, the Saints organization would be front and center for all the social events leading up to the game, including the huge NFL party arranged by Gayle Benson in New Orleans City Park.

Tom Benson clearly had decided to take the high road. Asked a few days before the Super Bowl how he thought the people of New Orleans would behave toward Roger Goodell during the big weekend, he struck a conciliatory note.

"They're going to treat him like I'm going to treat him—I'm going to give him a big hug," Benson said. Then, in a comment that seemed loaded with personal significance, he added, "One thing about the people here: they fight hard, but they forgive, too."10

Chapter 23

Basketball and a TV Station

If Tom Benson seemed unusually quiet during the months when his team's activities were under scrutiny by NFL commissioner Roger Goodell, it was in part because he was in the throes of another major deal. Just as he had known little about football before buying the Saints in 1985, Benson was not a big follower of professional basketball either. But that didn't stop him from entering the world of the National Basketball Association in 2012 by purchasing the New Orleans Hornets.

The NBA team had called New Orleans home for about a decade, since owner George Shinn had moved the team from Charlotte, North Carolina, and the Hornets took up residence at the newly built New Orleans Arena. The team had struggled to meet its early attendance goals and then in 2005 had to deal with the disruption brought about by Hurricane Katrina. The team spent two seasons in Oklahoma City following the storm and flood before returning to New Orleans, where it faced an even more difficult market given the post-storm decline in local population.

Shinn had started looking for a buyer in 2010, and several times it appeared that a deal might be close, particularly as local shipbuilding entrepreneur Gary Chouest, who had been an investor in the team, flirted with the idea of taking it over. Finally, the NBA, which had made clear that the league wanted the Hornets to remain in New Orleans, stepped in with a plan. The league would buy the team from Shinn and work on strengthening its financial position while searching for a new owner who would agree to keep the team in the city.

The NBA, under the leadership of Commissioner David Stern,

took the unprecedented step of buying the team in late 2010 and then began a campaign to grow the club's season-ticket base to the league's minimum benchmark of 10,000. Much as the NFL had done in 2006, the NBA tapped local business leaders for help in finding buyers for tickets and suites at the arena. Many of the same businesspeople who had stepped up to support the Saints now signed on with commitments to the Hornets. And the league attracted more corporate sponsors for the team than it had been able to claim since moving to the city.[1]

In addition, NBA representatives went to bat for the team at the state legislature. They negotiated a new lease for the Hornets that would keep the team in the state-owned arena through 2024 and provide $50 million of state-funded improvements to the basketball stadium, which sits directly across a street from the Mercedes-Benz Superdome. The deal also gave the team about $28 million worth of tax rebates over ten years, according to stadium finance expert Neil deMause.[2]

By the time the league approached Tom Benson to gauge his interest in buying the team, the state of Louisiana had already accommodated many of the demands he would likely have made in advance of a purchase. Though he had previously shown little interest in owning a basketball team, Gayle, who had been helping to reshape his local image, urged him to get involved. "I thought it was just time for Tom to step up and do that," she said later.[3]

All that was left for Benson to do was plop down $338 million and take over the team, and he obliged.

As he had done in 1985, Benson once again prevented a professional sports team from calling it quits in New Orleans. Local fans and city officials, who still recalled bitterly a buyer carting the New Orleans Jazz off to Utah in 1979, were grateful. "He really stepped up to the plate in a big way, because there was more than an idle threat that our team was going to get moved out of the city," New Orleans mayor Mitch Landrieu said of Benson.[4]

At the time of his purchase, Benson promised that he would change the name of the team from the Hornets to something better suited to its Louisiana home. In 2013, he and Gayle Benson announced the renaming of the team to the New Orleans

Pelicans, and they unveiled a new logo and uniforms in a blue, gold, and red color scheme.

The new owner, meanwhile, appeared more confident about the future of the local market than he had in the years when the fate of the New Orleans Saints was in question. "I think that our city's better off today than it was a few years back," Benson said in 2014. "Hopefully, we're playing a small part of that."[5]

From an administrative and marketing standpoint, Benson stood to benefit from having two professional teams in the city. He could spread the cost of certain back-office functions across two franchises. He already had a database to use in soliciting ticket sales, and the Saints had good relationships with potential corporate sponsors, with the ability to offer new package deals.

As for the action on the basketball court, Benson and Pelicans executive vice president Mickey Loomis, who plays a dual role with the Pelicans and Saints, stuck with General Manager Dell Demps and Coach Monty Williams, despite the fact that the team had logged a mixed record.

A highlight for the team to date had been the 2005 drafting of Wake Forest point guard Chris Paul, who ended up playing his first two seasons with the team in Oklahoma City. He quickly became a star and led the team to fifty-six wins in the 2007-8 season, helping the Hornets finish second in the NBA West Conference.[6] Paul also played in his first All-Star game in that year, in front of the hometown fans in New Orleans.

While Paul continued to shine, he suffered a string of injuries during the next few years, and the team's overall performance became inconsistent, never equaling its 2008 record. Early in 2012, the Hornets—then owned by the NBA—agreed to a trade that sent Paul to the Los Angeles Clippers and brought Eric Gordon, Chris Kaman, and Al-Farouq Aminu to New Orleans.

When Benson laid out $338 million in 2012, he acquired a team then valued at about $285 million, according to *Forbes*.[7] The magazine today pegs the team's value at $650 million—a seemingly big jump that nonetheless left the team at the bottom

From left, New Orleans Pelicans and Saints communications chief Greg Bensel; general manager Mickey Loomis; owner Tom Benson; Gayle Benson; Jennifer Lauscha, wife of Saints and Pelicans president Dennis Lauscha; and Dennis Lauscha at a basketball game. (AP Photo)

in the thirty-team league, where values of big-city clubs such as the New York Knicks, Los Angeles Lakers, and Chicago Bulls range from $2 billion to $3 billion.[8]

Valuations in the NBA have benefited in much the same way as they have in the NFL, based on rising popularity of the sport, high-dollar broadcasting rights, and increasing demand among wealthy individuals who would like to own a professional sports team. But until recent years, the league had not made systematic efforts, such as those of the NFL, to level the financial playing field among its teams.

Benson's purchase of the NBA team dovetailed nicely with a revenue-sharing plan that was in the early stages of implementation at the time. The aim of the agreement was to shift some of the revenue generated in the NBA's largest markets to its smallest cities, thereby helping those teams to sign quality players and making the league more competitive overall.[9]

On top of that, Benson lost no time in landing a name sponsor for the New Orleans Arena, where the Pelicans play. Under the 2014 agreement, the stadium built by the state of Louisiana in 1999 at a cost of $84 million would be called the Smoothie King Center, after the New Orleans-based beverage maker. Smoothie King owner Wan Kim reportedly shelled out $40 million for the ten-year deal.[10]

All of it seemed tailor-made for Tom Benson's approach to sports-team ownership. Always attuned to the bottom line, he has seen the operating income of the New Orleans Pelicans improve from a $6 million loss in 2011, the year before he purchased the team, to a $20 million profit in 2016.[11] The figure put the Pelicans at number thirteen among the thirty NBA teams in terms of operating income, based on estimates by *Forbes*.

In addition, the NBA negotiated rich new agreements with television broadcasters. A new nine-year agreement the league signed with ESPN and Turner Sports in the fall of 2014 carries a value of more than $23 billion. The networks will pay the league $2.6 billion annually, compared with the $930 million annual price that they paid under their deal signed in 2007.[12]

The benefits of the new agreement will accrue to owners and players, who stand to extract ever-higher salaries under a new collective-bargaining agreement between the league and the players association. New Orleans power forward Anthony Davis may snag the biggest rewards.

The Pelicans signed Davis in 2012, using one of the draft picks they received in trading away Chris Paul, and the six-foot ten-inch Davis proved his worth, being named to the NBA All-Star team twice and becoming a starter in the 2015 All-Star game. In anticipation of the NBA's salary cap rising substantially when the league's new TV rights deal kicked in, the Pelicans reportedly signed the twenty-two-year-old Davis to an unprecedented $145 million, five-year contract extension.[13]

While the team under Tom Benson's ownership is in the best shape, financially, in its history, the Pelicans have struggled on the basketball court. The team parted ways with Coach Monty Williams in 2015, and General Manager Dell Demps announced that NBA coaching veteran Alvin Gentry would replace him. But

New Orleans Pelicans power forward Anthony Davis goes for a basket in a game against the Philadelphia 76ers. (Cheryl Gerber Photo)

as Anthony Davis suffered injuries that left him on the bench, and with the talent behind him not thoroughly developed, a turnaround for the team was not yet in sight.

The selection of "Pelicans" as the new name for the NBA team in 2014 was apt, given that Louisiana's state bird is the brown pelican. But it may also have come about because Tom Benson had the name in his back pocket, so to speak.

Years before he became an NBA owner, Benson had tried hard to become the owner of a minor-league baseball team. A Class AA Southern Association team called the Pelicans had played in New Orleans between 1887 and 1959, and a couple of decades later, a Class AAA team of the same name, associated with the St. Louis Cardinals, had a brief run in the city.[14] In the early 1990s, Benson got a hankering to bring professional baseball to New Orleans, and he began making overtures to a AA team in

Charlotte, North Carolina. In 1992, he signed a letter of intent to purchase the Charlotte Knights, with plans to move the team to New Orleans and name it the Pelicans. He also came to an agreement with the University of New Orleans to have the team play its first local season in Privateer Park on the university's lakefront campus. Benson agreed to pay for improvements to the stadium and signed a one-year lease.

But before the team made the move, another investor who had been working to move a AAA team to New Orleans wrecked Benson's deal. John Dikeou, who owned the AAA Denver Zephyrs, needed to find a new home for the team because a major-league expansion team was starting up in Denver and the minor-league team had to go. After Dikeou filed a request with baseball's National League to be allowed to move to New Orleans, the league gave preference to the AAA Zephyrs, bumping the AA team.

Benson, who had not yet concluded his purchase of the Charlotte team, dropped the deal.

The New Orleans Zephyrs, which later came under new ownership, ended up with a new state-funded, 10,000-seat stadium called Zephyr Field, which lies next door to the New Orleans Saints headquarters and training camp on Airline Drive in Metairie.

The Saints headquarters and training camp stand along Airline Drive in suburban New Orleans. (Kathy Finn Photo)

Cross-Promoting

In his quest to find productive uses for his growing wealth, Tom Benson in 2008 took a turn that few could have predicted. It may have been part of his effort to demonstrate a lasting commitment to the city, or he may simply have been attracted by the potential for cross-promotional opportunities. In any case, Benson announced that he had signed an agreement to buy New Orleans television station WVUE for $41 million.

Its affiliation with News Corporation's Fox network made WVUE a good place for Benson to promote the Saints, as Fox held a big piece of the NFL's television broadcasting contract and carried the bulk of the Saints games. Under the league's contract that extends through 2022 and also includes CBS and NBC, Fox is paying an estimated $1.1 billion annually to carry the National Football Conference game package, which encompasses many of the NFL's biggest markets.[15]

NFL commissioner Roger Goodell quickly approved the deal, and the Federal Communications Commission also gave it a thumbs up.

Benson emphasized that his purchase from Indiana-based Emmis Communications Corporation would make WVUE the only locally owned New Orleans television station. "This community is going to get something from us having ownership of this station. I think it's going to show outsiders [that] hey, this is a good place to invest," Benson said in announcing the deal.[16]

As New Orleans television writer Dave Walker pointed out, Benson was buying the primary local distribution channel for his most valuable holding.[17] But Saints officials insisted Benson's goal was not simply to promote the team.

"It is going to be a TV station owned by locals," said Dennis Lauscha, then senior vice president of the Saints. "It's going to be trying to help out the locals, giving the locals the content that they want. That's the agenda. It's not a Saints agenda. . . . It's a local agenda."[18]

True to form, Benson's purchase of the television station came in the thick of other big deals that were also under way. In the spring of 2008, he was negotiating his $40 million acquisition of a downtown office building and a complex new lease with the state for the Saints in the Louisiana Superdome.

And the TV station purchase would not mark the last time he showed an interest in owning a piece of the news media. In 2012, around the same time he was preparing his bid for the New Orleans Hornets, owners of local daily newspaper the *Times-Picayune* announced that the paper would reduce its publishing frequency to three days a week. New Orleans readers were up in arms at the prospect of losing their only printed daily news source.

Benson sent a letter to the paper's owner, New York-based Advance Publications, and asked to meet to discuss purchasing the paper with a group of investors. But Advance chairman Steve Newhouse reiterated his earlier statement that the company would not consider selling the newspaper.[19]

Chapter 24

Anatomy of a Feud

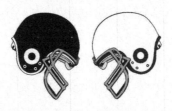

Isolating the moment when the Benson family core began to crumble is akin to pinpointing a tiny crack that led to an earthquake. In nearly any relationship that comes unglued, fault lines develop over a period of time through a pattern of behavior that can range from perceived slights to outright gestures of disrespect.

It is possible that Tom Benson unintentionally set the stage for trouble in 2001 when he began mentioning publicly that he was looking to his granddaughter Rita LeBlanc to one day succeed him as an owner and the public face of the New Orleans Saints.

Then again, the family foundation may have begun to weaken years earlier. In families that hold great wealth, it is not uncommon for competition to develop for the attention of the person who created or is the steward of the fortune. That competitiveness can help shape a family dynamic that endures for decades.

The Benson children and grandchildren had grown up with Tom Benson at the center of their lives. He was the person who had given them everything, the man they knew they could turn to anytime they needed help. They learned at a young age that he would provide for them always, not merely by making them heirs to his estate but by setting them up in one of his companies, as business owners, and eventually handing them the reins, if they so desired.

Tom Benson loved being able to give his family members everything they wanted and delighted in being the focus of their attention. No doubt he hoped to see all three of his and Shirley's children grow up to become his business partners. But as is often the case in family businesses, members of the younger generation were not equally inclined to take it on.

The Bensons' oldest child, Robert, did work in the automobile businesses after returning home from his service in the U.S. Navy. But he was more at home on the family's Texas ranch than in his dad's car dealerships. He liked working with the thoroughbred horses and taking them to racing events.

Tom and Shirley's youngest child, Tootsie, also loved the horses, and she grew into a fine rider, often showing her skills in equestrian competitions. Their shared fondness for horses helped form a bond between Tootsie and Robert, despite an eleven-year age difference. And if Robert was ambivalent about working in his dad's businesses, Tootsie was utterly averse. Neither of the siblings had the kind of ambition or innate business savvy that drove their father's career.

The Bensons' middle child, meanwhile, seemed to have a different temperament from either of her siblings. Eight years younger than Robert and three years older than Tootsie, Renee Benson did not care for horses, though she did like living on the ranch. Renee was less outgoing than other family members. Naturally reserved, she had a tendency to shy away from social settings, and living on the ranch made it easy to control her environment.

Both Renee and her brother had married and become parents in their early twenties. But whereas Robert and his first wife divorced after just a few years and he did not become deeply involved in his daughter's upbringing, Renee became the full-time mother of two children. Except for having a hand in managing the ranch, she would not involve herself much in her father's other businesses until her daughter and son were grown and she had divorced their father.

During her marriage to Russell LeBlanc, Renee Benson had to cope with the same tragedies that befell her father. Within an eleven-year period, she saw her mother die from complications of lupus, she lost her brother, Robert, to lung cancer, and she received the horrifying news that her sister, Tootsie, had taken her own life.

Five years after that event, Renee faced the end of her twenty-one-year marriage to LeBlanc. She would wed again in 1998, but her marriage to Roy McNett lasted just three years.

After the death of her mother, Shirley Benson, in 1980, Renee had been able to turn to her brother, sister, and father for comfort. But when Renee's brother succumbed to cancer in 1986, Tom Benson was married to his second wife, Grace, and they were spending much of their time in New Orleans.

By 1991, when Renee's sister, Tootsie, died in Missouri, her father and stepmother were even more deeply involved in New Orleans. If resentments within the family existed, they could easily have grown as Renee raised her two young teenagers in the remote environs of the Texas ranch.

By some accounts, Renee was unhappy from the beginning about her father's marriage to Grace in 1982, and she did little to disguise her feelings. Some say that Renee's children, Rita and Ryan LeBlanc, were more accepting of their grandfather's second wife than their mother was.

Members of Grace's family say that Renee was openly disdainful of the woman who had stepped into her mother's place. They even wonder whether Renee's "belittling" of her stepmother, which they say continued throughout the marriage of Tom and Grace, may have aggravated Grace's ill health as she struggled with Parkinson's disease.

In any case, by most accounts, Grace made it her mission to make Tom happy and was at his side whenever he wished, which may have rubbed Tom's daughter the wrong way. In 2001, when doctors discovered that Tom had blockages in arteries near his heart, Grace's own health was in decline. So when Tom underwent quadruple bypass surgery to address the problems, Grace's daughter, Susan Walker, became his hospital advocate and stayed near his bedside during his six-day hospitalization.

If Renee Benson or her children visited Tom during that period, "we never saw them," a member of Grace's family says.

After Grace passed away in 2003, Tom Benson moved quickly to fill the void in his life, and in doing so he put still greater stress on the family dynamic. Tom married Gayle Marie LaJaunie Bird less than a year after Grace died, and as his family would soon learn, Gayle was unlike Grace in key respects.

Though friends who knew both women saw them as kind and socially gracious, Gayle, who was twenty years younger than Grace, had spent much of her life trying to build a following in interior design, which many regard as a tough business. She had been through two marriages and a rugged second divorce, and she had defended herself repeatedly in court against creditors and unhappy clients.

Gayle had lived on her own for nearly two decades when Tom Benson met her. She was accustomed to managing her own life and doing things for herself.

After she married Tom Benson six months later, Gayle's life changed drastically, and not simply because of her transition from a middle-class existence into a life of great wealth. She had to adapt to Tom's lifestyle and the many demands that his life entailed. While friends say that her personality and social adeptness helped her slide with seeming ease into her new role as the wife of an NFL team owner, Gayle had never previously faced a family situation involving a spouse's adult offspring. She was only eight years older than Tom's daughter Renee, but she and Renee were vastly different people.

Gayle had come from modest roots, while her new stepdaughter had been born to wealth. Yet it was Gayle who seemed to have the polish and panache of a society maven.

Known throughout her life for being outgoing, well coifed, and meticulously dressed, Gayle exuded image consciousness, and her marriage to Tom Benson fueled her taste for designer clothes and expensive jewelry. As she spent more and more of her time at public events, board meetings, and the like, she sometimes changed her wardrobe of tailored suits and dresses several times a day, and almost never did she appear in public wearing heels less than three inches high.

Renee Benson, on the other hand, did not fit the stereotypical image of a woman who had grown up rich. She seemed to shun cosmetics and hairdressers, and she let her graying hair hang straight or pulled it into a ponytail. Her taste in clothing ran toward plain ranch wear and boots. She steered clear of big social events outside of church-related functions. She liked to drive a pickup truck.

When Tom and Gayle married in 2004, the wedding and related events likely were not Renee's cup of tea, but she and her children participated nonetheless.

Tom wanted a big San Antonio wedding that would bring his family and many Texas friends together, and Gayle planned an elaborate pre-wedding party at the New Orleans Museum of Art in City Park.

For the wedding, fashion designer Raoul Blanco dressed Gayle in an oyster-white silk dress with hand-beading, while her bridesmaids, including Renee Benson and her daughter, Rita LeBlanc, wore navy-blue silk.[1] Renee's son, Ryan LeBlanc, was among his grandfather's groomsmen, as was Tom Benson's only remaining brother, Larry.

To an observer who was not familiar with the family, the Benson clan on that day may have seemed the picture of unity. But as is often the case with family photos, the pictures didn't reveal the strains behind the smiles.

Some say that, given the previous testy relationship between Renee and Grace Benson, Tom's third wife had little chance of becoming his daughter's friend. And indeed, by one account, Gayle Benson found the going rough from the beginning. "It was contentious from day one," says Gayle's close friend, Angela Hill.

If the distance between New Orleans and San Antonio provided a buffer between Gayle and Renee during Tom and Gayle's first year of marriage, the cushion would soon shrink. Before the Bensons reached their one-year anniversary, Hurricane Katrina struck New Orleans and disrupted their lives, along with a million others. Displaced from team headquarters and the Louisiana Superdome, the New Orleans Saints scrambled to salvage the fall football schedule, and Tom Benson moved the team to San Antonio.

Renee Benson at the time owned a house in San Antonio, several miles from where her son and daughter-in-law, Ryan and Tracy LeBlanc, lived. The post-Katrina circumstances likely brought Gayle Benson into closer contact with Tom's daughter and grandson.

Their stay in Texas also may have brought Gayle closer to another of her husband's grandchildren. Dawn Benson Jones, who is the daughter of Tom's deceased son, Robert, lived with her husband, Chris, in Liberty Hill, Texas, a couple of hours northeast of San Antonio. By Dawn's account, they hosted Tom and Gayle in their home on a number of occasions.[2]

As Gayle Benson came into closer contact with Tom's family and friends in Texas, she may have worried privately over what her husband intended to do next with the Saints. What if he really did aim to take the team out of New Orleans permanently? Wouldn't he and Gayle have to relocate as well?

By the time the Saints returned to New Orleans at least temporarily in 2006, fears around the city about a possible Saints move had quieted somewhat. But Tom Benson had not committed to keeping the team in place permanently, and Gayle Benson may have felt motivated to do everything she could to keep the Saints, and herself, in her hometown.

During the next few years, as recovery and rebuilding moved into full swing in New Orleans, Gayle also went into action, finding ways to convince her husband to put the post-Hurricane Katrina ugliness behind him and make peace with the city. Gayle realized that she could play a key role in mending fences, in part simply by staying close to Tom in public and softening his persona. She also saw opportunities for her husband to endear himself to the city in more substantive ways.

In addition to his charitable causes throughout New Orleans, Benson pledged an $11 million gift that launched construction of the Tom Benson Stadium at the Pro Football Hall of Fame in Canton, Ohio. People took notice of Benson's stepped-up giving, and a number of organizations honored him with tributes and Good Samaritan awards.

As the Bensons spread more of their wealth around and generated local goodwill, Gayle Benson also expanded her own role as a board member in various organizations. And she was becoming a more familiar face at Saints headquarters.

From the time she and Tom began dating, players, coaches, and front-office personnel had grown accustomed to seeing Gayle at games. When Tom Benson cleaned house after the team's difficult 2005-6 season and brought in the new regime led by head coach Sean Payton and quarterback Drew Brees, the new hires quickly became accustomed to seeing "Mrs. Benson" strolling the halls at training camp and riding with her husband in his golf cart as he surveyed the practice field.

People around Saints headquarters seemed drawn to Gayle. A notable exception was Tom Benson's granddaughter, Rita LeBlanc.

After she graduated from Texas A&M University in 2001, the twenty-four-year-old LeBlanc, who called her grandfather Paw Paw, signed on full-time at Saints headquarters, where she would begin working in various departments. Rita's first few years on the job coincided with a difficult period for her grandfather, as Grace had begun her battle with Parkinson's disease and was gradually becoming weaker. With Grace less able to join Tom in public settings, it was Rita, a potential rising star in the ownership ranks of the NFL, who regularly appeared at her grandfather's side.

When Tom Benson brought Rita into the organization, he likely was feeling a growing urgency to secure the future of his sports franchise, which had quickly become the most valuable of his businesses and in many ways the most complicated one to own.

In order to keep the franchise in his family's hands, his options were limited. Renee Benson was his only surviving child, and she had never been inclined to become an active owner. He would have to look beyond Renee's generation, and of his three grandchildren, Rita was the only one who showed an interest.[3]

While Tom Benson had no intention of handing over the reins in the near term, he gave Rita a seat at the table that would ensure she would share in his spotlight as an NFL executive while she interned under his tutelage. By most reports, Rita took to her new role enthusiastically.

But after Grace Benson passed away and Tom found another love, a new Mrs. Benson would step in to share Tom Benson's spotlight.

Staff members at Saints training camp were anxious to get to know Gayle Benson and impress the boss's new wife. Perhaps inevitably, circumstances converged to set up a competition between Gayle and Rita for the attentions of Tom Benson and the respect of everyone who worked for him.

Their rivalry would grow, and while Tom may have become aware of it, defusing personal conflicts was not his strong suit. If people who worked for him had issues with one another, he expected them to resolve it and stay out of his hair, and he took somewhat the same approach with family members.

Another factor that would come to aggravate the relationship between Gayle and Rita was Tom's health.

Benson was a strong seventy-seven-year-old when he and Gayle met, but he was not without medical issues, and his history included major surgeries. He had undergone quadruple heart bypass surgery in 2001 and subsequently suffered bouts of atrial fibrillation, or an irregular heartbeat. Months after the heart surgery, he had an operation to relieve back pain.

Several years after Tom and Gayle married, doctors found a small cancerous mass on his left kidney and successfully removed it. Benson also began having vision difficulties, and doctors treated him repeatedly for macular degeneration. And he had knee problems that forced him to begin using a cane for support.

Over time, Benson counted more heavily on his wife to be at his side, and she came to see it as her responsibility to look out for him. Increasingly in public settings, such as when they strolled along the playing field before or after a Saints game in the Superdome, Gayle would keep a grip on Tom's arm, apparently to help steady him.

Despite the fact that life was becoming more challenging for him, Benson stayed in the game. He continued to scout for new opportunities to boost the team's revenue and kept up with commitments to the NFL.

But Gayle's increasing presence at Tom's side seemed to intensify the rivalry between her and Rita Leblanc. At a time when Rita may have hoped to take on a higher profile as her grandfather's protégée and business partner, everywhere she turned she saw

Gayle, and increasingly, it appeared that Gayle had Tom's ear.

It began to be clear, even to outside observers, that the two women not only disliked each other but could barely tolerate being within a few feet of one another. At Saints games, in front of television cameras, Tom, Gayle, and Rita would walk along the sidelines together, with Tom between his wife and granddaughter. While all wore happy faces and waved to the crowd, their body language spoke volumes: Gayle and Rita never made eye contact or even turned their heads toward one another. At times, even an outsider could see that their smiles were forced.

Gayle Benson kisses her husband as his granddaughter Rita LeBlanc looks on before a Saints game in December 2013. (AP Photo)

Whether the ongoing animosity between the two women had anything to do with what transpired in the front office in 2012 is anybody's guess, but it was in the spring of that year that local sports reporters noticed Rita's absence from Saints headquarters and sports-related events. Reporters cited insiders as saying that Tom Benson had placed his granddaughter on paid administrative leave because of issues including a difficult management style.[4] Though her apparent banishment lasted for at least three months, the Saints organization never provided an official explanation.

It's possible that an increasing competitiveness between Rita LeBlanc and Gayle Benson also coincided with a growing concerns in Rita's family about Tom Benson's spending. Tom and Gayle had bought nearly $7 million worth of residential property in San Antonio and New Orleans. During the years following the New Orleans Saints' 2010 Super Bowl victory, Tom shelled out tens of millions to replace his yacht and jet. In 2012, he paid $338 million to buy an NBA team.

In addition, the couple began funding their nonprofit Gayle and Tom Benson Charitable Foundation with annual multimillion-dollar contributions. Reports by the foundation to the Internal Revenue Service show that it distributed about $25 million from 2012 through 2014.[5]

Tom Benson's spending was hardly outlandish for a man of his means, and recent deals he had made with the state involving the Superdome were certain to provide a revenue boost from operations. But the increasing outflow of dollars was not lost on Renee Benson and her children, who were growing more wary of Gayle Benson and her influence over the family patriarch.

Sometime in 2012, following Rita LeBlanc's temporary banishment from Saints headquarters, Renee Benson apparently felt the need to keep a closer watch on the goings-on in New Orleans.

Though Renee had once owned a home in the Lakeview neighborhood of the city, that property had been sold years earlier. She went shopping for a residence that would put her close to Saints headquarters during her increasingly frequent visits from Texas, and she found what she wanted in suburban New Orleans.

In late 2012, she and her third husband, John Benham, whom she had married in 2006, paid $1.3 million for a large home set on one acre in River Ridge, ten minutes from the Saints training camp.[6] In the months to come, people at Saints headquarters would begin to notice that, in addition to Rita LeBlanc returning to her role with the team, both Renee and Ryan—who previously had visited the office only occasionally—began showing up more often, even settling into an office in the building for extended periods.

By some reports, the Benson family members' increased presence at Saints headquarters became a distraction for employees. A person close to the organization says that a brother-sister spat that erupted one day between Ryan and Rita turned into a

Tom Benson poses for a photo with his wife, Gayle, and granddaughter Rita LeBlanc before a game in November 2014. Several weeks later, he would cut all ties with Rita, her brother, and her mother. (AP Photo)

shouting match heard around the office, fueling concern through the ranks about where the organization was headed.

In the fall of 2014, Tom and Gayle Benson would celebrate their ten-year anniversary by renewing their vows at St. Louis Cathedral in New Orleans. They followed the ceremony with a reception for 1,000 guests at the New Orleans Museum of Art that was much like the party they had hosted before their wedding. The outside of the museum was dramatically lit for the occasion, and a harpist serenaded guests as they arrived at the door. Inside, members of the Louisiana Philharmonic Orchestra played as Tom and Gayle greeted friends, with Tom looking dapper in a pinstripe suit and Gayle wearing an ivory, mid-length dress by Vera Wang.[7]

Among the guests were many of Tom's cousins, nieces, and

nephews, as well as the daughters and grandchildren of his deceased wife Grace.⁸ Both Rita and Ryan LeBlanc attended the party. But despite the fact that she was then spending considerable time in New Orleans and owned a large home nearby, Renee was a no-show.⁹

Had Tom Benson's only surviving child become so seriously alienated that she refused to pay her respects on a momentous day for her eighty-seven-year-old father? Events of the next few months would leave little doubt that such was, indeed, the case.

Chapter 25

A Family Implodes

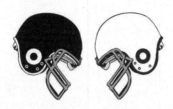

Several months after Tom and Gayle's tenth anniversary party, a lawyer would ask Renee Benson why she had not attended the celebration as other relatives of Tom had done. "I was not able to be free that day," she answered.[1]

Renee had missed the party despite the fact that she had for months complained that she and her children had been denied access to her father and received no information about his health because his wife, Gayle, was bent on keeping them away from him. The seeming contradiction between yearning to see her father and skipping his party was but one piece of a puzzle outsiders would scratch their heads over as the foundations of the Benson family began to give way.

People would also wonder about Gayle Benson's actions. Why, for instance, had she provided e-mail updates to Saints staff and her own friends regarding Tom's medical status following several knee surgeries but not included his daughter or grandchildren in the messages?[2]

At eighty-seven, Tom Benson's advancing age and declining health may have ignited the tinderbox that his family members' relationships had become. Some acquaintances of the family say that though Gayle Benson found herself at odds with Tom's closest relatives from the time she married him in 2004, the friction clearly intensified as he increasingly relied on her for help in navigating his infirmities and she stayed at his side nearly twenty-four hours a day—at home, at his office, at NFL meetings, and in a host of public settings.

As Gayle became as much Tom's caretaker as his wife and

companion, she was in a position to exert more control over how and with whom he spent time. Tom's daughter and grandchildren complained that they could not reach him by phone because all his calls went through Gayle, and she determined who would or would not speak with him.[3]

The November and December holidays added fuel to the fire as individuals on all sides complained of invitations not received or hospitality spurned. In addition, there was the matter of a heated exchange that occurred between Gayle Benson and Rita LeBlanc in Tom's suite at the Mercedes-Benz Superdome, during a December 21, 2014, game between the Saints and the Atlanta Falcons.

Accounts of the incident vary, but a New Orleans sportswriter, who cited as sources two individuals who were in the suite at the time, reported that Rita got into a confrontation with Gayle during which Rita put her hands on Gayle's shoulders and shook her repeatedly.[4] The incident became so ugly, one source said, that a guest rushed to the nearby suite of Saints president Dennis Lauscha and brought him in to calm things down.[5]

A cousin of Rita LeBlanc who also was in the suite later disputed the report, stating that Rita merely put her hands on Gayle's arms to get her attention and did not become aggressive.[6]

During a February 2015 court hearing, Tom Benson's lawyer Phil Wittmann questioned Tom's daughter Renee about the incident. Though Renee had not attended the game, she had heard about the exchange, which she refused to characterize as a confrontation. She would not confirm whether Rita had used profanity during the incident, and she said Rita was simply pleading for access to Tom. "My daughter asked—begged Gayle to let my dad see me," Renee said.[7]

For Tom Benson, who had become increasingly disturbed by the barrage of accusations flying among his family members, the suite incident may have been the last straw. According to a report by sportswriter Jeff Duncan, after the December 21 Saints game, Benson huddled in his Superdome office for more than an hour with Lauscha and lawyer Stanley Rosenberg.

Six days later, the simmering cauldron of jealousy, insecurity—and perhaps greed—that had come to characterize the core of the

Benson family reached the boiling point, and it bubbled over with irreversible results.

On December 27, 2014, at Tom Benson's direction, Rosenberg forwarded a letter to Tom's daughter and her two children, who were the primary heirs to his fortune and held board or executive titles in many of his businesses. The letter informed the three that Tom was fed up with their behavior and wanted nothing more to do with them and that they would have no further involvement in his sports teams, New Orleans real-estate holdings, auto dealerships, or television station.

Under the salutation "Dear Renee, Rita and Ryan," the letter said:

> During the over 80 years of my life, I have built a rather large estate which was intended to mainly be for you all as my family.
>
> Suddenly after I remarried you all became offensive and did not act in an appropriate manner and even had arguments among yourselves which created a very unpleasant family situation which I will not stand for. It made me very unhappy and uncomfortable. This situation cannot continue at my age.
>
> Because of the facts set out above and the heart break you have caused me I want no further contact with any of you and you will not be allowed to enter the Saints facilities or games, the basketball facilities or Pelicans games, the Benson Towers, the TV facilities or the automotive facilities in New Orleans and will have no right to give directions, or hire or fire any of the personnel.
>
> Sincerely yours, your father and grandfather,
> Tom Benson

It is impossible to imagine what Tom Benson expected to happen next. Presumably, his advisers helped him review the potential legal ramifications of his moves before he signed the letter. Rosenberg later confirmed that he had written the letter, roughly as Tom had dictated it to him.[8] And a nurse who was with Benson as he reviewed the letter said Benson read through it several times, crying as he did so, before finally signing it and having it sent.⁹ She testified that no one stood over him while he signed it, and he made the decision to do so on his own.

Shortly thereafter, representatives of Benson sent messages to Renee Benson and her children ordering them to stay away from all of the Benson auto dealerships and to turn in their company-owned vehicles.¹⁰ Rita Benson LeBlanc was given three days to clear her belongings out of her office at Saints headquarters, after which she would not be allowed back in the door.

As anguished as he must have felt at that point, Benson soon pushed matters even further, taking steps to remove the family members from ownership positions in his enterprises.

On January 11, he notified the steward of several trusts he had set up for his daughter and grandchildren in 2009, 2012, and 2014 that he intended to transfer key assets out of those trusts into his own hands and that he would replace those assets with other holdings and promissory notes. The assets he sought to move included nonvoting shares previously allocated to his heirs in the New Orleans Saints and Pelicans, along with interests in the Benson Tower office building, the adjacent Champions Square, and a nearby surface parking lot. Also included in the transfer was land on which Benson auto dealerships are located, and stock in all the dealerships themselves.¹¹

Benson in mid-January revealed publicly that he had created a new succession plan, which he had submitted to the NFL and NBA, that would put ownership and control of the Saints and Pelicans, and other Benson properties, into Gayle Benson's hands upon his death. "Rita will not be involved in the ownership or management of the Saints or Pelicans," Benson said in a release to the press.¹²

In a statement publicized by his staff on January 22, 2015, Benson explained that he had given careful consideration to his actions before taking the steps. "This is something I have thought about and prayed about for a while now," he said.¹³

"When family members are involved, decisions are always tougher. My family, as they have been their whole lives, will be very well taken care of, however, this is about making the correct decision as it pertains specifically to the future of the Saints and Pelicans and their long-term success in the city of New Orleans, where they belong," he said.

Benson also made clear his feelings about his wife. "My wife Gayle is my family too and a very important part of my life. . . . I am very proud of her. She is the most logical and natural person closest to me that will ensure the continuity, the stability and the success of our Saints and Pelicans in the city of New Orleans for a long time."

Benson was also uncharacteristically candid about his feelings with regard to his ownership of the sports teams. "I enjoy it, I truly do. I love being in the office and being around the coaches and players and staff and being a part of what they are doing. I have just come to a point in my life where I need to make some tough decisions on how things are going to be planned out," he said.

"Civil Death"

Benson's public statement was perhaps designed as a final, personal punctuation mark to his shocking decision to cut ties with his family and revamp their inheritance plan. But in fact, the fight was just getting started.

On the same day that Benson's staff released the statement, a lawyer for his daughter, granddaughter, and grandson filed what estate planners regard as the most drastic legal step an heir can take. Renee Benson and Rita and Ryan LeBlanc asked a New Orleans court to declare Tom Benson mentally incompetent and unfit to manage his affairs.

In their twenty-seven-page "petition for interdiction" of Tom Benson, his heirs laid out details intended to prove that both his health and mental acuity were in decline and that he had become a veritable puppet of his wife. "Gayle's influence over Tom Benson has grown, and she has increasingly isolated and alienated him from family, friends, business associates, and employees," his relatives said in the filing, which sought to have Renee appointed as the caretaker "of Tom Benson's property and person."[14]

They complained that Gayle intentionally omitted them from communications about Tom's health, failing to let them know that he was to have knee surgery in May 2014 and not informing them of follow-up procedures when complications developed. They also accused Gayle of insisting that Tom attend an NFL owners meeting in Atlanta immediately after one hospitalization, noting that during a presentation at that meeting he lost his balance, fell, and had to be hospitalized again as doctors checked him for a concussion.

Benson subsequently had several more health "scares" involving hospitalizations, and he made public appearances in which he seemed disoriented and unable to remember names and facts, the petition said. His relatives charged that Benson was overmedicated and that, "under the apparent supervision of Gayle," his diet often consisted of "candy, ice cream sodas, and red wine."

The petition accused Gayle Benson of orchestrating a "coup" that resulted in Tom's family being shut out of his life. "Gayle screens almost all, if not all, of Tom Benson's phone calls, emails, and regular mail [and] apparently has [him] under close watch and monitors whom he speaks with, what he says, and selects those whom she will permit to be near him," the petition stated.[15]

"Sadly, Gayle's apparent influence, combined with Tom Benson's physical and mental infirmities, has led to some alarming decisions purportedly made by Tom Benson in the managing of his affairs and in his relationships with his daughter and grandchildren," it continued.

Some estate lawyers refer to interdiction as "civil death," because if it is successful, it results in turning the management of a person's well-being and affairs over to someone else. "These cases are very hard for the person making the allegations to win, and they should be, because it has to do with denying an individual personal liberties," says New Orleans estate attorney Carole Cukell Neff.

In some cases, Neff notes, the parties requesting the interdiction do not actually aim to take charge of the individual who is the subject of the action. Rather, she says, they may hope to cast enough doubt on the person's competency to suggest that decisions the individual has made, which are unfavorable to their own interests, might be invalidated.

Even if a court refuses to order interdiction, a family may still pursue allegations of undue influence over the individual by a third party, in an effort to undo legal steps the individual took in the past. "Part of invalidating a change in the estate plan could be to show that maybe he is competent but is susceptible to influence by another person," Neff says.

Distrusted Trustee

Tom Benson's actions toward his daughter and grandchildren, which their petition termed "bizarre," gave rise to another case in Texas, where Renee Benson filed an additional lawsuit in Bexar County probate court seeking to have her father removed as the steward of a trust set up for her benefit many years earlier in the name of her mother, Shirley.

The Shirley Benson Testamentary Trust, completely funded by Tom Benson, held substantial assets initially set aside for Tom and Shirley's three children, but after two of them died, Renee was the only remaining beneficiary. Eventually, Renee's two children, along with her brother's daughter, Dawn Benson Jones, also would become beneficiaries through separate trusts set up for them.

Over time, Tom Benson added large business and real-estate holdings to the Shirley Benson trust. By the time of his falling out with his daughter and grandchildren, the trust held: 97 percent of Benson's Lone Star Capital Bank in San Antonio; a 50-percent interest in all five of his auto dealerships in Texas and Louisiana; a substantial portion of the Benson Farm and Ranch in Johnson City, Texas; the Uptown Blanco community project under development by Renee in Blanco, Texas; a house and several adjacent lots in Old Metairie where Rita LeBlanc has lived for some years; a vacation home near Lake Tahoe in Nevada; rights to a portion of some 1,500 acres of real estate in Blanco County, Texas; and several million dollars held in a Lone Star Bank money market account.[16]

Renee's San Antonio lawsuit came in response to actions Tom Benson took shortly after he sent the letter cutting ties with Renee, Rita and Ryan. Among other things, he ordered his longtime bookkeeper, Mary Polensky, who worked down the hall from Renee's office at Renson Enterprises, to quietly remove all of Tom's books and records from the building and to have no further contact with anyone at Renson Enterprises, including not only Renee and Ryan but also Tom Benson's longtime business associate Tom Roddy. Benson said he made the move because he was tired of his family members and Roddy going to Polensky to get information about Tom's businesses.

He also ordered his heirs and Tom Roddy removed as directors of Lone Star Capital Bank, and he transferred nearly $25 million out of Lone Star and into another bank.[17] In her lawsuit, Renee charged that the removal of such a large sum could have damaged Lone Star Capital Bank, which is an asset of the Shirley Benson trust, and she said her father's moves proved that she should replace him as trustee.

In courtroom testimony, she complained that Gayle Benson not only tried to keep family members away from Tom but remained constantly at his side during family visits, so that his relatives "never had any private quality time with" him.[18] Asked by a lawyer to explain her opinion of Gayle, Renee said, "I think she is an intelligent woman. She can put on stockings standing straight up. There are things I admire about her. But she has kept a lot of people away from my dad, including myself. And that bothers me."[19]

A San Antonio probate judge later temporarily suspended Tom Benson's control of the Shirley Benson trust and placed it in the hands of two receivers. Ironically, one of the receivers was lawyer Phil Hardberger, the former mayor of San Antonio who had tried to lure the New Orleans Saints to his city and lobbied Benson to keep the team there after Hurricane Katrina.

In a report that itemized the trust's holdings, Hardberger and the other receiver, Art Bayern, wrote, "The tangle of legal instruments through the years dealing with this vast wealth could give a legal scholar headaches." The receivers also took note of "the remarkable generosity of Mr. Benson to his family in the past."[20]

Benson's lawyers pointed out in court that, even though the original terms of the Shirley Benson trust had granted Tom Benson all of the income generated by its assets, he had never taken any income from it, instead paying all taxes due and allowing the income to accumulate unfettered for his daughter's benefit.[21]

In testimony, Renee Benson complained that her father had stopped making payments, such as the $10,000 a month she had received from the trust for more than twenty years and the $75,000 monthly management fee paid by Benson's car dealerships to her

Renee Benson dubbed her Blanco, Texas, community improvement project Uptown Blanco. A restaurant that operated there for several years has closed; a fabric store (far right) remains open. (Kathy Finn Photo)

company, Renson Enterprises. She also said that whereas her father had previously paid the insurance and property-tax bills for her Uptown Blanco project, he had ceased doing so after he cut ties with his family, and she had to make the latest payments herself.[22]

But Tom Benson's lawyer, Phil Wittmann, said that payments Renee had long received from the trust were at her father's discretion. In addition, Wittmann noted that Tom Benson had put some $20 million into the Uptown Blanco project and that it was losing $200,000 a year. Wittmann asked Renee whether, if she were the trustee of the trust, she would continue to pour money into a "bad investment."

"I may or may not," she answered.

In February 2015, Renee closed the restaurant she had opened several years earlier in one of the Uptown Blanco buildings. More than a year later, with the restaurant still closed, only one store, a quilting supplies shop, continued to operate in the otherwise dark complex.

Give and Take

The lawsuit Renee filed in San Antonio over the Shirley Benson trust played out simultaneously with the action she and her children had filed in New Orleans seeking to have Tom Benson declared mentally incompetent. At the same time, yet another case was under way in federal court in New Orleans, where Tom Benson had filed suit demanding that the asset substitutions he had directed in early January be allowed to proceed—removing the stock of his sports teams and other businesses from the individual trusts set up for Renee, Rita, and Ryan and replacing them with promissory notes.[23]

The steward of those trusts, San Antonio lawyer Robert Rosenthal, had balked at making the exchange because he said it was unclear that some $400 million worth of notes and $94 million in forgiven debt that Benson had offered were a fair trade for the assets he sought to remove. The case continued even after Benson increased his offer, with the family's lawyers demanding an independent valuation of the sports teams.[24]

As the lawsuits proceeded in Louisiana and Texas, they generated millions of dollars in attorney fees, which had to be a burr under Benson's saddle. He once said that one of the things he hated doing most is paying lawyers, and after a judge appointed temporary receivers to audit the Shirley Benson trust early in 2015, Benson complained loudly about the $600-an-hour fees the receivers planned to charge.[25]

Ultimately, Benson and his daughter settled that case before it went to trial, with Benson agreeing to allow Renee to take over as trustee. Other details of the settlement were not made public.

Meanwhile, following an eight-day trial of the interdiction case in Civil District Court in New Orleans, Judge Kern Reese, who had also interviewed and evaluated Tom Benson in a private meeting, ruled in Benson's favor. He said that Benson showed "memory lapses" not unusual in an octogenarian, but he found that Benson "is able to make reasoned decisions as to his person and his property."[26]

Renee Benson and Rita and Ryan LeBlanc appealed Reese's decision, but the Court of Appeal for the Fourth Circuit upheld the lower court's ruling. In March 2016, the family's lawyer, Randall Smith, asked the Louisiana Supreme Court to hear the matter. Smith's application to the state's high court hinged on his complaint that the lower court had not required Tom Benson to testify at his June 2015 trial. "If not overturned, the rulings of the lower courts will permit the truth to be concealed by manipulation of those in a weakened state," Smith said in a statement released to the press.

Through months of pursuing an interdiction of Tom Benson, Smith repeatedly said that his clients' primary interest was in protecting Benson and seeing to it that his estate would remain intact. In this case, as in many others, outside observers may always wonder whether the heirs might have chosen a less drastic path to their goals.

In May 2016, the Louisiana Supreme Court declined to hear the heirs' appeal of the Fourth Circuit ruling regarding Tom Benson's mental competency, thus ending that battle but leaving the family in a sea of bitterness. While Benson had prevailed in a crucial legal round, it seemed clear that his estate ultimately would be carved up in ways that he did not intend, which is not uncommon in disputes that arise in ultra-wealthy families. Wealth counselor Thayer Willis says that the kinds of family conflicts that erupt among the rich are not necessarily much different from tiffs that arise in families of modest means. Feelings of resentment, jealousy, and even entitlement can cause problems at any socioeconomic level, she says. But families with sparse resources may sweep the spats out of sight or try to ignore them in hopes of maintaining harmony, while members of rich families may be less inclined to let go.

"Where there is financial wealth, all of these challenges get amplified," Willis says. "People will fight a lot harder over a billion dollars than over $10,000."

Chapter 26

The Gloves Come Off

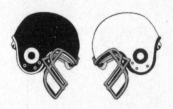

Perhaps when Tom Benson sent a letter banishing his family members from his businesses, and after he initiated an asset exchange to retrieve from their trusts business interests he had previously given them, he thought his actions would put an end to the saga of jealousy and distrust that had come to consume his family. Maybe he thought that, as had been the case through much of his life, once he made his decisions known, his family would simply fall into line.

When that didn't happen, Benson was shocked. "At first I couldn't believe it," he said a couple of months after Renee Benson and Rita and Ryan LeBlanc asked a New Orleans judge to declare him mentally incompetent.[1] "When your family attacks you, it's kind of hard to take, hard to understand."[2]

But maybe he should not have been surprised. Perhaps his family members over the years had learned a certain callousness from him. Hadn't he shown, more than once, his own willingness to sacrifice a friendship in favor of a financial benefit?

Maybe he could have reflected on his behavior toward Mike Persia III decades earlier, when Benson forced the young man out of the very family-owned business that had launched Benson on his own automobile career. And what about Tom Benson's relationships with friends and associates who had helped him acquire the New Orleans Saints and a local bank? How many of them remained his friends after being in business with him?

"I think Tom Benson demanded loyalty more than he gave it," former New Orleans Saints front-office executive Jim Miller says, when asked whether Benson stood by those who worked for him.

But Miller adds that such attitudes are common in the business world. "A lot of people put business before personal feelings," he says.

While it's possible that Benson's own insensitivity came back to bite him in the form of lawsuits by his family, his plight nevertheless generated sympathy in a city that often, in the past, had questioned his motives. No matter how they may have felt about Tom Benson over the years, many people—even those who once knew him and no longer associate with him—find it shocking that family members of a man in his late eighties, who gave them untold wealth and material comforts, would put him through the trauma of an expensive and highly personal court battle.

"It was beyond my comprehension how they could do that to him," says former New Orleans Saints and VooDoo marketing executive Mike Feder, who now lives in Arizona. "It seems very vindictive."

Benson's situation also drew sympathy from a former Louisiana politician and fellow octogenarian. Edwin Edwards, who is the same age as Benson and became well acquainted with him during and after Benson's efforts to buy the Saints in 1985, contacted Benson in the spring of 2015 after hearing of the lawsuits by the family.

The former four-term governor—who faced two federal trials during the 1980s and '90s and served eight years in prison after the last one—says he has always admired Benson. "I just wanted to let him know I was thinking about him."

Edwards was aghast that Benson's family took him to court. "It has to be a terrible burden for him to know that his heirs, who are going to profit so much from his efforts through the years, are that ungrateful," Edwards says. "It's ingratitude at its highest."

The lawyer for Benson's heirs, though, maintains that the family had no other choice after Tom Benson struck at them. In a statement released in late January 2015, attorney Randall Smith took issue with the "narrative" that Benson had deliberated long before making a "decision to reverse decades of plans to have Rita succeed him as the designated owner of the Saints" and make Gayle his successor instead.[3]

"All evidence suggests that Tom Benson, in a weakened mental and physical state, was unduly influenced to suddenly sever all relations with his daughter and grandchildren," Smith said in the statement. "The irrationality of the recent moves is well demonstrated by the bizarre communications and acts executing them."

Referring to a "coup" that he said began with Benson's letter severing ties with his daughter, granddaughter, and grandson, Smith stated: "The letter does not display a reasoned choice to change corporate governance, but a lashing out at those closest to [Benson]."[4]

Whether the actions of Renee Benson, Rita LeBlanc, and Ryan LeBlanc reflect a lack of appreciation or, as their lawyer insists, a deep love and concern for Tom Benson is a question outsiders will never be able to answer. But after his family members petitioned the court for a finding of mental incompetence, Benson's feelings on the matter became clear.

No More Sugarcoating

Throughout his life Benson had followed his mother's advice that when one member of the family found good fortune, other family members should share in it. As he built a profitable automobile business, he brought along with him all of his brothers, his father, cousins, step-children, and step-grandchildren and numerous nieces and nephews, who came to work in or own pieces of the sprawling enterprise.

When one or another of his brothers fell on financial hard times due to ill-advised business or investment decisions, Tom Benson bailed them out. And following the deaths of each of his three younger brothers, Benson was on hand to help their families.

Through it all, Benson's greatest loyalty was to his own children and grandchildren. Before his first wife died in 1980, he established the Shirley Benson Testamentary Trust for the benefit of their three children. Then, after Shirley passed away, he had to face the deaths of his son, Robert, and his daughter Tootsie. The losses likely intensified his determination to ensure a lifetime of opportunity for his remaining child and his three grandchildren.

Benson became particularly focused on doing so after the death of his second wife, Grace. As he reached his mid-seventies, he began bringing his heirs more directly into his businesses. He not only put Rita LeBlanc on the payroll of the Saints but also named her, her mother, and her brother as directors of his Texas bank.

Renee Benson and Ryan LeBlanc also headed a management company that provided services to Tom Benson's automobile dealerships, which paid their company millions of dollars in fees. And Benson would set up trusts designed to pass all of his businesses and other assets to Renee, Rita, and Ryan, as well as a portion to his third grandchild, Dawn Benson Jones, upon his death.

After investing so much of himself into providing for his family's long-term future, it likely was difficult, perhaps impossible, for Benson to give any credence to the idea that his family members might not measure up to his expectations. Even when he would get wind of problems one or another of them might be causing, he remained solidly in their corner.

In his Texas companies, he tried to ensure his family members' success by putting in place trusted associates, such as Tom Roddy, to provide oversight. He saw to it that his dealerships had stable management, and he relied on experienced financial managers to run his bank.

At Saints headquarters in New Orleans, Benson kept an eye on things himself. He had a close view of his granddaughter's on-the-job performance, and while he reportedly sometimes appeared displeased with what he saw, he kept his feelings under wraps. Some who worked in the New Orleans Saints organization say Benson often was frustrated by his granddaughter's absence from the office or a lack of focus on her job, but in public communications through the years, Benson stuck by Rita LeBlanc and talked her up as a worthy future successor to his sports teams.

Even after he put her into a three-month "timeout" for unspecified reasons in 2012, he downplayed the move publicly and welcomed her back into the fold by giving her a promotion. Benson showed over the years that, even if an ability to maintain a commitment to his friends and business associates sometimes eluded him, he was extraordinarily loyal to family members.

But in January 2015, after they filed suit to have him declared mentally unfit, the gloves came off. Tom Benson sent notice to Rita LeBlanc, her mother, and brother: stay away from all Benson-owned businesses and turn in your Benson-owned automobiles.

Subsequent communications by Tom Benson and his lawyers made clear that Tom would no longer sugarcoat any concerns he had about his heirs' capabilities. Following the court petition by Renee, Rita, and Ryan seeking a ruling on his competence, Benson's lawyers shot back with a filing expressing his disappointment in them.

"For years, Mr. Benson attempted to involve [his heirs] in various aspects of his business interests, and to groom them into the type of business persons that he could have confidence in to own and/or run those business interests when he died. Unfortunately, [they] never rose to the task," Benson's lawyers said.[5] "After years of concern and misgivings about [their] abilities to competently participate in (and eventually, perhaps, take over) the management of his businesses, Mr. Benson made the deliberate, reasoned, and difficult decision to change course and to name as his successor his loving wife, Gayle Benson, who has stood by his side and assisted him in his personal and business dealings for over a decade."[6]

Benson's lawyers took his complaints further as hearings proceeded in probate court in San Antonio over Renee Benson's effort to replace her father as trustee of the Shirley Benson trust.

Renee claimed in a hearing that in addition to becoming a member of the board of directors of Lone Star Capital Bank in 2002, she had responsibility—through her management company, Renson Enterprises—for hiring and firing top staff at all three of Tom Benson's San Antonio auto dealerships.[7] "She was responsible for reviewing and critiquing financial statements and month-end packages," along with overseeing many corporate departments and managing property rentals, dealership rents, and leases, her lawyers said in court filings.[8]

In 2010, Ryan LeBlanc, moved into the family's automotive operations, according to the attorneys, and had responsibility for reviewing and managing financial statements, sales statistics, service numbers, and human resources issues.

But testimony by a longtime Mercedes-Benz dealership manager cast doubt on the contributions of Tom Benson's heirs. In a February 2015 hearing, Richard Hood, who had managed Benson's

Mercedes-Benz dealership in New Orleans for some years before moving to San Antonio to take charge of that showroom, testified about the workings of Renson Enterprises.

While Renee Benson had previously said that Tom Benson's three San Antonio dealerships paid Renson a fee of $75,000 a month for various services, Hood stated that additional fees and commissions collected by Renson brought total payments by the dealerships to about $2 million a year.[9]

Renson had about eight employees, including Renee, Ryan, Tom Roddy, and another executive, along with IT human resources, and support staff.

When Tom Benson in January 2015 halted payments to Renson by his dealerships and Renson Enterprises shut down, the HR and IT employees shifted over to working directly for the three dealerships, Hood said. Benson asked Hood, who had worked for him for more than thirty years, to keep an eye on the Chevrolet and Honda dealerships as well as the Mercedes-Benz dealership that he managed.

Hood said that in his years at the Mercedes-Benz dealership, he had seen Renee Benson and Tom Roddy there only two or three times, whereas Tom Benson seemed to visit every time he was in town. Ryan LeBlanc had spent time at the dealerships as he was "learning about the business," Hood noted.[10]

Hood went on to say that the dealerships themselves could easily have handled the services for which they paid Renson $2 million a year, and they could have done it much less expensively. "We functioned last month with no Renson, and our profits were up 29 percent," he stated. "There's no task that Renson provided that we couldn't provide for ourselves."[11]

According to Hood's testimony, Renee Benson had wielded her hiring and firing authority over dealership management frequently. He said that the Benson Honda dealership had gone through seven general managers in eight years, and the Chevrolet dealership had four general managers in the same period. Meanwhile, Hood said, both of Benson's New Orleans auto dealerships have managers who have been in place for more than twenty years.

During that same hearing in February 2015, longtime Tom Benson friend and legal adviser Stanley Rosenberg also testified, discussing his business relationship and dealings with Benson over the years.

Rosenberg, who along with his wife, Sandra, had been close to Tom Benson for decades and had known all three of Tom's wives, weighed in on the claim by Renee Benson's lawyers that she and her father had been close until Gayle drove a wedge between them. Asked to describe Tom Benson's relationship with his daughter in the years before the court battle began, Rosenberg said it "was strained."[12]

"How long are you saying that their relationship has been strained?" a lawyer asked him.

"It's hard for me to guess an exact time, but over the years that I've known him. I've known Renee since she was . . . a little girl . . . and of course, I've known Tom forever," Rosenberg said.[13]

In February 2016, the feuding family reached a settlement agreement in the San Antonio case that shifted control of the Shirley Benson trust from Tom to his daughter.

Of the various legal proceedings that unfolded in two states and consumed the family for many months, the June 2015 trial in New Orleans over Tom Benson's mental competency had to be the toughest. Before the trial, he had to submit to court-ordered psychiatric evaluations by three doctors, who made extensive written reports of their findings to the court.

When the trial date arrived, the proceedings brought Benson face to face with Renee Benson, Rita LeBlanc, and Ryan LeBlanc for the first time in more than six months, as they sat on opposite sides of the courtroom during grueling personal testimony about the man responsible for the family's great wealth.

Because Civil District Court Judge Kern Reese had closed the courtroom to the public and press, and ordered that transcripts of the proceedings and other documents be kept under seal, details of what transpired during the eight days of trial are unknown except to the parties and their lawyers.

On each day, reporters who waited outside the courtroom watched family members and expert witnesses come and go,

The Gloves Come Off

Tom Benson's family members pause outside a New Orleans courthouse before a June 2015 trial to determine whether Benson was mentally competent. From left, Benson's grandson, Ryan LeBlanc; Benson's granddaughter Rita LeBlanc; attorney Randall Smith; and Benson's daughter Renee Benson. (Cheryl Gerber Photo)

with Renee Benson and Rita LeBlanc occasionally emerging from the room in tears. A handful of Saints and Pelicans employees, including the teams' president, Dennis Lauscha, also testified.

And in testimony that likely left Benson feeling wounded and betrayed, his longtime friend and business associate Tom Roddy spent several hours answering questions as a witness for Renee, Rita, and Ryan. Roddy would later emerge from the courtroom on the brink of tears.

During the trial, Tom Benson, still suffering from lingering knee problems, alternately used a cane or walker as he came and went, and he leaned heavily on the arm of his lawyer Phil Wittmann when he would pause to make a comment or give a thumbs up to reporters.

Benson, who never took the witness stand, sat through day after day of the trial as lawyers questioned his daughter and grandchildren, as well as his wife, Gayle, and as the three psychiatrists discussed details of his mental acuity.

Tom Benson gets assistance from his attorney, Phil Wittmann, as they approach the courthouse for the June 2015 trial in which Benson faced off with his family members. (Cheryl Gerber Photo)

While the judge would rule in Tom Benson's favor and deny his family's request for an interdiction, appeals would drag on for months, and it had to cross Benson's mind that the battle with his family could continue, in one form or another, for the rest of his life.

In characteristic displays of his tenacity, Benson occasionally expressed optimism and told reporters that he was feeling fine. But at the conclusion of the final day of the interdiction trial, looking tired and drained, he acknowledged his anguish in the highly personal legal struggle. "To have your kids turn against you—that's for the birds," he said to reporters as he left the courthouse.[14]

In late 2015, in the thick of the ongoing family battles, yet another legal problem slapped Tom Benson in the face. His longtime driver and personal assistant, who had been fired from his post in June 2015, filed a federal court complaint against the New Orleans Saints, alleging that the team had failed to pay him properly for hours he had worked.[15] Rodney Henry later amended the suit to add charges that Gayle Benson had slandered and discriminated against him and used the word "black" to describe him in lashing out at him verbally.[16]

Henry, an African American who worked for Tom Benson for about twenty years, claimed that his firing amounted to retaliation because he had given testimony in one of the suits brought by Benson's heirs, but the Saints and Benson took issue. "We deny any wrongdoing by anyone within the organization with respect to Mr. Henry's employment," Saints spokesman Greg Bensel said in response to Henry's complaint. "Just like any other employer, our organization sometimes has to make difficult decisions that are in the best interest of the company. Unfortunately, when those decisions are made, as is the case here, employees often take it personally and accuse their employers of wrongdoing in an effort to justify—in their own minds—why their employment was terminated."

After attorneys for the Saints, Benson, and Henry failed to

reach an out-of-court settlement, federal judge Carl Barbier in May 2016 ruled that, under the terms of Henry's employment, his complaints must go to arbitration before NFL commissioner Roger Goodell. Though Henry argued that Goodell could not be impartial given Benson's long association with the league, Barbier stuck by his order, telling Henry that if he still wished to pursue the question of Goodell's impartiality at the end of the arbitration, he could do so.

Chapter 27

In Search of Stability

Early in 2016, New Orleans Saints head coach Sean Payton held an unusual press conference. Despite the fact that the team had just finished a disappointing season, the event had a surprisingly upbeat tone.

Everything about the news conference, which Payton had called primarily to dispel rampant rumors that he planned to leave New Orleans, was atypical. For one thing, Tom and Gayle Benson, neither of whom would ordinarily show up for a postseason meetup with reporters, attended the event. They sat side by side, along with Saints president Dennis Lauscha and general manager Mickey Loomis, near the front of the room, close to Payton.

Second, the press conference went on for nearly an hour, which would be an aberration for almost any coach and likely was a first for Payton.

Third—and most noticeable—Payton had never before seemed so comfortable in his own skin. While the coach, during his ten-year run in New Orleans, was generally cordial and rarely showed a temper, his normal demeanor was nonetheless guarded. He tended to be self-protective in public settings, as though wary of revealing too much of himself.

But on this day, the coach sat relaxed and smiling—a broad, easy smile—as he faced a dozen reporters and patiently answered every single question they posed. Payton talked about the highs and lows of a season that had contained too many mistakes and missed opportunities, and he explained that he believed many of the rookie players would deliver a much stronger performance in the next season. Most of all he emphasized that, all rumors to the contrary, he intended to remain with the Saints for the long term.

It was hardly the first time a coach had spoken such words, particularly in the presence of his team's owner. But there was something about Sean Payton on this day that seemed to say he meant it.

He devoted a chunk of his time to speaking about strong feelings he had developed for New Orleans since arriving for the first time in the year after Katrina. He said that the city finally had him in its grip, and though it had taken a while, he felt truly at home. And he spoke of his colleagues at the Saints as though they were all part of his family.

Gauging reasons for Payton's unusual press conference is an exercise in conjecture, but it was difficult not to associate his manner with a change in the Saints organization. And the presence of Tom and Gayle Benson as he spoke seemed to reinforce the idea.

Though the coach and players had denied throughout the 2015 season that the bitter public explosion within the Benson family had had any effect on the team, the claim was not entirely believable. For more than a year, the family's vicious legal fights had been the stuff of local headlines, with many national news organizations paying attention as well. The players, coaches, and others could not have helped wondering what would happen if the court proceedings resulted in Tom Benson losing control of the team to his daughter and grandchildren.

While Tom Benson had never publicly acknowledged problems caused in the organization by his granddaughter, Rita LeBlanc, issues with her decision making and management style were a poorly kept secret. More than one staffer worried out loud about what would happen if and when her grandfather actually placed Rita in control of the Saints.

It is hard to believe that the concern and distraction caused by that ongoing uncertainty did not take a toll on the whole organization, including the players and coaches.

By more than one report, Sean Payton had tried at one point to insert a clause in his contract stating that, if he wished, he could become a free agent should Tom Benson no longer have control of the team. The NFL reportedly refused to allow the clause.[1]

Former staffers say that Drew Brees also had serious concerns about an ownership change, and though he did not express his feelings publicly, it seemed implicit in a comment he made shortly after Tom Benson announced that Rita would have nothing further to do with the team and that Gayle Benson would succeed Tom as controlling owner. "All I can say is, I absolutely love Gayle," Brees told a reporter at the 2015 Pro Bowl in Arizona. "I know she's one of our biggest fans. Her presence at practice with Tom all the time and the way she treats the wives and the players, she's first class."[2]

The unusual Sean Payton press conference in January 2016 seemed both a show of unity among owners and management and a message about the durability of the Saints organization. Payton acknowledged as much when he said: "The ownership, and the stability at the ownership position, is vital to having a chance. It doesn't guarantee success, but in many cases it can guarantee failure."

The importance of solid, predictable ownership is clear, Payton said, "when you look around the league and you pay close attention to who is winning."[3]

The extent to which Gayle Benson is qualified, in a business sense, to succeed her husband in owning the team became an issue in court filings by Tom's relatives. But the fact is, none of the individuals involved in the litigation has anything close to the experience and business savvy of Tom Benson, which means that in any case, the strength and stability of the management team running the organization will be crucial.

If Sean Payton's demeanor during the press conference was an indication, it seemed he was feeling good about the future of the team.

The months to come would bring more legal bickering as Tom Benson pressed his case against stewards of his heirs' trusts, seeking to retrieve from the trusts ownership shares in the Saints and Pelicans along with other holdings he had previously granted them. Though control of the sports teams was not at issue, since

Benson had always kept 100 percent of the controlling shares in his own hands, he badly wanted to "buy back" the nonvoting interests in the teams held by Renee Benson and Rita and Ryan LeBlanc, in order to remove them completely from the ownership ranks. Their non-controlling stakes amounted to almost 60 percent of the Saints and 95 percent of the Pelicans shares, and arriving at a fair valuation of the teams was central to resolving the case.

Just before the matter was slated to go to trial in June 2016, the parties reached a tentative settlement. While terms of the agreement remained under wraps, court documents filed days earlier provided hints about the sums at issue.

Filings showed that experts hired by each side placed the value of the New Orleans Saints in a range of about $1.23 billion to $1.65 billion, with Benson's expert giving the lowest estimate.[4] The figures bracketed a valuation published by Forbes.com, which in 2015 pegged the Saints' market value at $1.52 billion.

The estimated value of the New Orleans Pelicans, according to the heirs' expert, was about $588 million,[5] coming in lower than *Forbes'* January 2016 figure of $650 million. Court records did not show a calculation by Benson's expert for the NBA team, which Benson bought in 2012 for $338 million.

Also at stake in the case was ownership of the twenty-six-story Benson Tower office building and adjacent Champions Square entertainment plaza in downtown New Orleans. Records show that a national real-estate firm pegged the value of the property—acquired for $42 million in 2009 with state support that included a lucrative long-term lease on most of the office space—above $90 million.[6]

In the months leading up to the June 2016 agreement, some asset "trades" may have occurred among the parties. Property records in Bexar County, Texas, show, for instance, that Benson in March transferred to his heirs' trusts the deed to his $2.8 million San Antonio condominium.[7] His 2,300-acre Texas ranch and auto dealerships, held in part by the heirs' trusts, may also have come into play.

Once all parties sign off on the settlement and the portions related to the sports teams receive approval from the NFL and the NBA, as required by the leagues' rules, the final piece of the Benson family's legal battle will come to an end. With regard to Tom Benson's entire estate, valued above $2.5 billion, outsiders may never know exactly who ended up with what, as details will remain off-limits to the public. And fans of the Saints and Pelicans must content themselves with Benson's assurances, at the time the agreement was announced, that it is "business as usual" at the teams' headquarters.[8]

Whether Renee Benson and Rita and Ryan LeBlanc continue to hold any nonvoting shares in the Saints and Pelicans is a matter for speculation—though Rita LeBlanc in mid-2016 appeared confident that she would come away from the legal wrangling still owning a piece of the teams. In May 2016, LeBlanc talked with a reporter at *Street and Smith's Sports Business Journal* about her family's lawsuits and her future. In the article published the following month, she said, "No matter what happens in the litigation, I'll still be a partial owner."[9]

At the same time, LeBlanc seemed resigned to the likelihood that she would not again play an active role with the teams. Noting that "there are still things" she wanted to do in her professional life, she added, "but I can do them for other teams or other companies."

As the legal disputes wound toward a close, comments made by Tom Benson in a deposition, excerpts of which surfaced publicly in a court document, might have set his legal team wondering if his heirs might at some point mount a new challenge to his mental competency. The heirs' attorney and some news reporters made much of Benson's comment in the March 2016 deposition that his family members "tried to kill me"—a seemingly hysterical statement that, as became clearer in further questioning, probably merely reflected his distress at his heirs putting him under intense legal pressure at his advanced age.[10]

Still, Benson's deposition seemed to show confusion in his recollection of events, as when he stated repeatedly that it was his daughter Renee who was involved in a shoulder-shaking clash with Gayle Benson during a Saints game in 2014. News reports and court testimony by Renee Benson stated clearly that it was Rita LeBlanc who had a verbal clash with Gayle in the Superdome suite and that Renee had not attended the game.[11]

Chapter 28

Gauging Benson's Legacy

A small plaque that sits on Tom Benson's desk displays an adage that must seem more meaningful to him each day: *Tough times don't last, tough people do.*

After experiencing an extraordinarily exciting life that brought him both incredible highs and tragic lows, Benson could never have imagined that some of his biggest disappointments would occur as he approached ninety years of age.

Benson once told a friend: "You know, I don't think God is very happy with me."[1] At the time, he was referring to the untimely deaths of his two children and his first and second wives.

"I think it's uncommon for someone to have to deal with that," he said.[2]

Presumably, his friends in the Catholic Church are helping Benson find solace as he faces the reality of his broken family. But it is hard to imagine how he grapples with the possibility that he might never see his one remaining child, two of his grandchildren, and two great-grandchildren again.

Benson may find it comforting that the city where he was born and grew up, despite the criticism its citizens have flung at him at times over the years, seems largely respectful of the man who has had a large and lasting impact on New Orleans.

Even some of his staunchest detractors concede that Benson has been good for the city. "In spite of everything, I'm glad he's here and that he owns the teams," says a businessman who remains somewhat indignant that Benson once considered relocating the Saints.

"I think he's done a fine job and he's a steady hand. He had the guts to clean house when it was necessary, and he's made great hires that have had a huge impact on the Saints," says another observer who, while remaining critical of Benson's behavior after Katrina, terms him "a great owner" of the Saints.

The NFL, which has maintained solidarity with Benson, also continues to sing his praises. Pointing to his longtime leadership of the league's powerful Finance Committee, NFL commissioner Roger Goodell terms Benson's business and financial expertise "critical" in the resolution of many issues.

"Tom Benson has been an outstanding owner of the Saints and a strong leader and contributor on various league matters for many years," Goodell says. "He created moments in NFL history that the city of New Orleans and football fans across the country will never forget."

In the fall of 2014, before the teeth-gnashing within the Benson family had surfaced publicly, the Saints and Pelicans organization surprised Benson with a tribute that would catch him off guard. With the governor of Louisiana, the mayor of New Orleans, and the archbishop of the New Orleans Catholic diocese on hand, Saints head coach Sean Payton and general manager Mickey Loomis unveiled a fourteen-foot-tall bronze statue of Benson overlooking Champions Square just outside the Mercedes-Benz Superdome.

Uncharacteristically, Tom Benson was overcome. Handed a microphone as he fought back tears, he seemed almost not to believe what he was seeing.

"That's real nice," he managed. "I never did think this would happen."[3]

Gov. Bobby Jindal, who had been instrumental in putting taxpayer support behind the latest round of assistance for Benson in buying the nearby office building and other properties, weighed in on the impact of both Tom and Gayle. "It's no exaggeration to say the New Orleans Saints wouldn't be in Louisiana [and] the New Orleans Pelicans wouldn't be in Louisiana if it hadn't been for their leadership, their commitment or their generosity," Jindal said.[4]

In 2014, the New Orleans Saints and Pelicans unveiled this fourteen-foot statue of Tom Benson. It stands outside the Mercedes-Benz Superdome. (Kathy Finn Photo)

Mayor Mitch Landrieu, while joking that the Saints' 2010 Super Bowl victory overshadowed his election to office, added that he could not think of another sports team that is connected to its city the way the Saints are tied to New Orleans. "There is no other franchise in American sports history that is so intricately woven and bound to the success of its people," Landrieu said.[5]

It is a measure of Tom Benson's grit that, as his family came apart at the seams and threatened to consume the remainder of his life with bitterness and rancor, he and his wife dived into an entirely new enterprise.

Decades earlier, Tom and his son, Robert, raised and trained thoroughbreds on the Texas ranch. Benson's interest was rekindled when Gayle suggested they buy a horse. Benson decided that buying a handful of horses was a better idea, and he set about finding and hiring trainers to pick out promising yearlings.

The Bensons named their new business for Gayle Marie, and GMB Racing was born. Seemingly in no time, two of the Bensons' horses were headed for the Kentucky Derby.

Neither Mo Tom nor Tom's Ready would bring the Bensons a Derby win to go along with Tom's Lombardi Trophy, but the effort gave the couple an exciting departure from the drudgery of the ongoing feud with his heirs.

On their return to New Orleans from Louisville, Kentucky, Benson moved into the homestretch of the last remaining family lawsuit. His lawyers had gone into a frenzy in hopes of settling the suit and thus avoiding a trial that would publicly expose a plethora of sensitive financial information about the NFL, NBA, and Benson.

Benson may or may not have gotten much of what he wanted from his attempted asset exchange with his heirs. Either way, it was certain that he would return to work and continue looking ahead. That was the way he had reacted to every crisis, disappointment, and heartbreak throughout his life.

In the back of his mind, Benson may have remained concerned

that Gayle might face new battles with his heirs if she should outlive her husband. If Renee Benson and Rita and Ryan LeBlanc should choose to challenge Tom's will after he dies, there might be little to stop them.

At least Tom's relationship with his third grandchild, Dawn Benson Jones, and her family was still intact. And, critically to the continuation of an enjoyable lifestyle, Gayle, the woman who had become his twenty-four-hour companion and caretaker, remained at his side.

It appears that faith, hope, and an unwavering toughmindedness still imbue Tom Benson. With a little luck, he could become engaged in another big real-estate deal. And of course, another football season always lies ahead.

In the fall of 2016, the New Orleans Saints were preparing to celebrate the team's fiftieth anniversary. For thirty-one of the team's fifty years of existence, Benson had been at the helm. During those decades he absorbed abundant criticism, but he also enjoyed fans' adulation as his team delivered big wins.

As those same fans watched how the Saints owner handled his nearly two-years-long battle with his closest relatives, many felt sympathy. And they were more than a little awestruck by the resilience he continued to show.

Along with admiring Benson's strength and self-made success, people in New Orleans knew what the New Orleans Saints had meant to the viability of their city. And many—including some who once counted themselves among his harshest critics—looked at Tom Benson with nothing but gratitude.

Appendix

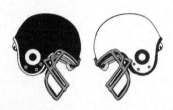

Tom Benson's Family: Ancestors

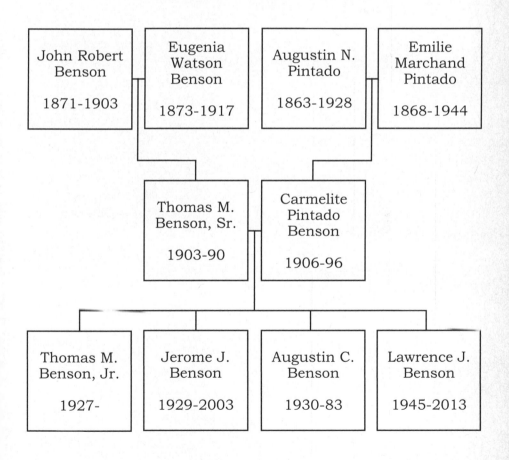

Tom Benson's Family: Descendants

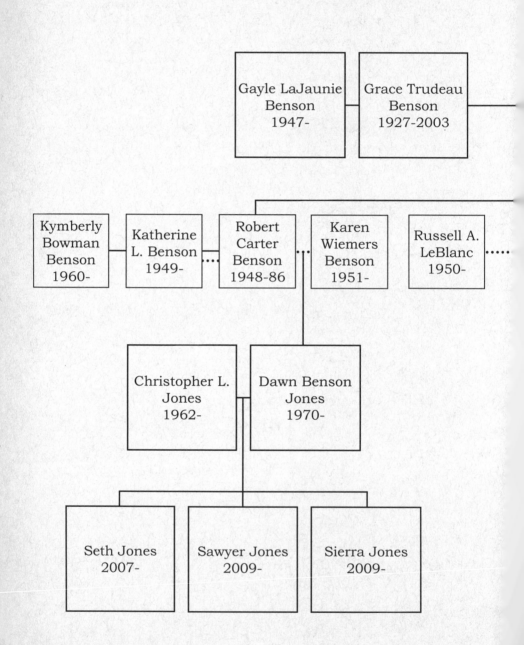

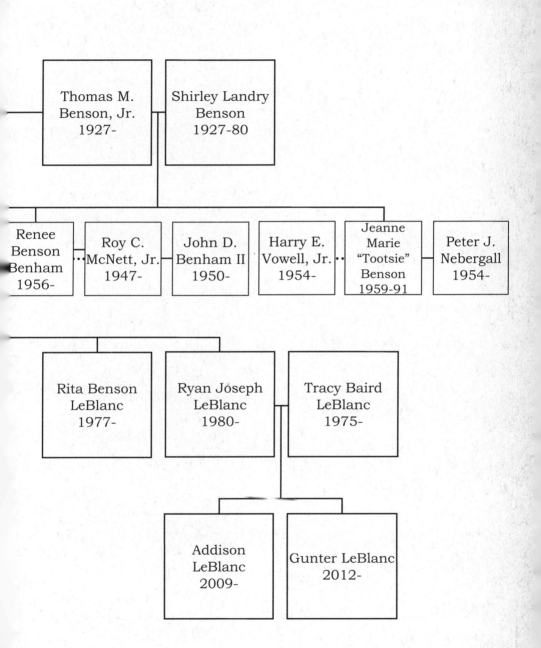

Timeline of Selected Events

July 12, 1927	Born in New Orleans
1944	Graduates from St. Aloysius High School
1945	Marries Shirley Mae Landry
1948	Begins working at Cathey Chevrolet (later acquired by Mike Persia, Sr.)
1956	Moves to San Antonio to manage a Persia-owned dealership
January 24, 1980	Shirley Benson dies from complications of lupus
May 1, 1982	Marries Grace Marie Trudeau
June 9, 1983	Brother, Augustin Benson, dies of colon cancer
June 3, 1985	Buys the New Orleans Saints
January 29, 1986	Robert Benson dies of lung cancer
April 10, 1990	Tom Benson, Sr., dies
April 13, 1991	Jeanne Marie "Tootsie" Benson dies
June 2, 1996	Carmelite Pintado Benson dies
April 3, 2001	Undergoes quadruple bypass heart surgery
June 17, 2003	Brother, Jerome Benson, dies
November 18, 2003	Grace Benson dies of Parkinson's disease
October 29, 2004	Marries Gayle Marie LaJaunie Bird
July 18, 2008	Purchases WVUE-TV
December 10, 2008	Undergoes surgery to remove cancerous mass from kidney
February 7, 2010	The Saints earn their first Super Bowl win
April 12, 2012	Buys the New Orleans Hornets (later renamed Pelicans)
October 28, 2013	Brother, Lawrence Benson, dies while traveling in Italy
December 27, 2014	Cuts all ties with Renee Benson and Rita and Ryan LeBlanc
January 21, 2015	Announces Gayle Benson will inherit much of his estate
January 22, 2015	Daughter, two grandchildren ask court to rule him mentally incompetent
May 2, 2016	Louisiana Supreme Court refuses to hear heirs' appeal of competency ruling
June 17, 2016	Reaches tentative agreement with heirs on final lawsuit

Tom Benson's Wealth: A Timeline

Year	Tom Benson's estimated net worth	Rank on Forbes *400* list of richest people in the United States
1985	$100 million	—
1989	160 million*	—
1992	180 million*	—
2011	1.0 billion	—
2012	1.2 billion	360
2013	1.3 billion	386 (tied with fourteen others)
2014	1.6 billion	383
2015	2.2 billion	307
2016	2.7 billion	—

*"The Texas 100," *Texas Monthly*, August 1989 and August 1992. Figures for 2012-15 from "The 400 Richest Americans," *Forbes*. Remaining figures from the author's research.

Tom Benson's Assets

Selected assets owned directly by Tom Benson or held in trusts for the benefit of his children and grandchildren:

Asset	Estimated Value
New Orleans Saints (NFL team)	$1.75 billion*
New Orleans Pelicans (NBA team)	650 million**
Benson Tower office building, New Orleans	91 million
WVUE-TV, New Orleans	51 million
Tom Benson Chevrolet, San Antonio	17.2 million
Benson Honda, San Antonio	17.4 million
Mercedes-Benz of San Antonio	11.4 million
Best Chevrolet, New Orleans	27 million
Mercedes-Benz of New Orleans	16.9 million
Mercedes-Benz Collision Center, Metairie, Louisiana	3 million
Lone Star Capital Bank, San Antonio	35 million***
Benson Farm and Ranch, Johnson City, Texas (2,300 acres of land, with three residences)	17 million
Uptown Blanco Arts and Entertainment District, Blanco, Texas	3.1 million
Primary home, Audubon Place, New Orleans	4 million
Vacation home, Rockport, Texas	2.3 million
Condominium, Alamo Heights, San Antonio	2.8 million
Vacation home, Lake Tahoe, Nevada	1 million
House and lots on Sena Drive/Elmeer Avenue, Old Metairie, Louisiana	2 million
Private jet, Bombardier Challenger 350, eight seats, twin engine, manufactured 2014	20 million
Turboprop, Beechcraft B300, nineteen seats, twin engine, manufactured 2013	5.7 million
Motor yacht, 140-foot, tri-deck, five-cabin, aluminum hull, built by Burger Boat Company, 2010	16 million
Surface parking lot, downtown New Orleans	3.1 million

*"The Business of Football," Forbes.com, September 2016.
**"The Business of Basketball," Forbes.com, January 2016.
***Estimate based on sale prices of comparable banks.
Auto dealership figures include land and improvements, where applicable.
Private jet and yacht valuations based on sale prices of comparable assets.
Other real estate and personal property figures from property records of the local jurisdictions.

Notes

Chapter 1
1. Elliot Harrison, "Super Bowl XLIV rematch: How the Saints took away Indy's ring," NFL.com, October 23, 2015.
2. Ibid.
3. Ibid.
4. Ibid.
5. Mike Triplett, "New Orleans Saints are Super Bowl champions," *New Orleans Times-Picayune*, February 8, 2010.
6. Teddy Kider, "Benson undergoes cancer surgery," *New Orleans Times-Picayune*, December 17, 2008.
7. Associated Press, "Saints owner Tom Benson undergoes back surgery," *America's News*, February 14, 2002.
8. Kider.
9. Elizabeth Merrill, "For two families, it's redemption time," ESPN.com, February 5, 2010.
10. Chris Rivette, letter to the editor, *New Orleans Times-Picayune*, October 19, 2005.

Chapter 2
1. Josh Peter, "Pride or profit?" *New Orleans Times-Picayune*, March 18, 2001.
2. Obituary of Tom Benson, Sr., *New Orleans Times-Picayune*, April 11, 1990.
3. Business filings with the Louisiana Secretary of State, 1985-98, and Ronette King, "Benson ready to sell to brother," *New Orleans Times-Picayune*, June 7, 1996.
4. Neal Morton, "Auto dealer was Rey Feo, known for generosity," MySanAntonio.com, October 30, 2013.
5. Ibid.
6. Obituary of Robert Watson Benson, Jr., *Ponchatoula (LA) Enterprise*, September 21, 2005.
7. Interview with a family member.
8. Tamarind Phinisee and Sandra Lowe Sanchez, "Auto magnate Tom Benson jumping back into bank biz," *San Antonio Business Journal*, March 9, 2003.
9. Allan Katz and Elizabeth Mullener, "The baffling Mr. Benson," Dixie Magazine, *New Orleans Times-Picayune*, September 1, 1985.

Chapter 3

1. U.S. City Directories, New Orleans, 1931-60, accessed through Ancestry.com.
2. Shaun Rein, "Think like a billionaire," Forbes.com, July 26, 2010.
3. U.S. Federal Census records, 1930, 1940, accessed through Ancestry.com.
4. Cynthia V. Campbell, "Tom Benson: The man," *Baton Rouge Advocate*, February 15, 1987.
5. Peter Finney, Jr., "Benson is Bro. Martin's $10 million man," *New Orleans Clarion Herald*, November 6, 2012.
6. U.S. Federal Census records, 1870, for Facundo Luis Pintado, and 1900, for Augustin Numa Pintado, accessed through Ancestry.com.
7. U.S. Federal Census records, 1870, for Jean Baptiste Bensa, and 1900, for John Robert Benson, accessed through Ancestry.com.
8. U.S. City Directories, New Orleans, 1945, 1949, accessed through Ancestry.com.
9. Campbell.
10. Ibid.
11. Peter.
12. Ibid.
13. Campbell.
14. Ibid.
15. Records of Student Registrar, Loyola University of New Orleans.
16. Peter.
17. Campbell.
18. Testimony of Renee Benson, February 2015, in Renee Benson v. Tom Benson, Probate Court, Bexar County, Texas.
19. U.S. Public Records, Directories and Death Records, accessed through Ancestry.com.
20. U.S. City Directories, New Orleans, 1954.
21. Mercedes-Benz of New Orleans Web site, automobile dealership history of Tom Benson.
22. U.S. Public Records, Directories and Death Records.
23. Peter.
24. Ibid.
25. Ibid.
26. Katz and Mullener.
27. Interview with an individual once close to the Benson family.
28. Ibid.
29. Ibid.

Chapter 4

1. Interview with Mike Persia III.
2. Peter.
3. Mercedes-Benz of New Orleans Web site.
4. Gold family memorial tribute to Arnold Gold, published by Porter Loring Mortuaries, San Antonio, September 2015.
5. Mercedes-Benz of New Orleans Web site.
6. Ibid.
7. Katz and Mullener.
8. Ibid.

9. Ibid.
10. Mercedes-Benz of New Orleans Web site.
11. Interview with Mike Persia III.
12. Gold family memorial tribute.
13. Peter.
14. Ibid.
15. Benson & Gold Chevrolet v. Louisiana Motor Vehicle Commission, 81-CA-0286, Sup. Ct. of La., 403 So. 2d 13 (1981).
16. Ibid.
17. John Hall, "Windfall to expand Benson dealerships," *New Orleans Times-Picayune*, December 22, 1995.
18. Mercedes-Benz of New Orleans Web site.

Chapter 5

1. Department of Banking notice, Texas Register, vol. 2, no. 96 (December 13, 1977), pp. 4741-802.
2. Phinisee and Sanchez.
3. Tamarind Phinisee, "Roddy shares wisdom from 45-year banking career," *San Antonio Business Journal*, December 2, 2011.
4. Mark Mensheha, "Benson Motors hires chair of the former Groos Bank," *San Antonio Business Journal*, July 14, 1996.
5. Phinisee and Sanchez.
6. FDIC and SEC reports based on filings by the company.
7. Phinisee and Sanchez.
8. Hall.
9. John Hall, "Benson has high hopes for Pontchartrain Bank," *New Orleans Times-Picayune*, June 21, 1985.
10. John Hall, "Pontchartrain deposits sold to First NBC," *New Orleans Times-Picayune*, July 20, 1991.
11. Ibid.
12. Ibid.
13. Lisa Y. Taylor, "Clear skies ahead," *San Antonio Business Journal*, February 3, 2002.
14. Mark Mensheha, "Camino Real appoints two banking vets to top posts," *San Antonio Business Journal*, May 18, 1997.
15. FDIC reports based on filings by Lone Star Capital Bank, December 31, 2014, and September 30, 2015.

Chapter 6

1. NewOrleansSaints.com, "Key moments in Saints history."
2. Joan Niesen, "Tulane Stadium left mark on New Orleans,"FoxSports.com, January 24, 2013.
3. NewOrleansSaints.com.
4. "Superdome managers make offer to buy Saints," *Philadelphia Inquirer*, December 23, 1984.
5. Obituary of H. R. 'Bum' Bright, *Los Angeles Times*, December 14, 2004.
6. John McQuaid, "Saints: Inside the sale," *New Orleans Times-Picayune*, May 26, 1985.

7. Ibid.
8. "Q&A with Tom Benson, Saints' new owner," *San Francisco Chronicle*, September 27, 1985.

Chapter 7

1. Opposition filings in Tom Benson v. Peter Glaser & Wendell Gauthier, 94-CI-09533, 150th J. D., Tex. (1994).
2. Ibid.
3. Tom Benson, letter to Wendell Gauthier, July 28, 1992, contained in Gauthier v. Benson, 95-1785, Civil District Court, Orleans Parish, Louisiana.
4. Ibid.
5. Affidavits filed in Benson v. Glaser & Gauthier.
6. Ibid.
7. Filings and exhibits contained in Benson v. Glaser & Gauthier.
8. Ibid.
9. Ibid.
10. Ibid.
11. Gauthier v. Benson.
12. Ibid.
13. Ibid.
14. Affidavits filed in Benson v. Glaser & Gauthier.
15. Ibid.
16. Gauthier v. Benson.
17. Philip Garrett affidavit in Benson v. Glaser & Gauthier.
18. Complaint filed in Peter Gauthier & Wendell Glaser v. Tom Benson, U.S. District Court, W. D., Tex. (1994).
19. Transcript of Benson's deposition in Benson v. Glaser & Gauthier.
20. Gauthier v. Benson.

Chapter 8

1. Austin Wilson, "Finks signs 3-year deal as Saints general manager," *Baton Rouge Advocate*, January 15, 1986.
2. Ben Brown, "Who dat in NFL playoffs? Prayers answered for New Orleans Saints," *USA Today*, December 29, 1987.
3. "Mike Ditka, football player and coach," Britannica.com.

Chapter 9

1. Mike Triplett, "New Orleans Saints owner revamps leading edge of the front office," *New Orleans Times-Picayune*, May 20, 2012.
2. Ken Belson, "At 88, Tom Benson conducts business," *New York Times*, September 19, 2015.
3. Filings contained in One Oak Park Limited v. Larry Benson, 89-12111, 131st J. D., Bexar County, Tex. (1989-92).
4. Ibid.
5. Intervention filed by Benson Motors Corporation in One Oak Park v. Benson.
6. Response of One Oak Park to Benson Motors' intervention in One Oak Park v. Benson.
7. One Oak Park v. Benson.

8. Ibid.
9. Mediator's report to the court in One Oak Park v. Benson (July 30, 1992).
10. WorldLeagueofAmericanFootball.com.
11. Larry Benson, Jr., LinkedIn profile, May 2016.
12. Online Web cast of the Larry Benson, Sr., memorial service and funeral, November 1, 2013, St. Francis of Assisi Catholic Church, San Antonio.

Chapter 10

1. U.S. City Directories, New Orleans, 1949.
2. Ibid., 1952, 1954.
3. Testimony of Renee Benson in Renee Benson v. Tom Benson.
4. Mercedes-Benz of New Orleans Web site.
5. Ibid.
6. David Hendricks, "Renee Benson suddenly faces uncertain future," *San Antonio Express-News*, February 6, 2015.
7. Testimony of Renee Benson in Renee Benson v. Tom Benson.
8. Maria C. Montoya, "The Saints heir apparent Rita Benson LeBlanc has a nose for books," *New Orleans Times-Picayune,* July 26, 2009.
9. Texas marriage and birth records, accessed through Ancestry.com.
10. Texas marriage, birth, and death records, accessed through Ancestry.com.
11. Testimony of Renee Benson in Renee Benson v. Tom Benson, and Texas death records.
12. Information provided by Tootsie Benson's husband, Peter Nebergall.
13. Ibid.
14. Records of Student Registrar, Stephens College, Columbia, Missouri.
15. Ibid.
16. Missouri State Police investigators' report on death of Tootsie Benson, April 15, 1991.
17. Ibid.
18. Adrian Quinlan, "Who is Renee Benson?" NOLA.com, February 6, 2015.
19. Testimony of Renee Benson in Renee Benson v. Tom Benson.
20. Ibid.
21. Ibid.
22. Texas marriage and divorce records, accessed through Ancestry.com.
23. Ibid.
24. Messages posted June 2006 on Wanderlodge Gurus, the NPR message board for Wanderlodge owners.
25. Property records for Blanco County, Texas.
26. Sheryl Smith-Rodgers, "Uptown Blanco," *Hill Country Magazine*, January 20, 2015.
27. *Blanco County News,* December 2006.
28. Smith-Rodgers.
29. YouTube video, "Planting trees in the Uptown Blanco Courtyard," by *Blanco County News*, February 25, 2011.
30. David Hendricks, "Renee Benson closes her Blanco restaurant," *San Antonio Express-News*, February 18, 2015.
31. Testimony of Renee Benson in Renee Benson v. Tom Benson.

32. Ibid.
33. Ibid.
34. Reply brief of Tom Benson in Tom Benson v. Renee Benson, 04-15-00087-CV, Court of Appeals (4th d, Tex.).
35. Katherine Sayre, "Judge asked to OK work on Benson home," *New Orleans Times-Picayune*, May 6, 2015.
36. Testimony of Renee Benson in Renee Benson v. Tom Benson.
37. Ibid.
38. Ibid.
39. Ramon Antonio Vargas, "Benson family feud documents shed light on professional lives," *New Orleans Advocate*, February 4, 2015.
40. Phinisee.
41. Business filings for Renson Enterprises, LLC with Texas Comptroller of Public Accounts, 2012.
42. Tom Roddy resume from State University of Texas, San Marcos, and bio as Public Finance Authority director in Texas State Directory.
43. Phinisee and Sanchez.
44. Hendricks, "Renee Benson suddenly faces uncertain future."

Chapter 11
1. Kim Shandrow, "Billionaire Mark Cuban on raising kids," Entrepreneur.com, July 15, 2015.
2. Montoya.
3. Information from Blinn College administrative office, Brenham, Texas.
4. Ramon Antonio Vargas, "Benson family feud documents shed light on estranged relatives," *New Orleans Advocate*, February 7, 2015.
5. Ibid.
6. Ibid.
7. Ryan LeBlanc, LinkedIn profile, 2015.
8. Texas marriage records, accessed through Ancestry.com.
9. "New Orleans Saints executive elected to board of Lone Star Capital Bank," *San Antonio Express-News*, May 4, 2006.
10. Business filings with the Texas Secretary of State.
11. WVUE-TV Ownership Report filed with Federal Communications Commission, 2009.
12. Receivers' report in Renee Benson v. Tom Benson.
13. Montoya.
14. Ibid.
15. Ibid.
16. Elizabeth Merrill, "Saints' Rita Benson LeBlanc stands out," ESPN.com, January 5, 2012.
17. Information from Texas A&M University administrative office.
18. Mike Triplett, "Saintly immersion—Rita Benson LeBlanc answered her calling," *New Orleans Times-Picayune*, March 26, 2006.
19. Ibid.
20. "Notes from Saints camp," *Baton Rouge Advocate*, August 8, 2002.
21. Jeff Duncan, "Two-teaming man: Saints and VooDoo owner Tom Benson," *New Orleans Times-Picayune*, March 7, 2004.

22. Texas marriage, birth, and divorce records, accessed through Ancestry.com.
23. Ibid.
24. Public statement released by Dawn Benson Jones.
25. Ibid.
26. Intervention filed in Renee Benson v. Tom Benson.

Chapter 12
1. Interview with a family member.
2. Testimony of Renee Benson in Renee Benson v. Tom Benson.
3. Katz and Mullener.
4. U.S. City Directories, New Orleans, 1952.
5. Jeff Duncan, "Tom Benson's wildly successful life has been marred by tragedy," *New Orleans Times-Picayune*, February 8, 2015.
6. Property records for Bexar County, Texas.
7. Brian Allee-Walsh, "Grace Benson, 76, activist, volunteer," *New Orleans Times-Picayune*, November 19, 2003.
8. Testimony of Renee Benson in Renee Benson v. Tom Benson.

Chapter 13
1. Associated Press, "9 partners sign to pay $64 million for Saints," *Lexington Herald-Leader*, March 13, 1985.
2. McQuaid.
3. "Pete Rozelle: Television, and the Modern NFL," Schmoop.com.
4. Ibid.
5. Figures based on 2014 financial results of Green Bay Packers, released by the team July 20, 2015.
6. IRS Form 990 (nonprofit report) filed by the National Football League for 2013.
7. Howard Bloom, "Roger Goodell deserves credit for NFL's growth," SportingNews.com, September 1, 2014.
8. John LaPlante, "Senate cuts would close Dome, Edwards says," *Baton Rouge Advocate*, June 18, 1986.
9. Jim Kleinpeter, "Some watch the game in luxury," *New Orleans Times-Picayune*, January 24, 1990.
10. Jimmy Smith, "Benson owns half of Saints," *New Orleans Times-Picayune*, May 25, 1989.
11. UPI, "Noel's consulting salary becomes issue at NFL trial," UPI Archives, August 12, 1992.
12. Garrett.
13. Associated Press, "Edwards signs bill to finance sports complex," *Baton Rouge Advocate*, June 16, 1993.
14. Randy McClain, "Saints owner, Foster say they see eye to eye," *Baton Rouge Advocate*, February 8, 2001.
15. Greg Thomas, "Favored stadium site off-limits, Morial says," *New Orleans Times-Picayune*, June 28, 2001.
16. Jeff Duncan, "New deal keeps Saints at home in the Dome," *New Orleans Times-Picayune*, September 27, 2001.
17. Josh Peter, "New stadium is still central to Saints' game plan," *New Orleans Times-Picayune*, September 27, 2001.

18. Stewart Yerton, "NFL chief: Ball in private sector's court," *New Orleans Times-Picayune*, November 11, 2001.

19. Tommy Craggs, "Leaked NFL documents: While owner cried hardship, Carolina Panthers had $112 million profit," *Deadspin*, March 7, 2013.

20. Mike Spofford, "Packers' financial picture remains strong," Packers.com, July 20, 2015.

21. Ibid.

22. Bob McGinn, "Packers report net income of $29.2 million on record revenue," *Milwaukee Journal Sentinel*, July 20, 2015.

23. Peter Finney, "No one is telling Benson to leave," *New Orleans Times-Picayune*, November 19, 2004.

24. Michelle Millhollon, "No new stadium: Study says find money, renovate Superdome," *Baton Rouge Advocate*, December 3, 2004.

25. Josh Peter, "Blanco tells Saints: Show us the money," *New Orleans Times-Picayune*, December 3, 2004.

26. Jeff Duncan, "Benson ready to make a deal," *New Orleans Times-Picayune*, November 18, 2004.

27. "Tagliabue: Saints situation bad," *Baton Rouge Advocate*, December 22, 2004.

28. NFL Team Valuations including revenue and operating income estimates for 2004, Forbes.com, 2005.

Chapter 14

1. Peter Finney, "Expect contentious contest between Benson, Blanco," *New Orleans Times-Picayune*, December 3, 2004.

2. Ed Anderson, "Blanco trying to set date for Saints talks," *New Orleans Times-Picayune*," August 26, 2005.

3. Ibid.

4. Ibid.

5. W. Scott Bailey, "Saints top administrator let go after Alamodome game," *San Antonio Business Journal*, October 18, 2005.

6. "Election endorsements," *Gambit Weekly*, April 18, 2006.

7. Brian Allee-Walsh, "Longtime Benson assistant resigns," *New Orleans Times-Picayune*, November 26, 2005.

8. Bailey.

9. Ibid.

10. Tom Osborn, "Mayor wants Saints in San Antonio," *San Antonio Express-News*, October 17, 2005.

11. Ibid.

12. Associated Press, "Attorney: Benson considering moving Saints west," *USA Today*, May 11, 2005.

13. Ibid.

14. Ibid.

15. Jeff Duncan, "'My plan right now is to stay in New Orleans,'" *New Orleans Times-Picayune*, May 25, 2005.

16. Tom Benson, "Open letter to our fans in Louisiana and the Gulf Coast," multiple Louisiana newspapers, October 26, 2005.

17. Ibid.

18. Robert Burns, "Uncaring, mean and greedy," letter to the editor, *New Orleans Times-Picayune*, October 19, 2005.

19. Brian Allee-Walsh, "Damage control: Saints owner seeks to terminate lease," *New Orleans Times-Picayune*, October 20, 2005.

20. Ibid.

21. Jeff Duncan, "Benson defends his actions in Saints ad," *New Orleans Times-Picayune*, October 27, 2005.

22. Posted by saintz08 on blackandgold.com, December 15, 2005

23. Les East, "NFL asks Saints to come home," *Baton Rouge Advocate*, December 23, 2005.

24. *New Orleans Times-Picayune*, October 25, 2005.

Chapter 15

1. Ed Anderson and Josh Peter, "Benson: No Saints decision made," *New Orleans Times-Picayune*, October 22, 2005.

2. Jeff Duncan, "Benson, La. to huddle in B.R. today," *New Orleans Times-Picayune*, October 30, 2005.

3. Ibid.

4. Interview with an individual who watched the events.

5. Associated Press, "Safety concerns might keep Benson from games," *Baton Rouge Advocate*, November 4, 2005.

6. Jeff Duncan, "Angry Benson vows not to set foot in B.R.," *New Orleans Times-Picayune*, November 3, 2005.

7. Ibid.

8. Jeff Duncan, "Deal gives Saints, La. more time to negotiate," *New Orleans Times-Picayune*, November 5, 2005.

9. Aaron Kuriloff and Darrell Preston, "Subsidies for Saints owner open New Orleans to Super Bowl," *Bloomberg Businessweek*, January 31, 2013.

10. Information provided by Paul Tagliabue.

11. Jed Lipinski, "New Orleans' International Matex purchased for $1 billion," NOLA.com, July 8, 2014.

12. Interview with a business owner who attended the meeting.

13. Ibid.

14. Ibid.

15. Interview with an individual who attended the dinner.

16. Statement released to press on February 14, 2006.

17. Joseph Nocera, "Take the money and stay," *New York Times*, February 5, 2006.

18. Howard Bloom, "Tom Benson—Will he keep the New Orleans Saints in the city?" *Sports Business News*, September 21, 2006.

19. Jeff Duncan, "Saints to play at home next year," *New Orleans Times-Picayune*, December 31, 2005.

20. East.

21. Nocera.

22. Property appraisal records for Bexar County, Texas, for 2015.

23. Duncan, "Benson ready to make a deal."

24. Duncan, "Benson, La. to huddle in B.R. today."

25. Peter Finney, "Benson has made Saints a hard sell, *New Orleans Times-Picayune*, November 21, 2005.

26. Jeff Duncan, "Paul Tagliabue: New Orleans' Katrina recovery 'greatest community moment,'" *New Orleans Times-Picayune*, August 21, 2015.
27. Ibid.
28. Interview with Paul Tagliabue.
29. Ibid.

Chapter 16
1. Information provided by Paul Tagliabue.
2. Interview with the business owner.
3. Ibid.
4. Interview with a business owner-activist.
5. Interview with a business owner.

Chapter 17
1. Interview with a friend of Tom Benson.
2. Chris Price, "Owner of New Orleans Saints picks granddaughter as his newest partner," *New Orleans CityBusiness*, August 9, 2004.
3. Elizabeth Mullener, "Owner in waiting: Hard work, not just pedigree, propelling Rita Benson LeBlanc," *New Orleans Times-Picayune*, July 26, 2009.
4. Ibid.
5. Ibid.
6. Jim Derry, "AFL honors Benson LeBlanc," *New Orleans Times-Picayune*, June 26, 2004.
7. Mullener.
8. Ramon Antonio Vargas, "Sources: Berating assistants, often missing from work," *New Orleans Advocate*, January 25, 2015.
9. Jeff Duncan, "Rita Benson LeBlanc's conspicuous absence," *New Orleans Times-Picayune*, April 22, 2012.
10. Ibid.
11. Franz Lidz, "Rita's Hail Mary Pass," *Portfolio Magazine*, September 17, 2007.
12. Ibid.
13. Triplett, "Saintly immersion."
14. Merrill, "Saints' Rita Benson LeBlanc stands out.".
15. Duncan, "Rita Benson LeBlanc's conspicuous absence."
16. "40 Under 40, Rita LeBlanc," *Street and Smith's Sports Business Journal*, March 12, 2007.
17. Duncan, "Rita Benson LeBlanc's conspicuous absence."
18. Triplett, "New Orleans Saints owner Tom Benson revamps leading edge of the front office."
19. Vargas, "Sources: Berating assistants, often missing from work."
20. Ian Rappaport, "Around the NFL," NFL.com, November 8, 2015.

Chapter 18
1. Gayle Benson, interview by Angela Hill, *The Open Mind*, WWL Radio, October 2, 2013.
2. Nell Nolan, "Artists, sailors and football fans," *New Orleans Times-Picayune*, November 5, 2004.
3. Gayle Benson, interview by Hill.

4. John Pope, "A winning team," *New Orleans Times-Picayune*, October 29, 2004.
5. Gayle Bird v. Thomas Bird, 1986, Civil District Court, Orleans Parish, La.
6. Ibid.
7. Katie Moore, *Eyewitness News*, WWL-TV, April 1, 2015.
8. "5 facts you might not know about Gayle Benson," *New Orleans Advocate*, January 23, 2015.
9. Lianna Patch, "Ben-eficience," *New Orleans Living*, September 2013.
10. Consolidated Freightways v. Gayle Bird, 92-CA-2799, La. 4th Circuit Ct. of Appeal, 626 So. 2d 445 (1993).
11. Larocca v. Bird, 1988, Civil District Court, Orleans Parish, La.
12. Bird v. Murray, Larocca, et al, 2-88-CV-04959, U.S. District Court, E. D., La.
13. Gayle Bird Interiors v. Fairmont, 1997, Civil District Court, Orleans Parish, La.
14. James Arcara v. Gayle Bird, 2000, Civil District Court, Orleans Parish, Louisiana, and counterclaim, 2000.
15. Moore.
16. WMC Mortgage v. Gayle Bird, 1999, Civil District Court, Orleans Parish, La.
17. In Re: Interdiction of Thomas Milton Benson, Jr., 2015, Civil District Court, Orleans Parish, La.
18. Ibid.
19. Ibid.
20. Ibid.
21. Nakia Hogan, "New Orleans Saints sell Superdome naming rights," *New Orleans Times-Picayune*, October 3, 2011.
22. Ibid.
23. Gayle Benson, interview by Hill.
24. "Saints owner agrees to buy Hornets," ESPN.com, April 13, 2012.
25. Ibid.
26. Ibid.
27. Morgan Packard, "The biggest party you never heard about," *New Orleans Magazine*, June 2013.
28. Ibid.
29. Ibid.
30. Katherine Sayre, "Who dat say they gonna," *New Orleans Times-Picayune*, January 24, 2015.
31. Property records for Orleans Parish, Louisiana.
32. Ryan Parry, "New Orleans Saints owner sued by daughter and grandchildren," U.K.DailyMail.com, February 4, 2015.

Chapter 19

1. U.S. Federal Census records, 2014.
2. Property records for Bexar County, Texas, 2015.
3. Texas death records.
4. Property records for Bexar County, Texas, 2016.
5. Obituary of Francis LaJaunie, Sunset Funeral Home, San Antonio, July 2010.

Chapter 20

1. Katz and Mullener.
2. Rick Eckstein and Kevin Delaney, *Public Dollars, Private Stadiums: The*

Battle Over Building Sports Stadiums (New Brunswick, NJ: Rutgers University Press, 2003).

3. Associated Press, "Superdome upgrade completed," ESPN.com, August 10, 2011.

4. Jim Watts, "The squeeze is on at the Superdome," *Bond Buyer*, March 5, 2008.

5. Sheila Kumar, "Louisiana lawmakers move forward with $400 million bond-restructuring scheme in Superdome bond deal," NOLA.com, December 21, 2012.

6. Rebecca Mowbray, "Benson family completes purchase of Dominion Tower," *New Orleans Times-Picayune*, September 15, 2009.

7. Ed Anderson, "Panel OKs sale of bonds to buy tower near Dome," *New Orleans Times-Picayune*, September 18, 2009.

8. Michelle Millhollon and Allen Johnson, Jr., "New Saints deal questioned," *Baton Rouge Advocate*, May 1, 2009.

9. Nakia Hogan, "N.O. scores 2013 Super Bowl," *New Orleans Times-Picayune*, May 20, 2009.

10. Ibid.

11. Financial Audit Services informational audit, "State of Louisiana Analysis of Benson Tower Lease," issued by Louisiana Legislative Auditor, September 3, 2014.

12. Memorandum of Understanding, Saints Stadium Agreement between Louisiana, the Saints, Louisiana Stadium and Exposition District, and SMG, dated April 30, 2009.

13. Ibid.

14. NFL Team Valuations and estimates of net worth of wealthiest Americans, Forbes.com, 1989-2016.

15. Ibid.

16. Ibid.

17. Ibid.

18. "The Texas 100," *Texas Monthly*, August 1989.

19. Benson, letter to Gauthier.

20. "The Texas 100," *Texas Monthly*, August 1992.

21. NFL Team Valuations, Forbes.com, 2007.

22. Estimates of net worth of wealthiest Americans, Forbes.com, 2011.

23. Ibid., 2016, and NFL Team Valuations, Forbes.com, 2015.

Chapter 21

1. Gayle Benson, interview by Hill.

2. Niesen.

3. Jennifer Armstrong, "New Orleans Saints' first lady Gayle Benson has come a long way as a fan," *New Orleans Times-Picayune*, August 14, 2009.

4. *New Orleans Saints 2016 Media Guide*.

5. John DeShazier, "Payton has the pedigree to succeed," *New Orleans Times-Picayune*, January 18, 2006.

6. Ibid.

7. Ibid.

8. Jeff Duncan, "A night to remember," *New Orleans Times-Picayune*, September 24, 2007.

9. Ibid.

10. Ibid.

Chapter 22

1. Victor A. Matheson and Robert A. Baade, "NFL Governance and the Fate of the New Orleans Saints: Some Observations" (Economics Department Working Papers, Paper 64, College of the Holy Cross, Worcester, MA, 2007).
2. Jeff Duncan, "Things have never been better for the New Orleans Saints," *New Orleans Times-Picayune*, November 8, 2009.
3. Greg Bishop, "Brees sees the stars aligning for New Orleans," *New York Times*, October 3, 2009.
4. Les Carpenter, "The New Orleans Superdome: a great American comeback story," *New York Guardian*, August 21, 2015.
5. Mike Florio, "The NFL's official announcement regarding bounty discipline," ProFootballTalk.NBCSports.com, March 21, 2012.
6. Ibid.
7. Ibid.
8. Steven Godfrey, "Scott Fujita rips Roger Goodell in statement," SBNation.com, October 10, 2012.
9. Michael David Smith, "Drew Brees: Everyone knows the bounty investigation was a sham," ProFootballTalk.NBCSports.com, November 29, 2012.
10. Judy Battista, "In step with New Orleans' comeback," *New York Times*, January 28, 2013.

Chapter 23

1. "Saints owner agrees to buy Hornets."
2. Neil deMause, "Hornets' new round of tax subsidies to total $78 million," FieldofSchemes.com, May 1, 2012.
3. Gayle Benson, interview by Hill.
4. Associated Press, "Benson gets All-Star treatment in New Orleans," NBA.com, February 12, 2014.
5. Ibid.
6. NBA team records, LandOfBasketball.com.
7. "The Business of Basketball," Forbes.com, January 2016.
8. Ibid.
9. John Lombardo, "Inside NBA's revenue sharing," *Street and Smith's Sports Business Daily*, January 23, 2012.
10. John Reid, "New Orleans Pelicans agree to arena naming rights deal with Smoothie King," *New Orleans Times-Picayune*, February 5, 2014.
11. "The Business of Basketball."
12. Kevin Draper, "What the NBA's insane new TV deal means for the league and for you," Deadspin.com, October 6, 2014.
13. Marc Stein, "Pelicans will re-sign Anthony Davis to 5-year, $145M extension," ESPN.com, July 1, 2015.
14. Edward Branley, "NOLA History: Baseball in New Orleans," GONola.com, July 7, 2011.
15. Matthew Futterman, Sam Schechner, and Suzanne Vranica, "NFL: The league that runs TV," *Wall Street Journal*, December 15, 2011.
16. Dave Walker, "Saints owner Tom Benson buys WVUE," *New Orleans Times-Picayune*, May 6, 2008.
17. Ibid.

18. Ibid.
19. Jaquetta White, "Tom Benson wants to buy *Times-Picayune*," *New Orleans Times-Picayune*, July 26, 2012.

Chapter 24
1. Pope.
2. Public statement released by Dawn Benson Jones.
3. Jeff Duncan, "Two-teaming man," *New Orleans Times-Picayune*, March 7, 2004.
4. Jeff Duncan, "Rita Benson LeBlanc's conspicuous absence."
5. IRS Form 990 filed by Gayle and Tom Benson Charitable Foundation for 2012, 2013, and 2014.
6. Property records for Jefferson Parish, Louisiana.
7. Sue Strachan, "Gayle and Tom Benson renew their wedding vows," *New Orleans Times-Picayune*, October 23, 2014.
8. Ibid.
9. Testimony in Renee Benson v. Tom Benson.

Chapter 25
1. Testimony of Renee Benson in Renee Benson v. Tom Benson.
2. Copies of family e-mails sent in fall of 2014, obtained by Associated Press and published by *New Orleans Advocate*, March 11, 2015.
3. Filings contained in Renee Benson v. Tom Benson.
4. Jeff Duncan, "Benson family feud got physical," *New Orleans Times-Picayune*, March 1, 2015.
5. Ibid.
6. Ramon Antonio Vargas, "Owner's niece was in suite at Dome," *New Orleans Advocate*, March 24, 2015.
7. Testimony of Renee Benson in Renee Benson v. Tom Benson.
8. Testimony of Stanley Rosenberg in Renee Benson v. Tom Benson.
9. In Re: Interdiction of Thomas Milton Benson, Jr.
10. Exhibits contained in Renee Benson v. Tom Benson.
11. Complaint filed in Thomas Milton Benson, Jr. v. Robert A. Rosenthal, U.S. District Court, E. D., La.
12. NewOrleansSaints.com, "Tom Benson restructures ownership, transfers control of Saints, Pelicans to his wife," January 22, 2015.
13. Ibid.
14. In Re: Interdiction of Thomas Milton Benson, Jr.
15. Ibid.
16. Receivers' report in Renee Benson v. Tom Benson.
17. Exhibits contained in Renee Benson v. Tom Benson.
18. Testimony of Renee Benson in Renee Benson v. Tom Benson.
19. Ibid.
20. Receivers' report in Renee Benson v. Tom Benson.
21. Testimony in Renee Benson v. Tom Benson.
22. Ibid.
23. Filings contained in Benson v. Rosenthal.
24. Ibid.
25. Exhibits contained in Renee Benson v. Tom Benson.

26. In Re: Interdiction of Thomas Milton Benson, Jr.

Chapter 26
1. Ken Belson, "Saints' owner marches out of step with his heirs," *New York Times*, March 6, 2015.
2. Ibid.
3. Public statement released by Randall Smith, January 26, 2015.
4. Ibid.
5. In Re: Interdiction of Thomas Milton Benson, Jr.
6. Ibid.
7. Testimony of Renee Benson in Renee Benson v. Tom Benson.
8. Ramon Antonio Vargas, "Benson family feud documents shed light on professional lives."
9. Testimony of Richard Hood in Renee Benson v. Tom Benson.
10. Ibid.
11. Ibid.
12. Testimony of Stanley Rosenberg in Renee Benson v. Tom Benson.
13. Ibid.
14. Ramon Antonio Vargas and Jaquetta White, "After his mental competency trial concludes," *New Orleans Advocate*, June 12, 2015.
15. Complaint filed in Rodney Henry v. New Orleans Louisiana Saints LLC, U.S. District Court, E. D., La.
16. Amended complaint in Henry v. New Orleans Saints.

Chapter 27
1. Rappaport.
2. Ted Lewis, "Drew Brees: 'I absolutely love Gayle Benson,'" *New Orleans Advocate,* January 21, 2015.
3. NewOrleansSaints.com, "Sean Payton's end-of-season press conference," January 6, 2016.
4. Filings contained in Benson v. Rosenthal.
5. Ibid.
6. Ibid.
7. Property records for Bexar County, Texas.
8. Public statement released by the New Orleans Saints, June 17, 2016.
9. Bruce Schoenfeld, "The days of Rita," *Street and Smith's Sports Business Journal,* June 27, 2016.
10. Filings contained in Benson v. Rosenthal.
11. Testimony of Renee Benson in Renee Benson v. Tom Benson.

Chapter 28
1. Comment following Benson's donation to establish the Shirley Landry Benson PACE Center in New Orleans, *New Orleans Clarion Herald*, June 5, 2004.
2. Ibid.
3. Andrew Lopez, "Saints, Pelicans owner honored with statue," *New Orleans Times-Picayune*, September 2, 2014.
4. Ibid.
5. Ibid.

Index

Acura, 23, 48
Advance Publications, 242
Aiello, Greg, 166
Aints, 58, 143
Airline Drive, 114, 135, 240
Airline Highway, 47
Airline Highway Saints training camp, 218
Alabama, 168
Alamodome, 138-39, 144-45
Alamo Heights, 156
Alamo Mission, 194
Albuquerque, 141
Algiers, 183, 192
Aminu, Al-Farouq, 236
Amoss, Tom, 190
Andersen, Morton, 76
Annunciation High School, 31
Aransas Bay, 114
Arcara, James, 184
Archdiocese of New Orleans, 218
ArenaBall, 168
Arena Football League, 140, 167, 169
Arizona, 267
Arizona Cardinals, 228
Arizona Coyotes, 127
Arizona Diamondbacks, 167
Atlanta, 259

Atlanta Falcons, 139, 222, 224, 256
Audubon Nature Institute, 153, 218
Audubon Place, 46, 152, 190, 192
Austin, 50, 109
Austin Wranglers, 169
automobile dealerships, 17, 22, 24, 27, 36, 38-39, 41-42, 48, 50, 54, 67, 83, 96, 101-2, 107, 112, 195, 198, 202, 212, 244, 257-58, 261-62, 266, 268-71, 280
Aymond, Gregory, 185

Baade, Robert, 225
Bahamas, 115, 134
Baird, Tracy, 107
Baltimore, 63
Baltimore Ravens, 119, 134, 233
banking, 19, 22, 40, 50, 52, 82, 101, 198, 202, 266, 269
banking regulators, 53
Barbier, Carl, 276
Barbot, Marilyn, 63, 86, 112, 114-15
Barbour, Haley, 135
Barnes, Elizabeth, 60, 67-69
baseball, 124, 239

Index

basketball, 235
Baton Rouge, 58, 137, 140, 144-46, 151, 157, 168
Bayern, Art, 262
Baylor University, 109
Bayou Lafourche, 91
Beaumont, Texas, 43, 45
being rich, 165
Benedict XVI, 218
Benham, John Daniel, II, 97-98, 252
Bensel, Greg, 137, 147, 275
Benson, Augustin, 22, 27, 35, 198-99
Benson, Carmelite Pintado, 22, 26, 29, 198-99
Benson, Dawn Marie, 92
Benson, Gayle LaJaunie, 13, 18, 117-18, 147, 152, 158, 178-90, 192-93, 195, 199-201, 216-18, 224, 233, 235, 245-53, 255-56, 258-60, 262, 267, 270, 272-73, 275, 277-79, 281, 285-86
Benson, Grace Trudeau, 23, 63, 86, 96, 111-18, 161, 178-79, 185-86, 199, 245-47, 249, 254, 268
Benson, Jeanne, 33, 90, 94-96, 113, 116, 198, 200, 244-45, 268
Benson, Jerome, 22, 27, 35, 52, 54, 60, 73, 198
Benson, Lawrence, 22, 27, 35, 60, 84-86, 181, 198-99, 247
Benson, Lawrence, Jr., 86
Benson, Leonard, 32
Benson, Mark, 23
Benson, Renee, 13, 32, 55, 91-92, 96-101, 103, 106, 109, 112-13, 116-18, 169, 177, 181, 185, 196, 198, 201, 244-47, 249, 252, 255-59, 261-64, 266, 268-73, 280-81, 286
Benson, Robert Carter, 32, 90, 92, 94, 109, 116, 189, 198-99, 217, 244, 248, 268
Benson, Robert W., Jr., 23, 52
Benson, Shirley Landry, 30-33, 35-36, 38, 40, 88-90, 92, 111-12, 114, 178, 195, 199, 243-44, 261, 268
Benson, Thomas Milton, Sr., 22, 26, 28, 198-99
Benson & Gold Chevrolet, 45-47, 83
Benson Automotive Group, 106
Benson Automotive World, 22-23
Benson Boogie, 224
Benson Chevrolet, 44
Benson Farm and Ranch, 24-25, 33-34, 45, 55, 94-95, 97-98, 103, 106-7, 109, 114, 189, 196, 198, 244-45, 261, 280, 285
Benson Field, 217
Benson Financial Corporation, 51-52, 54, 101
Benson Football, Inc., 65, 70
Benson Honda, 23
Benson Jesuit Center, 217
Benson Management Company, 198
Benson mausoleum, 199-201
Benson Memorial Library, 217
Benson Motors Company, 54, 85
Benson Motors Corporation, 101
Benson Tower, 174, 209, 258, 280
Benz-Saints, 71-73
Berger, Darryl, 153
Bexar County, 41, 261

billionaire, 213
Bird, Thomas, 182-84
Biscotti, Stephen, 119
Blanco, Kathleen, 130-31, 133, 135, 145-46, 148, 149-52, 158, 204, 225
Blanco, Raoul, 247
Blanco, Texas, 97-100, 261, 263
Blinn College, 106
BMW, 23, 48, 116
Bollinger, Donald, 153
Boston, 190
bounty scandal, 187, 232-33
Bowie, James, 194
Bowlen, Pat, 146
Boy Scouts, 30
BP oil spill, 188
Breeders' Cup, 190
Brees, Drew, 14-16, 18, 176, 212, 221, 225-27, 230, 233, 249, 278
Bright, H. R., 63
Bring New Orleans Back initiative, 160, 163
Brockenbraugh Court, 114, 162
Brooks, Aaron, 135
Brother Martin High School, 216-17
Bryan, James, 47-48
Buffalo Bills, 79, 126
Burger Boat Company, 115
Bush, Reggie, 221, 226
business leaders, 173

Cadillac, 42
Cagan, Joanna, 127
California, 137
Canada, 115, 190
Canadian Football League, 86
Canal Street, 27, 39
Canizaro, Joe, 153
Cannon, Steve, 107
Canton, Ohio, 248
Carmichael, Peter, Jr., 221
Carnival, 18
Carnival krewes, 161
Carolina Panthers, 128, 135, 146, 212
Cathey Chevrolet, 32, 38-39
Catholic Church, 31, 77, 112, 178, 216, 218, 282
Cattleman's National Bank, 55
CBS, 121, 241
Central Catholic High School, 92, 217
Champions Square, 174, 258, 280, 283
charitable giving, 216
Charlotte, North Carolina, 234, 240
Charlotte Hornets, 186
Charlotte Knights, 240
Chastant, Ledoux, Jr., 29-30
Chevrolet, 22, 32-35, 38-40, 42-48, 90, 106, 112, 194, 198, 271
Chicago, 58, 76, 146, 175
Chicago Bears, 80
Chicago Bulls, 237
Chouest, Gary, 234
Chrysler, 22
Chrysler/Plymouth, 42
Cicero, Jay, 162
Cincinnati Bengals, 57, 123
Citicorp, 72
City Council, New Orleans, 140
City Park, New Orleans, 189, 247
Civil War, 28
Claiborne Avenue, 29, 32
Clear Lake National Bank, 54-55, 101
clergy, 178
Cleveland, 222

Cleveland Browns, 232
Cole, Edward, 42
Coleman, James, Sr., 152
Coleman, Thomas, 152, 154-55, 159
College of the Holy Cross, Massachusetts, 225
College Station, Texas, 108
Colston, Marcus, 226
Columbia, Missouri, 94-96, 200
Commercial Bank, 51
Comptroller of the Currency, 53
condominium, 280
Consolidated Freightways, 183
Corpus Christi, 114
Coulon, Tim, 144
Court of Two Sisters restaurant, 183
Crescent City Bank & Trust, 153
Cuban, Mark, 103
Cut Off, 91-92

Dallas, 73, 196
Dallas Cowboys, 63, 210, 218, 227
Dallas Mavericks, 103
Davis, Anthony, 238-39
Dell, Inc., 109
Delmonico's, 180
Deloatch, Curtis, 224
Del Rio, Jack, 76
deMause, Neil, 126-28, 235
Demps, Dell, 236, 238
Denver, 146
Denver Zephyrs, 240
Detillier, Mike, 221-22
Detroit, 42, 155
Dikeou, John, 240
DirecTV, 121
Ditka, Mike, 80
Dodge, 48

Dominion Tower, 205
Duncan, Jeff, 126, 172, 256

Eckstein, Rick, 65-66, 203
Edwards, Edwin, 56, 58-59, 61-63, 81, 267
Elysian Fields Avenue, 26
Emmis Communications Corporation, 241
entrepreneurial activity, 163
Ernst, Brenda LaJaunie, 181, 192-93
ESPN, 238
ESPN.com, 174
ESPN's "Monday Night Football," 222
Exchange National Bank, 51

Fairmont Hotel New Orleans, 184
Favre, Brett, 230
Feder, Mike, 140, 167-69, 177, 267
Federal Communications Commission, 241
Federal Deposit Insurance Corporation (FDIC), 53-54
Federal Emergency Management Agency, 138, 150
Fielkow, Arnold, 132, 139-40, 145, 167-69, 173
Final Fours, 162, 174
Finks, Jim, 76-79
Finney, Peter, 129, 157
First Bank and Trust, 153
First National Bank of Commerce, 53
Flood, Great Mississippi River, 26
Florida, 134, 168, 190
Florida Avenue, 32, 38, 90
Forbes, 74, 132, 210, 212-15, 236, 238

Forman, Ron, 153
Foster, Mike, 124-25, 133, 148
Fountain, Pete, 78
Fourth Circuit Court of Appeal, 183, 264
Fox network, 241
Frederick, Harold, 30
Freeport-McMoRan, 82
French Quarter, 16, 32, 35, 38
Frischertz, Bernard, 52
Frischhertz Electric Company, 60
Fujita, Scott, 232

Galliano, 91
Gambit Weekly, 140
Ganis, Marc, 175
Gauthier, Wendell, 60, 69-73, 75, 123
Gayle and Tom Benson Cancer Center, 217
Gayle and Tom Benson Charitable Foundation, 216-17, 252
Gayle and Tom Benson Stadium, 217
Gayle Bird Interiors, Ltd., 183
General Motors Corporation, 42, 46
Gentry, Alvin, 238
Georges, John, 153
Georgia-Pacific Corporation, 88
Germany, 186, 189
Glaser, Peter, 60, 69-73, 75, 123
Gleason, Steve, 217, 224
GMB Racing, 189, 285
Gold, Arnold, 44, 83-84
Gold, Todd, 41, 83-84
Golden Meadow, 91
Goldstein, Nathan, 52
Goodell, Roger, 121, 146, 155, 181, 231-34, 241, 276, 283
Gordon, Eric, 236
Great Depression, 26

Greater New Orleans, Inc., 174
Greater New Orleans Sports Foundation, 162-63
Green Bay, 222
Green Bay Packers, 121, 128-29
Groos National Bank, 50-51, 67
Gruden, Jon, 218
Gulf Coast, 18, 30
Gulf of Mexico, 91, 134-36, 139, 188, 192
Gus Mayer Department Store, 27, 29

Hannan, Philip, 13
Hardberger, Phil, 140-41, 262
Hartley, Garrett, 15, 228
Haslett, Jim, 135, 218
Havana, Cuba, 28
Hebert, Bobby, 77
Henry, Rodney, 275
Henry B. Gonzalez Convention Center, 194
Herman, Fred, 59
Herman, Maury, 25, 35-36, 47-49, 52, 59, 69
Herman, Russ, 48-49, 59-60, 62, 69, 82, 203
Herman & Herman, 35, 47, 59, 70
Herman, Herman & Katz, 69
Hertz, Judah, 206-7
Hill, Angela, 179, 181, 184, 192, 247
Hock, Roy, 29
Hollis, Ken, 157
Holy Name of Mary High School, 183
Honda, 23, 42, 48, 106, 271
Hondo, Texas, 109
Hood, Richard, 270-71
horse racing, 189-90

horses, 34, 244, 285
horse trainers, 189
Houma, 50
Houston, 38, 57, 60, 67, 159
Houston Oilers, 58
Houston Texans, 159
Hunt, Lamar, 146
Hurricane Katrina, 17-18, 134-36, 139, 141-43, 145, 149-52, 155, 157, 160, 162-64, 168, 172-74, 178, 186-87, 192, 204-5, 216, 218, 222, 225, 234, 247-48, 262
Hurricane Rita, 149
Hyatt Hotel, 58

Immaculate Conception Memorial Chapel, San Antonio, 181
Indiana, 241
Indiana Pacers, 127
Indianapolis Colts, 13-16, 228
inducements, 207
Ingram Park Auto Center, 22, 86, 198
interior design, 182-83
Internal Revenue Service, 252
International Matex Tank Terminals, 152
Irsay, Jim, 13-14
Irvin, Michael, 233
Isuzu, 48

Jackson, Rickey, 76
Jacksonville, 63, 146
Jacksonville Jaguars, 119, 212
Japan, 115
Jeep/Eagle, 42, 48
Jefferson Parish, 46-48, 59
jet, 25, 213, 252
Jindal, Bobby, 187, 206, 283
John Paul II, 78

Johnson, Claudia, 196
Johnson, Lyndon Baines, 196
Johnson City, Texas, 24, 33-34, 55, 92, 106, 108, 114, 161, 196, 261
Jones, Christopher, 109, 248
Jones, Dawn Benson, 109-10, 248, 261, 269, 286
Jones, Jerry, 210, 212
Jones, Sam, 207

Kaman, Chris, 236
Kansas City, 146
Kansas City Chiefs, 58
Katz, Morton, 59, 69
Kelly Field National Bank, 51, 73
Kennebunkport, 190
Kennedy, John, 204
Kennedy, John F., 196
Kenner, 23, 46-47, 116
Kentucky Derby, 190, 285
Kenyon, Chris, 140, 168
Khan, Shahid, 119, 212
Kim, Wan, 238
Koerner, John, 153
Kowal, Connie, 140, 168
Kraft, Robert, 119, 146, 212
Kuharich, Bill, 78, 80

Lady Gayle Marie, 190, 213
Lady Grace Marie, 115, 190
Lafourche Parish, 91
LaJaunie, Francis, 192, 199
LaJaunie, Marie, 192-93
LaJaunie, Wayne, 181, 192
Lake Marina Tower, 114
Lake Pontchartrain, 114, 180
Lake Tahoe, 100, 261
L.A. Live (entertainment complex), 205
Lambeau Field, 129

Landrieu, Mitch, 146, 189, 235, 285
Land Rover, 48
Larose, 91
Las Vegas, 70
Laurel Street, 182
Lauscha, Dennis, 153-54, 166, 169, 175-76, 241, 256, 273, 277
lawsuits, 182, 185
Lay, Fred, 52-53, 82
LeBlanc, Rita Benson, 13, 55, 92, 98, 103, 107-9, 118, 142, 147, 166-77, 181, 185, 243, 245, 247, 249-52, 254-59, 261, 264, 266-69, 272-73, 278-81, 286
LeBlanc, Russell Anthony, 91-92, 97, 103, 106, 244
LeBlanc, Ryan, 13, 55, 98, 103, 106-7, 109, 118, 147, 169, 177, 181, 185, 195, 247, 252, 254, 257, 259, 261, 264, 266, 268-73, 280-81, 286
LeBlanc, Tracy, 248
Lee, Harry, 59
Liberty Hill, Texas, 248
Lincoln/Mercury, 48
Little, Michael, 29
Lone Star Capital Bank, 55, 107, 261-62, 270
Loomis, Mickey, 153-54, 173, 181, 218, 221, 232, 236, 283
Los Angeles, 61, 108, 141, 205
Los Angeles Clippers, 236
Los Angeles Lakers, 237
Louisiana, 22-23, 35, 38-39, 42, 48, 50, 52, 56, 59, 63, 81, 91-92, 100, 106, 116, 119-20, 122, 124-25, 129-30, 132-33, 136, 138-39, 142, 145-46, 148-51, 155-56, 168, 186, 192-93, 198, 204-6, 225, 235, 238-39, 261, 264, 267, 283
Louisiana Derby, 190
Louisiana Legislature, 56-57, 62, 123, 163, 207, 227, 235
Louisiana Motor Vehicle Commission, 35-36, 47-49
Louisiana Philharmonic Orchestra, 189, 253
Louisiana Recovery Association, 163
Louisiana Stadium and Exposition District, 124
Louisiana State University, 145-47, 151, 198
Louisiana Superdome, 67, 69, 71, 77-78, 81-82, 122-25, 127, 129, 131, 133-34, 136, 138-39, 141, 143-44, 148-51, 155, 157-58, 160, 162-63, 172-74, 186, 198, 204-7, 209-10, 213, 222, 224
Louisiana Superdome Commission, 204, 206
Louisiana Supreme Court, 48, 264-65
Louisville, Kentucky, 285
Loyola University of New Orleans, 23, 31, 217
Lurie, Jeff, 146
Lyndon B. Johnson High School, 106

McCarthy, Brian, 224
McCaskey, Mike, 146
McClelland, Chalmer, Jr., 67
McNair, Robert, 152, 159
McNett, Roy, Jr., 97
Maine, 115
Major League Baseball, 139
makeover, Benson's, 216

Index

Mandeville, 116
Manning, Archie, 58
Manning, Peyton, 14-15
Mardi Gras, 18, 143, 161
Marksville, Louisiana, 56
Marrone, Doug, 221
Martin Behrman Senior High School, 182-83
Mass, 178-79
Matheson, Victor, 225
Mazda, 22, 42
MCC Group, the, 60
Mecom, John W., Jr., 57-60, 62, 75-76
Mercedes-Benz, 42, 48, 83, 106, 186, 189, 210, 270-71
Mercedes-Benz Superdome, 57-58, 61, 63, 178, 181, 186, 210, 225, 227-28, 230, 233, 235, 242, 247, 250, 252, 256, 281, 283
Metairie, 114, 116, 133, 138, 143, 157, 240
Metairie Road, 39
Miami, 16-19, 30, 117
Miami Dolphins, 145-47, 209
Michigan, 42
Microsoft, 121
Mike Persia Chevrolet, 35, 45-46, 198
Miller, Jim, 77-79, 81, 266
Minneapolis, 52
Minnesota, 76
Minnesota Vikings, 119, 228, 230-31
Mission National Bank, 55
Mississippi, 135
Mississippi Gulf Coast, 168
Mississippi River, 28, 114, 152, 183
Missouri, 62, 94, 96, 245

Mitsubishi, 48
Montvale, New Jersey, 106
Moore, Lance, 15
Mora, Jim, Sr., 76-79
Morial, Marc, 125
Morstead, Thomas, 15
Mo Tom, 285
Mount Sacred Heart Catholic School, 91
Murphy, Mark, 129

Nagin, Ray, 135-36
National Basketball Association, 103, 124, 127, 164, 172, 186-87, 234-39, 252, 258, 280, 285
National Football Conference, 241
National Football League, 14, 56-57, 65-66, 69, 74-79, 85, 94, 108-9, 115-17, 119-29, 131-32, 138-39, 142, 144-47, 151-56, 158-59, 161-62, 164-67, 172-74, 181, 187-89, 202-4, 206-7, 210, 216, 218, 221-22, 224-27, 230-35, 237, 241, 246, 249-50, 255, 258-59, 276, 278, 280, 283, 285
National Football League Finance Committee, 124, 283
National Hockey League, 127
National League Baseball, 240
National Weather Service, 134
NBC, 241
NCAA, 162, 174
Nebergall, Peter, 94-95
Neff, Carole Cukell, 260-61
Nevada, 261
New England, 146
New England Patriots, 119, 212
Newhouse, Steve, 242
New Jersey, 108
New Mexico, 141

New Orleans, 16-19, 22, 25-36, 38-39, 42-47, 49-50, 52-54, 56, 59, 61, 63-64, 70, 76, 80, 83, 90-92, 98, 100, 107, 110-12, 114-15, 120, 122, 124-26, 130-64, 167-74, 179, 184, 186-90, 193, 196, 198, 204-7, 209, 216, 218, 221-22, 224-28, 232-36, 238-42, 245, 247-48, 252-54, 256-57, 260, 264, 266, 269, 271-72, 275, 277-78, 280, 282-83, 285

New Orleans Advocate, 153

New Orleans Arena, 162-63, 179, 186, 234-35, 238

New Orleans Business Alliance, 174

New Orleans Business Council, 160, 174

New Orleans Centre, 205

New Orleans Convention and Visitors Bureau, 153-54

New Orleans Hornets, 131, 164, 172, 186-88, 234-36, 242

New Orleans Jazz, 235

New Orleans Louisiana Saints Limited Partnership, 65

New Orleans Museum of Art, 180, 185, 189, 218, 247, 253

New Orleans Pelicans, 107, 164, 188, 236, 238-39, 257-59, 273, 279-81, 283

New Orleans Saints, 13-19, 24, 30, 52, 54, 56-81, 83, 85, 92, 96, 107-9, 113-17, 119-20, 122-27, 129, 131-35, 137-61, 163, 166-78, 180-81, 186-87, 190, 192, 198, 202, 204-7, 209-10, 212-18, 221-22, 224-28, 230-36, 240-43, 247-52, 255-59, 266-67, 269, 273, 275,
277-81, 283, 285-86

New Orleans Times-Picayune, 126, 129, 242

New Orleans VooDoo, 167-68, 267

New Orleans Zephyrs, 124, 240

News Corporation, 241

New York, 83, 108, 126, 146, 189, 242

New York City, 172, 190

New York Knicks, 237

New York Times, 156

NFC South Division, 226

NFL.com, 177

NFL Employee Benefits Committee, 174

NFL International Committee, 174

NFL Players Association, 144

Nissan, 22, 42, 48

NOCCA Institute, 218

Nolan, Dick, 58

North Carolina, 186

North Johnson Street, 27, 35

North Park, San Antonio, 195

North Rampart Street, 32, 38, 42, 46

Northshore Volkswagen, 116

Norwest Banks, 52, 54, 67, 101

Oakland, 61, 63, 137

Oakland Raiders, 135

Ochsner Health System, 217

oil and gas industry, 51, 56-57, 161, 205

O'Keefe, Sean, 146

Oklahoma City, 187, 234, 236

Old Metairie, 114, 162, 190, 261

Oldsmobile, 42

Olympic trials, 162

One Oak Park, Ltd., 84-85

One River Place, 75, 114

Ormsby Chevrolet, 40, 44
Our Lady Star of the Sea Catholic Church, 31
Our Lady Star of the Sea Elementary School, 28

Palm Beach, Florida, 115
Parcells, Bill, 218
Paul, Chris, 236, 238
Payton, Sean, 15, 18, 176, 187, 212, 218, 221, 225-26, 231-32, 249, 277-79, 283
Peake, Martin, 23, 116
Peake, Miriam "Mimi" Walker, 23, 113, 116
Peake BMW, 23, 116
Pensacola, Florida, 134
Perry, Stephen, 154-55
Persia, Mary Bradford, 43-44
Persia, Mike, Jr., 38-39, 43
Persia, Mike, Sr., 32-33, 38-40, 43-44
Persia, Mike, III, 43-46, 266
Philadelphia, 146, 150
Philadelphia Eagles, 115, 226
philanthropy, 164
Phillips, O. A., 58, 76
Phoenix, 63, 168
Pittsburgh, 146
Pittsburgh Steelers, 123
Polensky, Mary, 261
Pontchartrain Hotel, 57
Pontchartrain State Bank, 52-54, 82
Pontiac, 22, 42
Pontiac Lane, San Antonio, 195
Porter, Tracy, 16
Poydras Street, 56-57, 143
prenuptial agreement, 185
Pritzker, A. N., 58, 60
Privateer Park, 240

Pro Bono Project of New Orleans, 217
Pro Football Hall of Fame, 248

Rappaport, Ian, 177
real estate, 22-24, 40-41, 51, 53-54, 83, 153, 202, 206, 257
Reese, Kern, 264, 272
Rein, Shaun, 27
Reis, Chris, 15
renewing vows, 185
Renson Enterprises, LLC, 100-101, 261, 263, 270-71
Richardson, Bill, 141
Richardson, Jerry, 128, 146, 212
River Ridge, 252
River Walk, San Antonio, 194
Rizzo, Pete, 33
Roaring Twenties, 26
Robinette, Garland, 184
Rockport, Texas, 114, 162, 192
Roddy, Tom, 50-51, 54-55, 101, 120, 262, 269, 271, 273
Rooney, Dan, 146
Rosenberg, Stanley, 41, 60, 67, 72, 141-42, 256-57, 271-72
Rosenblum, Paul, 60
Rosenthal, Robert, 264
Ross, Stephen, 209
Rozelle, Pete, 57, 78, 120-21

Saban, Nick, 147
St. Aloysius High School, 28, 31
St. Anthony Catholic School, 183, 217
St. Anthony's Seminary, 33-34
St. Charles Avenue, 28
St. Claude Avenue, 39
St. Joseph's Academy, 112
St. Louis, 62
St. Louis Cardinals, 239

St. Louis Cathedral, 179, 185, 253
St. Louis Rams, 232
St. Mary's University, 22, 198
St. Roch Avenue, 31
Saints Business Council, 154, 173
Salomone, Nace, 182
San Antonio, 22-24, 32-35, 38, 40-42, 44, 46, 48, 50, 54-55, 60, 63, 67, 70, 83-84, 86, 90-92, 95, 98, 99-102, 106-7, 109-12, 114, 117, 120, 137-42, 144-146, 148, 156-58, 161-63, 172, 180-81, 186, 192-96, 198-200, 217, 247-48, 252, 261-64, 270-72, 280
San Antonio Riders, 85-86
San Antonio River, 194
San Diego, 181
San Diego Chargers, 221
San Francisco 49ers, 233
San Francisco Chronicle, 64
San Francisco University, 43
San Jose, California, 135
San Juan, Puerto Rico, 70
San Pedro Avenue, San Antonio, 34-35, 40-41, 46, 194-95
San Pedro State Bank, 50
Santa Anna, Antonio Lopez de, 194
savings and loan industry, 51
Schneider, Fred, 60, 67-68
Searcy, Viola, 91, 95, 112
Seattle Seahawks, 123
SEC, 162
Shinn, George, 164, 186-87, 234
Shirley Benson Testamentary Trust, 261-62, 264, 268, 270, 272
Shockey, Jeremy, 15

Sicily, 28
Simpson, O. J., 222
Singer, Karl, 73-74
SMG, 150, 155, 157, 162
Smith, Randall, 182, 264-65, 267-68
Smoothie King Center, 238
Sokolski, John, 33
Solomon, Gary, Sr., 153
South Carolina, 48
Southern Methodist University, 51
Spicer, Susan, 189
stadium finance, 203
Stall, Al, 190
Stanford University, 109
Staples Center, 205
Stern, David, 187, 234
Stewart, Dallas, 190
Stram, Hank, 58
Street and Smith's Sports Business Journal, 174, 281
subsidies, sports, 203
succession, 258
Sunset Memorial Park, San Antonio, 199
Super Bowl, 14, 16, 18-19, 76, 80, 117, 131, 133, 151, 155, 174, 189, 205-6, 209-10, 213, 222, 226-28, 230, 233, 252, 285
Super Bowls, 162
Suzuki, 22

Tagliabue, Paul, 78, 117, 126, 131, 144-48, 150, 152-55, 157-60, 163, 173, 181, 218, 222, 232
Tampa Bay Buccaneers, 123
television rights, 129, 238, 241
television station, 257

Index

Tennessee Titans, 232
Texas, 22-23, 25, 32, 35, 38,
    42-43, 45, 48, 50-52, 54-55,
    58, 65, 70, 80, 83, 92, 94-95,
    98-101, 103, 106-8, 112, 116,
    119-20, 140, 159, 161, 174,
    189, 196, 198, 244-45, 247-48,
    261, 264, 269, 280
Texas A&M University, 108, 249
Texas Banking Commission, 50
Texas Christian University, 43
Texas Hill Country, 24, 33
Texas Monthly, 74
Texas White House, 196, 198
Thibodaux, 91
Thomas, Pierre, 15, 226
Thornton, Doug, 150, 156, 158,
    162, 173, 222, 230
Three *R*s, 185
Tiger Stadium, 145-47, 151, 157
Tom Benson Chevrolet, 22, 40, 90
Tom Benson Stadium, 248
Tom's Ready, 285
Touro Infirmary, 70
Toyota, 48
Treme, 125
Tulane University, 57, 190, 217
Turner Sports, 238

UBS Financial Services, Inc., 45
United Distributors, Inc., 60
United States Navy, 31, 92, 244
University of Missouri at
    Columbia, 94
University of New Orleans, 240
University of Texas, 23, 116
University of the Incarnate Word,
    San Antonio, 181, 217
Upshaw, Gene, 144
Uptown New Orleans, 28
U.S. Football League, 76

Utah, 235

Valence Street, 184
Van Wyck, Bronson, 189
Veterans Memorial Boulevard, 47
Vietnam War, 92
Villanova University, 65, 203
Vilma, Jonathan, 231-32
Vince Lombardi Trophy, 17-18,
    213, 230, 285
Vitt, Joe, 221, 232
Vitter, David, 146
Volkswagen, 23, 48, 116

Wake Forest, 236
Walker, Dave, 241
Walker, Melvin, 112
Walker, Susan, 23, 113, 116-17,
    245
Walker, Tim, 112
Walker Acura, 116
Walker Volkswagen, 23, 116
Wall Street, 26
Wanderlodge RV, 97
Wang, Vera, 253
Washington, D.C., 142
Wayne, Reggie, 16
Weaver, Wayne, 146
Wells Fargo, 52
West Bank, 182, 192
Whitman, Miriam, 24
Whitney National Bank, 112
Who dat, 15, 224
Wiemers, Karen, 92, 109
Wilf, Zygi, 119
Williams, Gregg, 230-32
Williams, Monty, 236, 238
Williams, Ricky, 80
Willis, Thayer, 20-21, 88-89, 165,
    265
Wisconsin, 140

Wittmann, Phillip, 143, 182, 256, 263, 273
Women in Sports and Events group, 174
Worcester, Massachusetts, 225
World League of American Football, 85
World Trade Center, 83
World War II, 31
WVUE-TV, 107, 241
WWL Radio, 221

WWL-TV, 147

yacht, 25, 115, 180, 190, 213, 252
Yaeger, Joe, 60
Young Leadership Council, 162
Yulman Stadium, 217

Zelia, LLC, 207
Zephyr Field, 221, 240